Hawaiian archipelago

Australasian fauna

New Zealand subfauna

Palearctic subfauna

Oriental fauna

...fauna

Madagascan subfauna

A map on Fawcett's equal area projection (centred on London) showing the areas presently occupied by the principal world faunas and subfaunas, with blend zones.

The northern tree-line, shown as a broken line, corresponds closely with the edge of the tundra climatic zone of the coastal arctic; other areas of tundra climate are found in central Asian and Siberian highlands. In the holarctic region desert or steppe climates reign in the south-west United States, north Africa, and Asia south of around 50° N including most of the central highlands; a Mediterranean climate in most Mediterranean countries and the Pacific United States; a temperate climate in most of the east United States, Pacific Canada and Alaska, Japan, south Korea, south-eastern China and western Europe south of Oslo; and a boreal climate in the rest, north to the tree-line, including some northern United States and most of Canada, eastern Europe, Fenno-Scandia, Siberia and northern China.

The principal rivers and inland waters mentioned in the text are numbered.

1	Alazeya	30	Lena
2	Amur	31	Loire
3	Anadyr	32	Mackenzie
4	Aral Sea	33	Mississippi
5	Azov Sea	34	Niger
6	Baikal, Lake	35	Nile
7	Balkhash, Lake	36	Ob
8	Baltic Sea	37	Oder
9	Black Sea	38	Onega, Lake and River
10	Caspian Sea	39	Pechora
11	Congo	40	Po
12	Danube and	41	Rhine
12a	Sava	42	Rhône
13	Dnepr	43	St Lawrence
14	Dnestr	44	Seine
15	Don	45	Syr Darya (Aral Sea)
16	Dvina (North)	46	Tigris
17	Dvina (South)	47	Tunguska, Upper
18	Ebro	47a	Tunguska, Stony
19	Elbe	47b	Tunguska, Lower
20	Euphrates	48	Ural (River)
21	Ganges	49	Ussuri
22	Guadalquivir	50	Vilyui, Upper
23	Hwangho		(trib. of Lena)
24	Indigirka	51	Vistula
25	Indus	52	Volga
26	Irtysh	53	Weser
27	Khatanga	54	Yangtze
28	Kolyma	55	Yenisei
29	Kuskokwim	56	Yukon

THORBURN'S BIRDS

Michael
       Xmas '69.
Good luck to Anne &t.

            Father.

THORBURN'S
BIRDS

Edited with an introduction and new text by

James Fisher

EBURY PRESS

MICHAEL JOSEPH

Designed and produced by

George Rainbird Ltd, Marble Arch House,
44 Edgware Road, London, W2

for

Ebury Press, Chestergate House,
Vauxhall Bridge Road, London, SW1
and Michael Joseph Ltd, 26 Bloomsbury Street, London, WC1

Printed and bound by

Jarrold and Sons Ltd, Norwich

House Editor: Mary Anne Norbury
Designers: Ronald Clark and Anthony G. F. Truscott
Cartographer: John Flower

Front endpaper on Fawcett projection by permission of
the Royal Geographical Society, back endpaper by
permission of Wm. Collins, Sons & Co.

First published 1967

Text © James Fisher 1967
Illustrations by Archibald Thorburn,
first published 1915–18 in *British Birds*,
© George Rainbird Ltd

Introduction

Of the great picture book here revived it has been lately (1953) written by Sacheverell Sitwell that it brought 'the long succession of Fine Bird Books to an end'.

I am not certain that this is so, for a new style of monographs and general folios has developed since the Second World War that has brought justice to the beautiful work of our great twentieth-century bird artists with modern and sophisticated printing techniques. This has enabled a far wider public to enjoy the works of Axel Amuchástegui, D. M. Reid Henry, Fenwick Lansdowne, George Lodge, Roger Tory Peterson, Peter Scott, Charles Singer and Charles Tunnicliffe – to name an exalted few – than were ever able to purchase the classic nineteenth-century folios with the works of the earlier generation of masters.

Archibald Thorburn, in fact, gives us in his work the bridge between the last flourishment of the hand-coloured lithography of the nineteenth century and the chromolithography and letterpress colour reproduction of the twentieth. His field was the natural history of western Europe, its animals and in particular its birds; and he had developed such skills by the time he was thirty that his work became regarded then as the best ever to have come from the hand of a British bird artist. Not excluding Edward Lear, John Gould and his team, even Joseph Wolf (Gould's strong man of the birds of prey), Thorburn is still felt to be the best of the nineteenth century; his figures in Lord Lilford's *Coloured figures of the birds of the British Islands* (1885–98), which he began to paint in 1887, are still reproduced in several bird book series today, and prove it to a wide public.

What the wide public scarcely realises is that Thorburn did even better, greater work, and in particular the *British birds* offered here, which shows him as the first great bird artist of the twentieth century as well as the last of the nineteenth. He was born 1860 May 31 at Lasswade, in Midlothian near Edinburgh, the fifth son of the famous miniaturist Robert Thorburn. Sir Hugh Gladstone, historian alike of Dumfries and ornithology, tells us that Robert Thorburn was said to have been discovered drawing in chalks on the pavements of Dumfries and became an art pupil at Dumfries Academy. He came up to London in 1836, was elected an Associate of the Royal Academy in 1848, returned to Scotland in 1858 and died in 1885, having painted Queen Victoria three times, and the famous portrait of Prince Albert that Victoria always kept upon her table.

Archibald Thorburn was well coached by his father in his youth, when he was educated in Dalkeith and Edinburgh and was sent for a time to art school in London's St John's Wood. Like his father, Archibald became recognised as a painter of some calibre around the age of thirty, and had his first work published in 1883 in James Edmund Harting's *Sketches of bird life* – two monochrome plates. His first major assignment was for Walter Swaysland, whose *Familiar wild birds*, a popular book, came out in four volumes in 1883–88 with 144 coloured lithographs. At once he became a marked man; and when the competent bird illustrator J. G. Keulemans fell ill in 1887 he was called in by Lord Lilford as a major contributor to Lilford's *Coloured figures*. Eventually he produced 268 of the 421 plates of this classic work.

In the 1890's Thorburn was often 'hung' in the Royal Academy, contributed plates to W. H. Hudson's *British birds* and more importantly to the supplement of Dresser's *Birds of Europe*, and married Constance Mudie (in 1896). The turn of the century found him busy, well travelled within Europe though with a predilection for Scotland, in demand as an illustrator of sporting and scientific books (especially those of fellow-artist John Guille Millais, son of 'Bubbles' Millais) and even the by then widespread Christmas card. Monographers of birds on the Continent began to use him. When the First World War began he was quietly settled at Hascombe, Godalming, Surrey and working at full pressure on pictures, some vast, for private customers, the Royal Society for the Protection of Birds (of which he was a lifelong supporter) and the first book which was entirely his own.

Thorburn eventually wrote and illustrated four titles of his own: the present volume – *British birds* – *A naturalist's sketch book* (1919), *British mammals* (1920–21), and *Game birds and wild-fowl of Great Britain and Ireland* (1923). All were published in London by Longmans, Green. His *British birds* had a fourth edition in 1925–26 in a new octavo format, in four volumes, each with 48 new colour plates as opposed to 20 in the first edition. It was not a great circulation success, even though the ornithological critics of the day preferred it (incorrectly in my opinion) to the original quarto edition. There is something in the boldness of Thorburn's design and execution of the 1915–16 quarto *British birds* that distinguishes it from any of its predecessors and most of its successors. All his work was good; but the birds of the great quarto are the alivest birds he ever did, and living in their natural niches, as we can see from the deftest of environmental hints and representations.

As the publication sequence of the quarto *British birds* is somewhat complex, a chronology of it which may help the librarian and private collector appears to be as follows:

1915 March. First edition, volume one, vii+1143 pp., 20 colour plates (1–20), 1050 copies+105 copies on large paper.

1915 October. First edition, volume two, vi+72 pp., 20 colour plates (21–40), 1050 copies+105 copies on large paper.

1916 March. First edition, volume three, vi+87 pp., 20 colour plates (41–60), 1550 copies+105 copies on large paper.

1916 July or August. Second edition, volume one, pagination and plates as first, 500 copies.

1916 September. Second edition, volume two, pagination and plates as first, 500 copies.

1916 November. First edition, volume four, vii+107 pp., 20 colour plates (61–80), 1550 copies+105 copies on large paper.

1917 October or November. Third edition, volume one, pagination and plates as first, 500 copies.

1917 December. Third edition, volume two, pagination and plates as first, 500 copies.

1918 January. Second edition, volume three, pagination and plates as first, 500 copies.

1918 February. Second edition, volume four, vii+117 pp., 22 colour plates (61–80, 80A and 80B), 500 copies; and supplementary part to first edition, volume four, 11 pp., 2 colour plates (80A, 80B), number of copies not recorded but would not have been over 1550+105 on large paper.

It will be seen that formally the first edition, including the supplement, should be dated 1915–18, the second 1916–18, and the third 1917– (volumes one and two only; volumes three and four of the second edition were published with an adjusted print order).

After the war Thorburn continued to paint not only for himself and his private customers but also for other distinguished ornithologists, notably C. W. Beebe whose *Monograph of the pheasants* was published in 1918–22. To the end of his days Thorburn painted a regular annual Christmas card for the R.S.P.B., and the last picture he ever painted was of a goldcrest, which he did when lying in bed in his last painful illness. He died at Hascombe 1935 October 9; his last scientific job was published posthumously – plates to Sir Geoffrey Archer's and Miss Eva Godman's *Birds of British Somaliland* (1937). If re-editions, re-workings and re-exploitations be included, Thorburn has enjoyed more posthumous publication than any other bird artist except Audubon.

In the original quarto *British birds* Thorburn was not up to date, or even very precise, with the systematic arrangement and scientific names of his birds. As the systematic arrangement of the British birds is being revised as I write I have used a recent classification (Fisher and Peterson 1964) and have rearranged the plates to follow it as far as possible, with full notes on the necessary departures. I have cited, for the benefit of scientific ornithologists and the owners of the original editions, the vernacular and Linnean names as used by Thorburn, and have employed the convention of citing the authority for the Linnean name, and the date on which that authority first published it with a satisfactory description. A Linnean species name consists of two parts: the first word, which bears a capital, is the name of the genus, which is often shared by several, or sometimes many, closely related birds; the second word, which starts with a small letter, is an adjective describing it, and the two together constitute the name of the species. When the first describer used the second word as an adjective qualifying another genus, to which he believed the species should belong at that time but from which it has since been transferred, his name (and date) are placed in brackets. Second adjectives, or third Linnean words, are descriptive of valid geographical races, or subspecies.

Thorburn's original text was, frankly, somewhat superficial, and I decided to write a new text bringing to the fore some of our present knowledge of distribution and status, including conservation status of the British birds as up to date as possible, with copious use of the deep geographical studies of Charles Vaurie (1959, 1965) and Karel H. Voous (1960), to which the whole world of ornithology is in eternal debt. It seemed to me that this was the most useful thing to do, for the Witherby *Handbook* and the Bannerman *Birds of the British Isles* stand as definitive accounts of the less changeable general habits of our birds and are unlikely to be materially out of date in this respect for years. The distribution of birds, on the other hand, changes so fast that every published statement, however small the gap between writing and publishing, is to a greater or lesser extent false. Some idea of the extent of these changes can be gauged from the fact that Thorburn figured 407 species fifty years ago. Six of these have been rejected from the British-Irish List since his day – largely as a consequence of the re-examination of the notorious 'Hastings Rarities', said to have been observed or collected between 1892 and 1930 in the Hastings area of east Sussex and west Kent, and analysed by E. M. Nicholson and others in 1962. Six more were known to Thorburn but not figured by him. Thirteen more are now known to have occurred by 1914 but were apparently unknown to Thorburn. Forty-eight others were, or are likely to be, admitted to the List as having been recorded (or recognised as having become feral after introduction) between 1914 and 1967. Pending the appearance of the new British-Irish List late in 1967 my belief is that it may contain 468 species, including some whose status as truly feral (or gone-

6

wild) after introduction, or as truly vagrant, will not have been easy for the List Committee to make a proper decision upon. I have had the advice of many colleagues over the birds now listed in this book, notably I. J. Ferguson-Lees of *British Birds* journal; but the list is entirely my responsibility and may not coincide in some particulars with that which the British Ornithologists' Union is about to publish.

The endpapers of this book show the British-Irish counties and vice-counties, and the world showing the the main geographical zones now occupied by the great bird faunas. In the text I have used full counties (as before the London reorganisation) except in northern Scotland where the Hebridean units are treated as 'counties' in a self-evident way, and have referred to them as co. and st. when they are not strictly a shire but counties or a stewartry carrying the name of the principal town, or in Ireland, not so much out of pedantry as for economy. In my treatment of the world distribution of the birds the expression 'system' as applied to a river, lake or sea should be taken to mean the general area drained by the river and its tributaries, or by the rivers (and their tributaries) of the cited lake or sea. Designations of parts of systems, e.g. 'upper Ob system' should be taken in their broadest sense – in this case as meaning 'the upper systems of the Ob and its tributaries', rather than 'the system of the upper Ob and its tributaries', or 'the system of the Ob and its upper tributaries'.

An attempt has been made, following Fisher (1952) and Parslow (1967), to indicate the geometric or logarithmic order of the populations of British-Irish breeding birds, as follows:

Present book's 'order':	1....	2......	3.........	4............	5...............	6...........	7
J. L. F. Parslow's expression:	very scarce....	scarce....	not scarce....	fairly numerous...	numerous....	abundant	
Total estimated number of breeding pairs lately in Britain and Ireland:	1–9..	10–99..	100–999..	1000–9999....	10,000–99,999....	100,000 to 999,999......	a million or more

An easy mnemonic is that order 4 means an estimated number of breeding pairs in 4 figures. The use of the nines in the right-hand column is in simple celebration of this system; nobody could ever claim with certainty that a wild population was 999 as distinct from 1,000 pairs!

Bibliography

Since the publication of the great Witherby *Handbook of British Birds* which began in 1938 no fully authoritative textbook on the birds of Britain and Ireland has been published apart from David Bannerman's heroic and voluminous *The Birds of the British Isles* (1953–63). Some lists have been published (British Ornithologists' Union 1952, Fisher 1966) and the B.O.U. is to bring a new one out in 1967: also P. A. D. Hollom has brought the *Handbook* up to date in potted form (1952 and later editions, rare birds 1960). The surveyor of the status of British birds has, as main quarries apart from the above, the admirable journal *British Birds* published by Witherby, *Bird Study* published by the British Trust for Ornithology (incorporating *Bird Migration*), *Birds* published by the Royal Society for the Protection of Birds (formerly *Bird Notes*), *Scottish Birds* published by the Scottish Ornithologists' Club, and the *Irish Bird Report* published by the Irish Ornithologists' Club; also the *Bulletin of the British Ornithologists' Club* and the B.O.U.'s learned *Ibis*. For reasons of space I have been unable to cite here many papers published in these journals by authors mentioned in my text who have made valuable studies of individual species. The flourishing network of local natural history and ornithological societies and bird observatories that publish regular bird material is analysed in detail in my *Shell Bird Book* (1966); special mention must be made of *Nature in Wales* published by the West Wales Naturalists' Trust. County bird books, and county lists in local journals published since the *Handbook* and cited in the *Shell Bird Book* are not listed below, though I refer to the important works of Baxter and Rintoul (1953) on Scotland, and Kennedy (1961) and Ruttledge (1966) on Ireland. The deep analysis of the status of our British-Irish breeding birds by J. L. F. Parslow (1967) had four parts published when this book went to the printer in 1967 August, and its lucid array of information and conclusion has been something to be grateful for.

In the alphabetical-by-author list that follows an **asterisk** * indicates that a publication has had an edition or editions in years since the year or years cited (which are those of the first edition). A **dagger** † indicates a publication in which Archibald Thorburn was personally involved in a way summarised (if not self-evident) at the end of the particular citation. When the number of pages is cited the 'preliminary pages' (the small Roman numerals) are ignored.

ALEXANDER, W. B. and FITTER, R. S. R. (1955). American land birds in western Europe. *Brit. Birds* 48 (1): 1–14.

AMERICAN ORNITHOLOGISTS' UNION (1957). Checklist of North American birds. Baltimore, A.O.U., 691 pp.

† ANKER, Jean (1938). Bird books and bird art an outline of the history and iconography of descriptive ornithology. Copenhagen, Levin and Munksgaard, 251 pp.

† ARCHER, Sir Geoffrey Francis and GODMAN, Eva M. (1937). The birds of British Somaliland and the Gulf of Aden. London, Gurney and Jackson, 2 vols, 626 pp. Contains Thorburn's last published plates.

ARMSTRONG, Edward A. (1955). The wren. London, Collins *New Naturalist*, 312 pp.

ATKINSON-WILLES, G. L. ed. (1963). Wildfowl in Great Britain. London, H.M. Stationery Office, 368 pp.

BANNERMAN, D. A. (1953–63). The birds of the British Isles. Edinburgh and London, Oliver and Boyd, 12 vols, c 4300 pp., illustrated by George E. Lodge.

BAXTER, E. V. and RINTOUL, L. J. (1953). The birds of Scotland their history, distribution and migration. Edinburgh and London, Oliver and Boyd, 2 vols, 816 pp.

*† BEEBE, C. W. (1918–22). A monograph of the pheasants. London, Witherby, 4 vols, 913 pp.
Some of the finest of the 90 colour plates by Thorburn.

*† BENSON, S. Vere (1937). The observer's book of British birds. London, Warne, 224 pp.
The most popular book containing many Thorburn plates from Lilford (1885–98).

BRITISH ORNITHOLOGISTS' UNION (1952). Check-list of the birds of Great Britain and Ireland. London, British Ornithologists' Union, 106 pp.

BROWN, P. E. and DAVIES, M. G. (1949). Reed-warblers. East Molesey, Foy, 127 pp.

* BROWN, Philip and WATERSTON, George (1962). The return of the osprey. London, Collins, 223 pp.

BUXTON, E. J. M. (1950). The redstart. London, Collins New Naturalist, 180 pp.

*† COWARD, T. A. (1920–26). The birds of the British Isles and their eggs. London, Warne, 3 vols, c 1070 pp.
The most useful current general British bird book that still uses the Thorburn plates from Lilford (1885–98).

† COWARD, T. A. (1922). Bird haunts and nature memories. London, Warne, 214 pp.
A fine Thorburn frontispiece of a noctule, dated 1919 October 10.

† COWARD, T. A. (1927). Bird life at home and abroad with other nature observations. London and New York, Warne, 242 pp.
Colour frontispiece by Thorburn as 'flamingoes at home'.

† DRESSER, Henry Eeles, SHARPE, Richard Bowdler and HAY, Arthur Viscount WALDEN (1871–96). A history of the birds in Europe, including all the species inhabiting the western palæarctic region. London, 9 vols (includ. suppl.), originally publ. in 93 parts, 5144 pp.
Colour plates by Thorburn in the supplement of 1895–96.

† [DREWITT, C. M.] (1900). Lord Lilford . . . a memoir by his sister [Hon. Mrs F. Dawtrey Drewitt]. . . . London, Smith Elder, 290 pp.
Seven plates in monochrome by Thorburn of Lilford Hall, Northamptonshire and living birds in its aviaries.

* FISHER, James (1947–). Bird recognition. Harmondsworth, Penguin Books. 3 vols of 4 published to date.

FISHER, James (1952 c June). Bird numbers a discussion of the breeding population of inland birds of England and Wales. S. E. Nat. 57: 1–10.

FISHER, James (1952 Oct.). The fulmar. London, Collins New Naturalist, 496 pp.

FISHER, James (1966). The Shell bird book. London, Ebury Press and Michael Joseph, 344 pp.
The list of British-Irish birds in this book was preprinted in 1966 July for the 14th International Ornithological Congress.

FISHER, James and LOCKLEY, R. M. (1954). Sea-birds: an introduction to the natural history of the sea-birds of the North Atlantic. London, Collins New Naturalist, 320 pp.

FISHER, James and PETERSON, Roger Tory (1964). The world of birds. London, Macdonald, 288 pp.

FITTER, R. S. R. (1963). Collins guide to bird watching. London, Collins, 254 pp.

FITTER, R. S. R. and RICHARDSON, R. A. (1952). The pocket guide to British birds. London, Collins, 240 pp.

† GLADSTONE, H. S. (1917). Handbook to Lord Lilford's coloured figures of the birds of the British Islands. London, Bickers, 69 pp.

† GLADSTONE, H. S. (1936). Obituary. Archibald Thorburn. Scot. Nat. 1936 (217): 1–7.

GODFREY, W. Earl (1966). The birds of Canada. Ottawa, Nat. Mus. Canad. Bull. no. 203 (Biol. Ser. no. 73); 428 pp.

GORDON, Seton (1955). The golden eagle. London, Collins, 246 pp.

† GRIMBLE, Augustus (1896). The deer forests of Scotland. London, Kegan Paul, etc., 324 pp.
8 monochrome illustrations by Thorburn.

† GRIMBLE, Augustus (1901). Deer-stalking and the deer forests of Scotland. London, Kegan Paul, etc., 343 pp.
8 monochrome illustrations by Thorburn.

† GRIMBLE, Augustus (1902). The salmon rivers of Scotland. London, Kegan Paul, etc., 400 pp.
Illustrations by Thorburn.

† GRIMBLE, Augustus (1902). Shooting and salmon fishing and Highland sport. London, Kegan Paul, etc., 275 pp.
16 monochrome illustrations by Thorburn.

† HARTING, J. E. (1883). Sketches of bird life, from 20 years observation of their haunts and habits. London, 292 pp.
Two monochrome plates by Thorburn, the first of his to be published.

† HARTING, J. E. (1898). The rabbit. London, etc., Longmans Fur, Feather and Fin series, no. 6; 256 pp.
Monochrome frontispiece by Thorburn.

* HOLLOM, P. A. D. ed. (1952). The popular handbook of British birds. London, Witherby, 424 pp.

HOLLOM, P. A. D. (1960). The popular handbook of rarer British birds. London, Witherby, 133 pp.

*† HUDSON, W. H. and BEDDARD, Frank E. (1895). British birds. London, etc., Longmans, 363 pp.
8 colour plates by Thorburn.

† IRBY, L. Howard L. (1895). The ornithology of the straits of Gibraltar. London, Porter, 2nd ed., 326 pp.
8 colour plates by Thorburn.

KENNEDY, P. G. (1961). A list of the birds of Ireland. Dublin, Eire Stationery Office, 102 pp.

† KOENIG, A. [F.] (1911). Avifauna Spitzbergensis. . . . Bonn, author, 294 pp.
Colour frontispiece of little auks painted by Thorburn in 1910.

* LACK, David (1943). The life of the robin. London, Witherby, 200 pp.

LACK, David (1950). Swifts in a tower. London, Methuen, 239 pp.

*† LILFORD, Lord (1885–98). Coloured figures of the birds of the British Islands. London, Porter, 36 parts in 7 vols, 974 pp.
Thorburn was brought in to the work of illustration in 1887 January and his first plate was published in part 7, vol. 2 in 1888 September. He ended by doing the bulk of the work, with 268 colour plates of the total of 421.

† LILFORD, Lord (1895). Notes on the birds of Northamptonshire and neighbourhood. London, Porter, 2 vols, 706 pp.
24 monochrome plates of birds and Northamptonshire scenery by Thorburn.

† LITTLE, Alicia Bewicke [Mrs Archibald] (1900). Our pet herons. [Roy.] Soc. Protect. Birds Leafl. no. 35; 4 pp.
Thorburn monochrome drawing of little egrets.

LOCKLEY, Ronald M. (1942). Shearwaters. London, Dent, 238 pp.

LOCKLEY, Ronald M. (1953). Puffins. London, Dent, 186 pp.

† L[ODGE], G[eorge] E. (1935). Obituary. Archibald Thorburn. Brit. Birds 29 (6): 172

† L[ODGE], G[eorge] E. (1936). Archibald Thorburn. Ibis (13) 6 (1): 205–06.

LOWE, Frank A. (1954). The heron. London, Collins New Naturalist, 177 pp.

*† MacPHERSON, H. A. and others (1894). The partridge. London, etc., Longmans Fur and Feather series, no. 1; 276 pp.
9 monochrome plates by Thorburn.

† MacPHERSON, H. A. and others (1894). The grouse. London, etc., Longmans Fur and Feather series, no. 2; 293 pp.
10 monochrome plates and 1 vignette by Thorburn.

*† MacPHERSON, H. A. and others (1894). The pheasant. London, etc., Longmans Fur, Feather and Fin series, no. 3; 265 pp.
9 plates (10 in 2nd ed. 1896) and 1 vignette, in monochrome, by Thorburn.

† MacPHERSON, H. A. and others (1896). The hare. London, etc., Longmans Fur, Feather and Fin series, no. 4; 263 pp.
3 monochrome plates by Thorburn.

† MacPHERSON, H. A. and others (1896). The red deer. London, etc., Longmans Fur, Feather and Fin series, no. 5; 328 pp.
6 monochrome plates by Thorburn.

† MATSCHIE, Paul (1900). Bilder aus dem Tierleben. Stuttgart, Union, 476 pp.
  Some text-figures by Thorburn.

† MILLAIS, J. G. (1902). The natural history of the British surface-feeding ducks. London, Longmans, 168 pp.
  8 colour plates by Thorburn.

† MILLAIS, J. G. (1904–06). The mammals of Great Britain and Ireland. London, etc., Longmans, 3 vols, 1048 pp.
  30 colour plates by Thorburn done between 1893 and 1905.

† MILLAIS, J. G. (1909). The natural history of the British game birds. London, etc., Longmans, 142 pp.
  Some of the 18 colour plates by Thorburn.

† MILLAIS, J. G. (1913). British diving ducks. London, Longmans, 2 vols, 305 pp.
  15 colour plates by Thorburn.

† MILLAIS, J. G. (1917, 1924). Rhododendrons . . . and the various hybrids. London, etc., Longmans, 2 vols, 532 pp.
  2 colour plates by Thorburn.

† MILLAIS, J. G. and others (1912). British gamebirds and wildfowl. London, The Gun at Home and Abroad, 2 vols, 455 pp.
  Some illustrations by Thorburn.

MOUNTFORT, Guy (1957). The hawfinch. London, Collins *New Naturalist*, 176 pp.

† MULLENS, W. H. and SWANN, H. Kirke (1916–17). A bibliography of British ornithology. . . . London, Macmillan, 691 pp.

MURTON, R. K. (1965). The wood pigeon. London, Collins *New Naturalist*, 256 pp.

NETHERSOLE-THOMPSON, Desmond (1951). The greenshank. London, Collins *New Naturalist*, 244 pp.

NETHERSOLE-THOMPSON, Desmond (1966). The snow bunting. Edinburgh and London, Oliver and Boyd, 316 pp.

NICHOLSON, E. M., FERGUSON-LEES, I. J. and NELDER, J. A. (1962). The Hastings rarities. *Brit. Birds* 55 (8): 281–384.

† NISSEN, Claus (1953). Die illustrierten Vogelbücher ihre geschichte und bibliographie. Stuttgart, Hiersemann, 223 pp.

† OWEN, J. A. (1896 Sep.). The Lilford vivaria. *Pall. Mall Mag*: 48–61.
  6 monochrome illustrations by Thorburn.

PARSLOW, J. L. F. (1967). Changes in status among breeding birds in Britain and Ireland. *Brit. Birds* 60 (1): 2–47; (3): 97–123; (5): 177–202; (7): 261–85.

* PETERSON, Roger, MOUNTFORT, Guy and HOLLOM, P. A. D. (1954). A field guide to the birds of Britain and Europe. London, Collins, 318 pp.

† PYCRAFT, W. P. (1934). Birds of Great Britain and their natural history. London, Williams and Norgate, 206 pp. Colour frontispiece by Thorburn (from Hudson and Beddard 1895).

RUTTLEDGE, Robert F. (1966). Ireland's birds their distribution and migrations. London, Witherby, 207 pp.

SAVAGE, Christopher (1952). The mandarin duck. London, Black, 78 pp.

† SHAW, L. H. de Visme and others (1903). Snipe and woodcock. London, etc., Longmans *Fur, Feather and Fin* series, no. 10; 298 pp.
  4 monochrome plates by Thorburn.

† SITWELL, Sacheverell, BUCHANAN, Handasyde and FISHER, James (1953). Fine bird books 1700–1900. London and New York, Collins and van Nostrand, 120 pp.

SMITH, Stuart (1950). The yellow wagtail. London, Collins *New Naturalist*, 178 pp.

SNOW, D. W. (1958). A study of blackbirds. London, Allen and Unwin, 192 pp.

SPENCER, K. G. (1953). The lapwing in Britain. London, etc., Brown, 166 pp.

SUMMERS-SMITH, J. D. (1963). The house sparrow. London, Collins *New Naturalist*, 269 pp.

*† SWAYSLAND, Walter (1883–88). Familiar wild birds. London, Cassell, 4 vols, 640 pp.
  144 coloured lithographs by Thorburn; his first major publishing assignment.

† THORBURN, Archibald (1896). Sabine's gull in Cornwall. *Zoologist*: 475–76.

*† THORBURN, Archibald (1915–16 [and 1918]). British birds. London, etc., Longmans, 420 pp.
  82 colour plates by the author; for collation of editions see p. 6. The basis of the present book.

† THORBURN, Archibald (1919). A naturalist's sketch book. London, etc., Longmans, 72 pp.
  60 plates by the author, 24 in colour.

† THORBURN, Archibald (1920–21). British mammals. London, etc., Longmans, 2 vols, 108 pp.
  50 colour plates by the author.

† THORBURN, Archibald (1923). Game birds and wild-fowl of Great Britain and Ireland. London, etc., Longmans, 80 pp.
  30 colour plates by the author.

† THORBURN, Archibald (1925–26). British birds. London, etc., Longmans, 4 vols, 638 pp.
  Bibliographically the fourth edition of Thorburn (1915–16), with an octavo format and 192 new colour plates by the author.

† THORBURN, A. (1935). Kittiwakes nesting in Dunbar. *Scot. Nat.* 1935 (212): 50.
  Thorburn's last published material; and one of his few contributions to a scientific journal.

TINBERGEN, Niko (1953). The herring gull's world. London, Collins *New Naturalist*, 255 pp.

† [TREVOR-BATTYE, Aubyn] (1897). Archibald Thorburn and his work. *The Artist (Lond.)* 20 (211): 318–30.
  17 monochrome reproductions of Thorburn's drawings and paintings.

† TREVOR-BATTYE, Aubyn *ed.* (1903). Lord Lilford on birds. . . . London, Hutchinson, 312 pp.
  13 monochrome plates by Thorburn.

TUCK, Leslie M. (1960). The murres. Ottawa, Dep. Northern Affairs and National Resources, 260 pp.

VAURIE, Charles (1959, 1965). The birds of the palearctic fauna. London, Witherby, 2 vols, 1546 pp.

VOOUS, K. H. (1960). Atlas of European birds. London, Nelson, 284 pp.

* WITHERBY, H. F., JOURDAIN, F. C. R., TICEHURST, N. F. and TUCKER, B. W. (1938–41). The handbook of British birds. London, Witherby, 5 vols, 1882 pp.

Plate 1 (Thorburn's plate 77)

Order GAVIIFORMES

Family GAVIIDAE, divers or loons

Red-throated Diver   B4
Gavia stellata (Pontoppidan 1763)
T4 p. 85 and pl. 77 **mid left** (winter and summer)
as *Colymbus septentrionalis*, Linnæus

Origin doubtless arctic; breeds in the tundra and north boreal zones of virtually all the north, winters through temperate zone at sea on continental shelf and in some inland waters.

Breeding population of Britain-Ireland order 3; has bred in Scotland in every central, western and northern Highland county and has its British headquarters in Hebrides, Orkney and Shetland; colonised the Lowlands (Ayr co. and probably Kirkcudbright st.) in the 1950's. In Ireland first found breeding in co. Donegal in 1884 where 1 or 2 pairs persist. Has increased lately, after nineteenth-century decline under human pressure. Regular winter visitor and spring passenger.

Black-throated Diver   B1
Gavia arctica (Linnaeus 1758)
T4 p. 84 and pl. 77 **bottom** (summer)
as black-throated diver, *Colymbus arcticus*, Linnæus

Origin probably holarctic; breeds in the tundra and north boreal zones of most of the north, winters through northern temperate zone in inland waters and off coast.

British breeding population (Scotland only) order 2; has bred in central, west and north Highlands and the western and northern isles; colonised Arran and Lowland Ayr co. in the 1950's. Vulnerable to disturbance and evidently has its most stable population in the north Highlands. Winter visitor, mainly in east.

Great Northern Diver   B2
Gavia immer (Brünnich 1764)
T4 p. 83 and pl. 77 **top** (summer and winter)
as great northern diver, *Colymbus glacialis*, Linnæus

Origin doubtless nearctic, where it breeds in tundra, boreal and north temperate zones of Alaska, the Canadian mainland, south Baffin Island, Newfoundland and Gulf of St Lawrence islands south to the northern United States and in the west north-eastern California; also Greenland, extending into palearctic region importantly in east Greenland and Iceland – sporadically to Spitsbergen, Bear Island and perhaps Jan Mayen; winters mainly at sea in boreal and north temperate zones.

May have bred in Shetland; a pair with 3 'scarcely fledged' young were seen in Unst in 1843 August or September, and similar family parties on a loch near Aith in 1932, off Nesting 1933 August 20, and in Basta Voe, Yell, 1946 August 26. Eggs believed to be of this species were taken in Yell in 1858 and 1859. Winter visitor, mainly to north; juvenile non-breeders quite often summer.

White-billed Diver   B3
Gavia adamsii (G. R. Gray 1859)
T4 p. 83 and pl. 77 **mid right** (summer)
as white-billed northern diver, *Colymbus adamsi*, G. R. Gray

Origin probably arctic, where it breeds round the north, except in eastern Canada and Atlantic sector, almost entirely north of range of great northern diver; winters in coastal seas very seldom beyond boreal zone.

A rare vagrant: twenty records since the first near Embleton, Northumberland 1829 December; Shetland 7; rest of Scotland 6; England 7: 8 February; 12 November–February; 8 April–June.

Pl. 77.

Great Northern Diver. (summer & winter).

Red-throated Diver. (summer & winter).   White-billed Northern Diver.

Black-throated Diver.

Plate 2 (Thorburn's plate 78)

Order PODICIPEDIFORMES

Family PODICIPEDIDAE, grebes

Dabchick or **Little Grebe**   B9
Podiceps ruficollis (Pallas 1764)
T4 p. 88 and pl. 78 **bottom right** (summer and winter)
as little grebe, *Podicipes fluviatilis* (Tunstall)

Origin doubtless Old World; mainly resident in waters of
temperate and tropical Old World including Africa as far as
the Papuan area of the australasian region, and breeds in
southern boreal Europe whence winters to south, mostly in
inland waters and estuaries.

Breeding population of Britain-Ireland order 4; has bred
in every county except two in the present century after a
recovery at the end of the last. Has disappeared from some
urban and industrial areas, though has colonised new gravel
pits and suburban park lakes. Our stock does not winter out
of the countries. Continental birds winter, usually near the
east coast.

Black-necked Grebe   B8
Podiceps nigricollis C. L. Brehm 1831
T4 p. 88 and pl. 78 **top right** (summer)
as black-necked or eared grebe, *Podiceps nigricollis*, C. L.
Brehm

Origin doubtless Old World; breeds in temperate and subtropical Europe and central Asia, and western North America
where also reaches boreal zone; outposts in north China,
tropical east Africa, and southern Africa; northerly populations winter some distance south. Has colonised parts of
north-west Europe, including Britain and Ireland in present
century.

Breeding population of Britain (but fifty years old) order
2 presently; the occupation of Ireland lasted from 1915 to
1957 and was based on co. Roscommon, though in its hey-day
the Irish group reached *c* 250 pairs *c* 1930 and spread into
other counties; it was driven out by drainage operations. A
pair had attempted to breed Achill Island, co. Mayo 1906.
In England, and lately Wales, breeding has been very
sporadic though it has taken place in up to a dozen English
counties; its nesting in Scotland has been more stable (though
not more than 20 pairs in two or three main sites) in the
central Highlands. Winter visitor, and passage migrant
through England particularly; rare in Ireland.

Slavonian Grebe   B7
Podiceps auritus (Linnaeus 1758)
T4 p. 87 and pl. 78 **bottom left** (winter and summer)
as Slavonian or horned grebe, *Podiceps auritus* (Linnæus)

Origin clearly holarctic – where breeds virtually throughout
boreal zone, migrating south to nearest suitable estuaries and
coasts in winter.

Breeding population of Britain-Ireland order 2: first
colonised Scotland in 1908 (Inverness co.); spread into
Sutherland and Caithness and has bred in Ross; lately has
bred in Moray and Aberdeen co.; but present population,
with headquarters in Inverness co., probably still under 50
pairs. Stock does not leave the country in winter. Winter
visitor and passage migrant in Britain, very rare in Ireland.

Red-necked Grebe   B6
Podiceps griseigena (Boddaert 1783)
T4 p. 87 and pl. 78 **top left** (summer)
as red-necked grebe, *Podiceps griseigena* (Boddaert)

Origin clearly holarctic; breeds through boreal and north
temperate zones though not in central Siberia and scarcely
in North Atlantic border countries, though migrates to
Atlantic (and Pacific) continental shelves in winter.

Winter visitor, to east England regularly and to Lowlands,
rest of England and Wales more rarely, and rarest in Ireland
and northern Scotland.

Great Crested Grebe   B5
Podiceps cristatus (Linnaeus 1758)
T4 p. 86 and pl. 78 **mid right** (summer)
as great crested grebe, *Podiceps cristatus* (Linnæus)

Origin doubtless Old World, where breeds mainly in temperate and some subtropical zones in Eurasia and North
Africa, in open-country Africa south of the Sahara, and has
outposts in southern Australia and New Zealand; disperses to
neighbouring inshore and sea-shelf waters in winter. Has
expanded into boreal Europe in the present century.

Breeding population of Britian-Ireland order 4; was much
persecuted in the nineteenth century (partly for plume
trade); in 1860 bred only in England when *c* 42 pairs.
Recovered rapidly under protection in last four decades;
census of 1931 found *c* 1150 breeding pairs in England and
Wales, and *c* 80+ (incomplete coverage) in Scotland. British
population in 1965 was 2000+ pairs. In Ireland has increased
and spread well in last fifty years. Has bred in present century
in every English county, most counties of Ireland and Wales,
all of the Lowlands and a number of those in the Highlands.
British-Irish birds winter within the four countries on large
inland waters and sheltered coasts.

Pied-billed Grebe
Podilymbus podiceps (Linnaeus)
Not illustrated

A neotropical-nearctic species distributed from Canada
through the Americas to central Argentina; migratory and
wandering.

Three English records: 1 Blagdon Lake, Somerset 1963
August 17–October 23, reappeared 1966 May 15, July *c* 18–
November 2, 1967 March or April–May; 1 Beaverdyke
Reservoir near Harrogate, Yorkshire 1965 June 9–November
24.

Pl. 78.

Black-necked or Eared Grebe.
Red-necked Grebe.   Great Crested Grebe.
Slavonian or Horned Grebe. (summer & winter)   Little Grebe (summer & winter).

Plate 3 (Thorburn's plate 80)

Order PROCELLARIIFORMES

Family DIOMEDEIDAE, albatrosses

Black-browed Albatross B10
Diomedea melanophris Temminck 1828
T4 p. 98 and pl. 80 **top left**
as black-browed albatross, *Diomedea melanophrys*, Boie

Breeds on islands in the southern hemisphere, the nearest in the South Atlantic being the Falkland archipelago: has a number of vagrant occurrences in the North Atlantic north to Greenland.

Seven records 1897–1967: England 4; Ireland 2; Scotland 1; the first Linton, Cambridgeshire 1897 July 9; in April, July, August, September and October. There are also at least eight records 1894–1966 of unidentified albatrosses which might have been of this species – England 4; Scotland 2; and Ireland 2. The Scottish proved bird joined the gannets on the Bass Rock, East Lothian in 1967 June and was still around later in that summer; other vagrants had previously attached themselves to gannetries in Faeroe and Iceland.

Family PROCELLARIIDAE, petrels and shearwaters

A modern systematic order is B26, 23, 25, 24, 22, 20 (pl. 3), 19, 21 (pl. 4), 16 (pl. 3), 17–18 (pl. 4).

Fulmar B26
Fulmarus glacialis (Linnaeus 1761)
T4 p. 97 and pl. 80 **bottom left**
as fulmar, *Fulmarus glacialis* (Linnæus)

Holarctic; but doubtless of antarctic origin; ancestor of present northern fulmar is probably antarctic fulmar *Fulmarus glacialoides* (A. Smith 1840), to which Pacific race of fulmar seems closer than Atlantic races, which may have arrived and evolved there during the Pleistocene Ice Ages. Pacific race breeds in Kuriles, Komandorski Islands, Aleutians, in the Bering Sea on Hall, St Matthew and the Pribilov Islands, and in the Semidi Islands south of the Alaska Peninsula. Atlantic races' colonies on Smith Island south of Ellesmere Island, Devon and Baffin Islands, west and east Greenland, Jan Mayen, Bear Island, Spitsbergen, Franz Josef Land and William Island off the North Island of Novaya Zemlya are probably the oldest, and from these arctic climes the fulmar has colonised south into the boreal zones; the huge St Kilda colony is probably at least a thousand years old, but those of Iceland, Faeroe, the rest of Britain, Ireland, Norway and France have all been founded in last two hundred years or so and continue to increase and spread. Disperses in winter into full North Atlantic Ocean.

Breeding population of Britain-Ireland order 6; c 130–140,000 pairs 1959. Apart from St Kilda, Britain-Ireland was probably colonised from Faeroe in 1878 (Foula, Shetland), and the old St Kilda colony (now c 38,000 pairs) may not have contributed importantly to the spread, which was probably the consequence of a steady provision of whale offal and then trawler offal by our and others' fishermen. Fulmars first bred in the Outer Hebrides in 1887, Orkney in 1900, on the Highland mainland in 1903, the Irish mainland in 1911, the English mainland in 1922, the Isle of Man in 1936 and Wales in 1940. Ireland and Britain, in 1959, were almost ringed by 487 colonies on islands, cliffs and even inland crags, buildings and ruins, and at 222 other places birds were prospecting colony sites but not proved to lay eggs. Colonisation is slower in the north, now, than in the south, but the population is still increasing at c 3 per cent a year and approximately doubled in each decade of the 1930's and 1940's. The increase is still geometric though it was slower in the 1950's than before. Disperses to open oceans outside breeding season, and to some large distance during it.

Kermadec Petrel B23
Pterodroma neglecta (Schlegel 1863)
T4 p. 96 and pl. 80 **bottom right**
as Schlegel's petrel, *Æstrelata neglecta* (Schlegel)

A South Pacific petrel, breeding from Lord Howe Island, the Kermadecs, the Austral Islands and Tuamotu Archipelago to Juan Fernandez.

One found dead near Tarporley, Cheshire 1908 April 1.

Diablotin or Capped Petrel B25
Pterodroma hasitata (Kuhl 1820)
T4 p. 95 and pl. 80 **top right**
as capped petrel, *Æstrelata hæsitata* (Kuhl)

Formerly bred in the West Indies on Guadeloupe, Dominica, Martinique and Jamaica, where now believed extinct. Surviving breeding-place found in 1963 on Morne la Salle, Haiti.

One caught alive on heath at Southacre, near Swaffham, Norfolk 1850 March or April.

Gould's or Collared Petrel B24
Pterodroma leucoptera (Gould 1844)
T4 p. 95 and pl. 80 **mid**
as collared petrel, *Æstrelata brevipes* (Peale)

Breeds from Australia widely into the Pacific Ocean.

One (of the New Hebrides-Fiji race) shot between Borth and Aberystwyth, Cardigan co. 1889 end November or early December.

Bulwer's Petrel B22
Bulweria bulwerii (Jardine and Selby 1828)
T4 p. 96 and pl. 80 **mid right**
as Bulwer's petrel, *Bulweria bulweri* (Jardine and Selby)

Breeds in the Pacific; and in the North Atlantic in the Cape Verdes, Canaries, Madeira and the Azores.

Three English records of birds found dead, on the River Ure at Tanfield, Yorkshire 1837 May 8; near Beachy Head, Sussex 1903 February 3; and near Scarborough, Yorkshire 1908 February 28; and 1 Irish record, 1 seen off Cape Clear, co. Cork 1965 August 26.

Cory's Shearwater B20
Procellaria diomedea Scopoli 1769
Not illustrated

Breeds on Mediterranean coasts and islands and in Azores, Canaries and Cape Verdes, whence disperses over neighbouring seas, often beyond shelf, reaching southern and western British and Irish coasts more often than has been supposed, and, rarely, Scotland.

Manx Shearwater B16
Puffinus puffinus (Brünnich 1764)
T4 p. 94 and pl. 80 **top mid**
as Manx shearwater, *Puffinus anglorum* (Temminck)

Has a scattered, cosmopolitan breeding distribution mainly on islands in temperate seas, with several races, including one in Mediterranean; some British birds winter off South Atlantic coast of Brazil.

Breeding population of Britain-Ireland probably order 6, on west coast isles of all four countries. In Pembroke co. c 20,000 pairs Skokholm, c 35,000 Skomer, stable or increasing; but some evidence of decline in north Scotland colonies, though that of Rhum is presently vast. There is no recent *proof* of a decline in England (West Country only), or Ireland where the status needs further examination and the largest colony is probably on Puffin Island, co. Kerry where c 10–20,000 pairs 1955. The dark Mediterranean race is fairly regular off the south English and the Irish coasts and may reach eastern England in autumn.

PL. 80.

Black-browed Albatross. (scale ½)   Manx Shearwater.   Capped Petrel.
Collared Petrel.

Fulmar.   Bulwer's Petrel.
                                                        Schlegel's Petrel.

Plate 4 (Thorburn's plate 79)

Family PROCELLARIIDAE, petrels and shearwaters (*continued*)

Great Shearwater   B19
Puffinus gravis (O'Reilly 1818)
T4 p. 93 and pl. 79 **bottom right**
as great shearwater, *Puffinus gravis*, O'Reilly

Breeds on Tristan da Cunha in South Atlantic, whence a 'winter' visitor in our summer and autumn to all western coasts, much more rarely in the North Sea.

Sooty Shearwater   B21
Puffinus griseus (J. F. Gmelin 1789)
T4 p. 93 and pl. 79 **lower mid right**
as sooty shearwater, *Puffinus griseus* (J. F. Gmelin)

Breeds in New Zealand, Tasmania, Tierra del Fuego and Cape Horn islands, the Falklands and islands of south Chile, whence a 'winter' visitor in our autumn off most British and Irish coasts.

Little Shearwater   B17 and B18
Puffinus assimilis Gould 1838
T4 p. 94 and pl. 79 **bottom left**
as little dusky shearwater, *Puffinus assimilis*, Gould

Breeds in the Atlantic, Pacific and Indian Oceans.
    Twelve records. The race *Puffinus assimilis baroli* (Bonaparte 1857) of Madeira, the Canaries and the Azores has been recorded 1853–1965 10 times; in England 6; Wales 1; Ireland 3; the first off Bull Rock, co. Cork 1853 May 6, in April–May (6) and August–October. The race *Puffinus assimilis lherminieri* Lesson 1839, of Bermuda and the West Indies, has been found (alive) once, at Galley Hill, Bexhill, Sussex 1936 January 7. At least 2 birds of undetermined race were seen at Cape Clear, co. Cork 1965 September 5. The Welsh and two Irish records referred to *Puffinus assimilis baroli* above were sight and not specimen records.

Family HYDROBATIDAE, storm petrels

Wilson's Storm Petrel   B11
Oceanites oceanicus (Kuhl 1820)
T4 p. 91 and pl. 79 **lower mid left**
as Wilson's petrel, *Oceanites oceanicus* (Kuhl)

Breeds on the Antarctic continent and islands; winters into the North Atlantic, particularly on the western side.
    At least eleven records 1838–1914: the first found dead near Polperro, Cornwall 1838 November; England 8; Scotland 1; Ireland 2; all October–December.

Frigate Petrel or **White-faced Storm Petrel**   B15
Pelagodroma marina (Latham 1790)
T4 p. 91 and pl. 79 **upper mid left**
as frigate-petrel, *Pelagodroma marina* (Latham)

Breeds in the Pacific, Indian and Atlantic Oceans, in the last on Tristan da Cunha and Gough Island, the Cape Verdes and on the Salvages south of Madeira. Two records: 1 found dead Walney, Lancashire 1890 November; young female caught alive Colonsay, Inner Hebrides 1897 January 1.

British Storm Petrel   B14
Hydrobates pelagicus (Linnaeus 1758)
T4 p. 89 and pl. 79 **top left**
as storm-petrel, *Procellaria pelagica*, Linnæus

Breeds only in south Iceland, Faeroe, Britain, Ireland, Atlantic coast of Europe and western Mediterranean; dispersive in Mediterranean, but rest of population winters some distance south in open ocean, and some elements may reach the subantarctic South Atlantic.
    Breeding population of Britain-Ireland possibly order 6, though census very difficult. All headquarters are on west coasts including Pembroke co., with big colonies in Scilly, the western and northern isles; it appears to be decreasing in the south, including islands of Ireland. Probably a number of colonies remain to be discovered. Disperses widely to open ocean outside breeding season.

Leach's Storm Petrel   B12
Oceanodroma leucorhoa (Vieillot 1817)
T4 p. 90 and pl. 79 **top right**
as Leach's fork-tailed petrel, *Oceanodroma leucorrhoa* (Vieillot)

Origin probably in North Pacific; the quite heavy breeding populations of the Newfoundland neighbourhood and smallish groups of south Iceland–Faeroe–Scotland may well have arrived in Pleistocene Ice Age times; has lately (since 1930's) colonised or recolonised Faeroe, and recolonised Shetland where it was eaten by Vikings a thousand years ago.
    Breeding population (Scotland only) certainly order 4, based mainly on St Kilda, the Flannans (lately spreading), Sula Sgeir and North Rona (a recent rapid increase) with outposts (possibly sporadic) rather lately discovered in Foula (Shetland) and at least two other Outer Hebridean islands. In Ireland breeding was proved on Kerry islands in 1886–89 and on Mayo islands in 1899–1906 and suspected on another Mayo island in 1946–47 and another Kerry island in 1965; but these occurrences may have been sporadic. Disperses into open ocean outside the breeding season, sometimes reaching the equator.

Madeiran Storm Petrel   B13
Oceanodroma castro (Harcourt 1851)
T4 p. 90 and pl. 79 **upper mid right**
as Madeiran fork-tailed petrel, *Oceanodroma castro* (Harcourt)

Breeds in the Pacific and the Atlantic, in the latter on Ascension, St Helena, the Cape Verdes, Madeira and the Azores. Two records: 1 picked up dead Milford, Hampshire 1911 November 19; 1 at Blackrock Light, off co. Mayo 1931 October 18.

Pl. 79.

Storm-Petrel.   Leach's Fork-tailed Petrel.
Frigate-Petrel.   Madeiran Fork-tailed Petrel.
Wilson's Petrel.   Sooty Shearwater.
Little Dusky Shearwater.   Great Shearwater.

Plate 5 (Thorburn's plate 39)

Order PELECANIFORMES

Family SULIDAE, gannets and boobies

Gannet   B27
Sula bassana (Linnaeus 1758)
T2 p. 69 and pl. 39 **top** (adults and young)
as gannet, *Sula bassana* (Linnæus)

Has (in the broad sense) what may be a relict cosmopolitan distribution, with subspecies or closely related species in South Africa, Tasmania and Bass Strait islands, and New Zealand. The North Atlantic gannet has presently 30 colonies in Québec, Newfoundland, Iceland, Faeroe, Britain, Ireland, Norway, the Channel Islands and France, with a breeding population in the early 1960's probably between 130,000 and 150,000 occupied nests. The bird is dispersive along the sea-shelf, the juveniles migrating further south than the adults, from Europe into the Mediterranean and some distance down the north-west African coast.

In the early 1960's between 90,000 and 110,000 nests were occupied at the British-Irish colonies: in England, Bempton in Yorkshire (the only mainland site); in Wales, Grassholm in Pembroke co. (15,500 in 1964); in Scotland the Scaur Rocks, Wigtown co.; Ailsa Craig, Ayr co. (11,700 in 1963); the Bass Rock, East Lothian (evidently known as a gannetry from the late seventh century, *c* 7,500 in 1966); St Kilda (*c* 30,000–45,000 in 1959) and Sula Sgeir (*c* 5,000 in 1965) in the Outer Hebrides; Sule Stack, Orkney (*c* 2800 in 1960); Noss and Herma Ness in Shetland (each *c* 4000–5000 in 1965); in Ireland the Little Skellig, co. Kerry (*c* 17,700 1966): the Bull Rock, co. Cork and Great Saltee, co. Wexford. Britain and Ireland certainly house over two-thirds of the world's breeding gannets, whose population has roughly doubled since it reached its lowest *c* 1890 as the consequence of human persecution and exploitation on both sides of the Atlantic. The controlled taking of young on Sula Sgeir (a very ancient custom) is permitted by law; elsewhere in Britain (and indeed, now, throughout its range, with some legal fowling permission also in Iceland and Faeroe) the gannet enjoys lawful protection.

Family PHALACROCORACIDAE, cormorants

Cormorant   B28
Phalacrocorax carbo (Linnaeus 1758)
T2 p. 68 and pl. 39 **bottom left** (young and adult)
as common cormorant, *Phalacrocorax carbo* (Linnæus)

Origin doubtless Old World; has a coastal, and a scattered but substantial inland distribution, in Eurasia (including the oriental region), Africa, Australia and New Zealand, ranging from the tropics to some boreal and even tundra zones, and with outposts (probably Pleistocene) in west Greenland and the Gulf of St Lawrence neighbourhood of eastern North America; northern coastal populations winter south, rest are dispersive, on sea-shelves.

Breeding population of Britain-Ireland order 4; breeds in well-knit social colonies on cliffs and sea-islands, and still in places inland in Wales, Scotland and Ireland, though no longer inland in England. Was heavily persecuted and reduced in the last century, and though decreasing in some north and south areas, including Ireland, is increasing on the east coast from the Firth of Forth to the Farne Islands in Northumberland, south of which it has recolonised in Yorkshire but breeds no further south in eastern England, and no longer on Channel coast east of Isle of Wight.

Adults do not disperse far outside the breeding season; but the young show a significant autumn movement to the south-west.

Shag   B29
Phalacrocorax aristotelis (Linnaeus 1761)
T2 p. 69 and pl. 39 **bottom right** (young and adult)
as shag, or green cormorant, *Phalacrocorax graculus* (Linnæus)

Origin doubtless in the eastern North Atlantic; breeds on coasts of western Europe, Mediterranean and palearctic north-west Africa north to Iceland, Faeroe, northernmost Norway and Kola: northern populations winter south, rest are dispersive, on sea-shelves.

Breeding population of Britain-Ireland order 5; breeds in all four countries where, after the almost axiomatic nineteenth-century decline it has in the last decades entered a period of steady increase and colonisation at least in Britain, especially noticeable in the Firth of Forth and north-east England, but also marked in parts of the Irish Sea. Most shags winter near their breeding grounds, but some disperse.

Family FREGATIDAE, frigate birds

Magnificent Frigate Bird
Fregata magnificens Mathews 1914
Not illustrated

Breeds in the Pacific and the Atlantic, in the latter in the Cape Verdes, on islands off Brazil, Venezuela, Nicaragua and México and in the Antillean West Indies from Tobago to the Bahamas.

One record: an immature female found exhausted on Tiree, Inner Hebrides 1953 July 9. Three unidentified frigate birds, most probably of this species, have been seen off Forve, Aberdeen co. 1960 August 30; at the Calf of Man 1963 September 28; and off Hauxley, Northumberland 1965 September 19.

Gannet. (adults & young).

Cormorant. (adult & young).

Shag. (adult & young).

Plate 6 (Thorburn's plate 40)

Order CICONIIFORMES

Family ARDEIDAE, herons

A modern systematic order is B38, 39, 37, 36, 34 (pl. 7), 35, 33, 32, 30, 31 (pl. 6).

Purple Heron   B31
Ardea purpurea Linnaeus 1766
T2 p. 71 and pl. 40 **top right**
as purple heron, *Ardea purpurea*, Linnæus

Origin possibly oriental; now distributed in temperate-tropical zones through most of the oriental region, the western European and North African palearctic (where evidently relict but lately recovering), the west-central and far eastern palearctic (not Japan), and much of Africa south of the equator, including Madagascar; only northerly elements appear to be migratory.

An annual vagrant, least often in the winter, to eastern England particularly, Wales, Scotland and Ireland rarely.

Heron   B30
Ardea cinerea Linnaeus 1758
T2 p. 70 and pl. 40 **bottom left**
as common heron, *Ardea cinerea* (Linnæus)

Origin probably palearctic; in which region very widespread, into boreal zone, and presently spreading north-west in Europe; widespread also in most of the oriental region; in the ethiopian region has a curiously patchy and apparently relict distribution. In Europe range is rather fragmented in south-west with groups in Iberian Peninsula on Guadalquivir and Douro, in south France, Majorca, Corsica and north Italy, but more continuous from central France, north edge of Alps and Balkans north to Ireland, Britain, west coastal Norway and the Oslo area, south Sweden, southernmost Finland and Lake Ladoga; only the more northerly birds are migratory.

Breeding population of Britain-Ireland order 4; nests in all but 9 counties of the four countries, with a rather stable population since the first census year of 1928 fluctuating (mainly as a consequence of hard winters) around a mean between over 3000 and under 8000 nests; a decline in the south Highlands, Lowlands and northern England may be partly due to illegal persecution by anglers. Our native stock sedentary; continental birds visit regularly for winter and on passage.

Little Egret   B32
Egretta garzetta (Linnaeus 1766)
T2 p. 72 and pl. 40 **mid left**
as little egret, *Ardea garzetta*, Linnæus

An Old World distribution, temperate to tropical, obviously of a relict type in Africa, where very scattered, and Europe, where now mainly confined to Mediterranean, Danubian and Black Sea wetlands; widespread in western Asian palearctic, the oriental region and Papuan islands; extends to northern and eastern Australia.

An annual summer vagrant to England, rarer in Wales, Scotland and Ireland.

Great Egret   B33
Egretta alba (Linnaeus 1758)
T2 p. 71 and pl. 40 **bottom right**
as great white heron, *Ardea alba*, Linnæus

A cosmopolitan warm temperate-tropical species, found in such zones (though often in a local, scattered pattern) in all major continents, though in Europe now practically reduced to the Danubian system.

Ten records 1821–1951; England 8; Scotland 2; the first Hornsea Mere, Yorkshire 1821 winter; most of the rest May–October.

Cattle Egret   B35
Ardeola ibis (Linnaeus 1758)
T2 p. 72 and pl. 40 **top left**
as buff-backed heron, *Ardea bubulcus*, Audouin

Origin African or Indian; with a wide distribution in Africa outside deserts and the more massive tropical forests, and in the oriental region, and with outposts round the western Mediterranean, Mesopotamian and south-eastern palearctic. Colonised northern South America in *c* 1911 and since then Central America, the West Indies and eastern North America; and has also lately colonised northern Australia, possibly after introduction; outside breeding season tends to be a dispersive migrant, a habit doubtless connected with its evident talent for rapid colonisation.

Four records (others may have escaped from captivity): immature female near Kingsbridge, Devon 1805 October; male shot Breydon Marshes, Norfolk 1917 October 23; 4 seen just north of Pagham Harbour, Sussex 1962 April 27 (1 seen again April 29); and 1 seen Lancing, Sussex 1962 April 28.

Pl. 40.

Buff-backed Heron.

Little Egret.

Purple Heron.

Common Heron.

Great White Heron.

Plate 7 (Thorburn's plate 41)

Family ARDEIDAE, herons (*continued*)

Squacco Heron   B34
Ardeola ralloides (Scopoli 1769)
T3 p. 1 and pl. 41 **mid right**
as squacco heron, *Ardea ralloides*, Scopoli

Origin doubtless ethiopian, with a wide distribution in non-desert Africa and a (now decreasing) range in Europe mainly round the Mediterranean and Black Seas, extending east into western Asia; the European element winters in tropical Africa.

A rare vagrant, chiefly to southern England, has been recorded in Wales, Scotland and Ireland.

Night Heron   B36
Nycticorax nycticorax (Linnaeus 1758)
T3 p. 3 and pl. 41 **top right**
as night heron, *Nycticorax griseus* (Linnæus)

A cosmopolitan, with a wide distribution from temperate to tropical zones over the world, though rather scattered in Africa and absent from Papua, Australia and New Zealand; European breeders winter in tropical Africa.

An annual passage vagrant to England, chiefly in the south and east; rare in Wales, Scotland and Ireland.

Little Bittern   B37
Ixobrychus minutus (Linnaeus 1766)
T3 p. 4 and pl. 41 **mid right left** (♂)
as little bittern, *Ardetta minuta* (Linnæus)

An Old World species of the palearctic wetlands of Europe and western Asia, Africa, and coastal zones of Australia, ranging from tropical forest to boreal areas; the palearctic element winters in tropical Africa.

Never formally proved to have bred in Britain, this bird probably did so sporadically in eastern England in the nineteenth century and in southern England in 1947 and perhaps also in 1956. Possibly England may be due for a further colonisation as part of the now clear process of invasion of our protected wetlands by several species which breed (as the little bittern does) in the wetlands of Holland and the Rhine system. Otherwise an annual passage vagrant to England, particularly in the south and east, rarer in Wales and rarer still in Scotland and Ireland.

American Bittern   B39
Botaurus lentiginosus (Rackett 1813)
T3 p. 7 and pl. 41 **bottom right**
as American bittern, *Botaurus lentiginosus*, Montagu

Breeds from Canada south to the southern United States; a rare vagrant to England, Wales, Scotland and Ireland, most often to south England and Ireland.

Bittern   B38
Botaurus stellaris (Linnaeus 1758)
T3 p. 5 and pl. 41 **bottom left** (2 birds)
as common bittern, *Botaurus stellaris* (Linnæus)

Origin doubtless palearctic, in which region occupies most of the temperate zone and some southern boreal areas; an outpost in southern Africa. The western palearctic population winters round the Mediterranean and in tropical Africa south of the Sahara.

Breeding population (England only) order 2; became extinct in *c* 1886 as a consequence of persecution and wetland drainage, recolonised East Anglia in 1911 and slowly re-established a stock in protected marshes. Since the 1940's has expanded from Norfolk–Suffolk, has bred in 9 counties, and now has a stable colony in the Lancashire R.S.P.B. sanctuary of Leighton Moss. Winter visitor also to England and Wales, less often to Scotland and Ireland, wanders far in hard winters.

Family THRESKIORNITHIDAE, ibises and spoonbills

In a modern systematic order this could follow the next family.

Glossy Ibis   B43
Plegadis falcinellus (Linnaeus 1766)
T3 p. 10 and pl. 41 **top left**
as glossy ibis, *Plegadis falcinellus*, Linnæus

Origin doubtless Old World; a breeding range through the temperate-tropical western palearctic, ethiopian and oriental regions and eastern Australia, very spotty, and obviously relict, on the 1960 map of Dr K. H. Voous, who believes that the breeding population of the West Indies and south-eastern United States may possibly have been derived from a trans-atlantic flight earlier than, and similar to that of the cattle egret, whose wandering dispersive habits are shared by the glossy ibis. In western Europe regular breeding is now virtually confined to the Po valley in Italy and the Danubian system.

An irregular autumn passage visitor to England and Ireland; rare in Wales and Scotland.

Pl. 41.

Glossy Ibis.
Common Bittern.

Night Heron.
Little Bittern.   Squacco Heron.
American Bittern.

Plate 8 (Thorburn's plate 42)

Family THRESKIORNITHIDAE, ibises and spoonbills (*continued*)

Spoonbill   B42
Platalea leucorodia Linnaeus 1758
T3 p. 12 and pl. 42 **top left**
as spoonbill, *Platalea leucorodia*, Linnæus

Origin probably palearctic; breeds in the oriental region only in India and Ceylon, and in Africa only on islands off Mauretania, the southern Red Sea and Somaliland. In the palearctic the regular breeding range is scattered within the broad temperate zone, and in western Europe presently confined to two neighbouring areas of south Spain, the delta of the Rhine in the Netherlands, and the Danubian and some other Black Sea river systems.

Bred in England and Wales to the eighteenth century; now a non-breeding visitor, often in summer, to south and sometimes east England; rare in Wales, Scotland and Ireland.

Family CICONIIDAE, storks

In a modern systematic order this could precede the previous family.

White Stork   B40
Ciconia ciconia (Linnaeus 1758)
T3 p. 8 and pl. 42 **bottom left**
as white stork, *Ciconia alba*, Bechstein

Origin doubtless palearctic; breeding range, which just extends from the temperate into the boreal zone in Europe, is confined to the palearctic, including Morocco and Tunisia, and extends east from Europe through Asia Minor; an outpost race breeds in Turkestanian Russia and (sometimes) China. The European population has lately fluctuated and generally declined, and the species is now extinct as a breeder in Switzerland and Italy and virtually so in Sweden and France. Nearly the whole population winters in South Africa.

Nested in Scotland in the fifteenth century; now a rare vagrant, most often to south and east England; recorded from Wales, Scotland and Ireland.

Black Stork   B41
Ciconia nigra (Linnaeus 1758)
T3 p. 9 and pl. 42 **bottom right**
as black stork, *Ciconia nigra*, Linnæus

Origin doubtless palearctic; has evidently colonised a few wintering grounds in Africa south of the Sahara, as a breeder, only in present century. Has, or had, a wide summer distribution throughout the continental palearctic into the southern boreal zone, but the breeding range in most westerly Europe is now clearly of relict type and confined to parts of Spain and Portugal. In the last hundred years it has become extinct in nearly all western Germany, and since 1940 also in Denmark and Sweden. The European birds winter in Africa south of the Sahara.

A rare vagrant to England, most often in the summer; 1 Scottish record.

Order PHOENICOPTERIFORMES

Family PHOENICOPTERIDAE, flamingos

Greater Flamingo   B44
Phoenicopterus ruber Linnaeus 1758
T3 p. 13 and pl. 42 **top right**
as flamingo, *Phoenicopterus roseus*, Pallas

A relict distribution: the New World race breeds now only in the West Indies, Venezuela, Yucatán and the Galápagos Islands; the Old World race has very isolated colonies (probably about a score in all) in central Russia, Persia, Afghanistan, north-west India, north-west Africa, Kenya and South Africa. Only two colonies survive in Europe, of which that in the marismas of the Guadalquivir in southern Spain breeds only sporadically, and the famous Camargue colony in the delta of the Rhône in southern France regularly. Movements from the breeding stations are dispersive and irregular.

A rare vagrant to England and Wales; has been recorded in Scotland and Ireland.

Spoonbill.
    White Stork.

Flamingo.
    Black Stork.

Pl. 42.

Plate 9 (Thorburn's plate 45)

Order ANSERIFORMES

Family ANATIDAE, wildfowl

A modern systematic order for the ducks on Plates 12–17 is B74, 73, mandarin duck, 45, black duck (pl. 12), 46, Baikal teal (pl. 13), 49 (pl. 12), 50, 51 (pl. 14), 52 (pl. 13), 47 (pl. 14), 48, 53 (pl. 13), 54, 57 (pl. 14), 58, ring-necked duck, 56, 55 (pl. 15), 67, 68 (pl. 16), 66 (pl. 17), 65 (pl. 16), 61 (pl. 15), 62, 63, 64 (pl. 17), 60, Barrow's Goldeneye, 59 (pl. 15).

Mute Swan   B84
Cygnus olor (J. F. Gmelin 1789)
T3 p. 26 and pl. 45 **bottom** (♀ and young)
as mute swan, *Cygnus olor* (J. F. Gmelin)

Origin doubtless palearctic; with a clearly relict distribution, outside Europe now possibly only in Afghanistan; from north Persia along the rivermouths west of the Caspian, and east into central Siberia; in the rivermouths of the Aral Sea; in Transbaicalia; and in Ussuriland. In Europe colonies persist in northern Black Sea rivermouth systems, notably the Danube delta; but the surviving strongholds are in the western Baltic area in south Sweden and from Estonia to Denmark, and – greatest of all – in Britain and Ireland. Introduced feral groups breed elsewhere in Europe and now in the eastern United States, Australia and New Zealand.

Fossil evidence proves the mute swan to be a fully native resident bird and not, as often pronounced, a feral introduction. Breeding population of Britain-Ireland order 4; 1955–56 census established *c* 4000 breeding pairs in Britain (not Ireland). The population has generally increased during the present century, and it now nests in virtually every Irish and British county except Shetland (where a few introduced pairs have bred) and north-west Sutherland.

Whooper Swan   B85
Cygnus cygnus (Linnaeus 1758)
T3 p. 24 and pl. 45 **top right** (and flock behind)
as whooper swan, *Cygnus musicus*, Bechstein

Origin doubtless palearctic, though closely related to the trumpeter swan, *Cygnus buccinator* Richardson 1832, of North America. As a regular breeder now virtually confined to the boreal and southern tundra zone from Norwegian Lapland to Sakhalin and Kamchatka, and to Iceland. Winters south, along coast and inland, but not normally beyond the palearctic region.

Bred in Highland Scotland (earliest record Sutherland 1651), in Orkney, Caithness and Ross perhaps not after eighteenth century; latest records seem to be Shetland (pricked birds) 1910–18, Perth co. 1919–21, west Highlands 1921, Inverness co. 1939, all obviously sporadic. Winter visitor (many from Iceland) to regular haunts in England, Wales, Ireland and Scotland, least commonly in the south and most in the Outer Hebrides.

Whistling and Bewick's Swans   B86
Cygnus columbianus (Ord 1815)
Whistling swan, *Cygnus columbianus columbianus*

The North American black-billed counterpart of Bewick's swan, reported several times in Britain, but doubtless escaped from captivity or wrongly identified.

Bewick's swan, *Cygnus columbianus bewickii* Yarrell 1830
T3 p. 25 and pl. 45 **top left**
as Bewick's swan, *Cygnus bewicki*, Yarrell

Some authorities regard Bewick's swan as a full species, and not a race of the whistling swan. Both forms have a mainly tundra breeding distribution, the whistler in the lower river systems of the Bering Sea and Arctic Ocean from the Alaska Peninsula to Hudson Bay, and on some neighbouring islands from St Lawrence to Baffin; and Bewick's in the summer wet-lands from the Murmansk Peninsula along the Russian Arctic Ocean to beyond the Kolyma, and on the islands of Kolguev, south Novaya Zemlya and Vaigach. Bewick's swan migrates south, but not beyond the palearctic; many of the western breeding elements fly to Holland and Britain.

Winter visitor to England, especially in a belt from the Fen country to the Severn, to Wales and south-west Ireland, rarer elsewhere and in Scotland.

Pl. 45.

Bewick's Swan.   Whooper Swan.

Mute Swan (adult & young).

Plate 10 (Thorburn's plate 43)

Family ANATIDAE, wildfowl (*continued*)

Grey Lag Goose B75
Anser anser (Linnaeus 1758)
T2 p. 14 and pl. 43 **top right**
as grey-lag goose, *Anser cinereus*, Meyer

Origin doubtless palearctic, and confined to this region, breeding north to the boreal zone, and beyond it in Iceland. Breeding distribution is now relict in Europe and west Asia, though the Siberian race has a fairly continuous distribution through Siberia and north China, with outposts surviving in Persia, Iraq and Afghanistan. The European race now has headquarters of wild (not feral) breeding birds only in Iceland, Scotland, the Norwegian and most of the Baltic coastal areas, Denmark, northern Germany, most Black Sea river systems including the Danube, northern Greece and possibly Asia Minor. Formerly the species bred over virtually all Europe and into Algeria. Grey-lags mostly winter south of their summer range, leaving Iceland and other subarctic zones altogether, but not beyond the palearctic region.

Breeding population (now only truly wild in Scotland) order 3; wild stock became extinct in Ireland (last Leinster and co. Down) in eighteenth century and in the English fens (last possibly Deeping Fen, Lincolnshire) *c* 1831. There is no evidence that it bred in Wales. During the nineteenth century and into the twentieth it withdrew under human pressure to north Scotland so rapidly that by 1956 the wild stock was estimated at but *c* 175 pairs, mostly in the Outer Hebrides, where South Uist is its headquarters. Since then the situation has improved, and the native wild stock is slowly recovering in the Outer Hebrides, on islands off Wester Ross and in Sutherland and Caithness. Feral introductions have supported some of these populations, and have established free breeding groups lately in Galloway, the English Lakes and some other areas.

Winter visitor (many from Iceland) mainly to Scotland; also to north-west England, Wales and eastern Ireland; rare elsewhere. The winter population is probably between 10,000 and 20,000.

White-fronted Goose B76
Anser albifrons (Scopoli 1769)
T3 p. 16 and pl. 43 **top left**
as white-fronted goose, *Anser albifrons* (Scopoli)

An holarctic bird, breeding in the tundra zone inland to, and in places into the boreal zone all round the Arctic Ocean and the northern part of the Bering Sea from the Kanin Peninsula in European Siberian Russia eastabout to north-east Keewatin, Canada, and on a few neighbouring islands, with an outpost race in west Greenland. Migrates in winter mostly to central and southern palearctic, but occasionally beyond it to México, West Indies, northern India and Burma; Irish winterers mostly of west Greenland race, British winterers of west Russian race.

Some Greenland birds winter in western Scotland and Wales, many Russian birds in the Severn, Norfolk, Solway, north Argyll and the Hebrides. In recent years the wintering Greenland population has been of the order of 20,000, the Russian birds' population between 4000 and 8000.

Lesser White-fronted Goose B77
Anser erythropus (Linnaeus 1758)
Not illustrated

Origin doubtless palearctic; breeds in high boreal and low tundra zones mostly in hills, from Norwegian Lapland through Siberia to Anadyr. Normally winters in the palearctic region east of Hungary, and in oriental region in northern India and China.

An annual vagrant since 1945, usually caught up in whitefront packs, to Severn, and sometimes Norfolk and Kirkcudbright st.; has been recorded in Wales.

Bean Goose and **Pink-footed Goose** B78
Anser fabalis (Latham 1787)
Bean goose, *Anser fabalis fabalis*
T3 p. 17 and pl. 43 **bottom right**
as bean-goose, *Anser segetum*, J. F. Gmelin

Species' origin is doubtless palearctic; the five races of the Continent ('bean geese') breed in the tundra and taiga zones broadly from northern Scandinavia to Siberian Amur and Anadyr, and winter south within the palearctic region, the typical race named above in Europe.

Pink-footed goose, *Anser fabalis brachyrhynchus* Baillon 1833
T3 p. 18 and pl. 43 **bottom left**
as pink-footed goose, *Anser brachyrhynchus*, Baillon

This well-marked race breeds only in east Greenland and central Iceland (whose populations winter almost entirely in Britain) and Spitsbergen (whose population winters almost entirely near the continental North Sea coast south of Denmark).

The bean goose winters mainly in Solway, Northumberland and Norfolk, is rare in Wales and Ireland. Pink-feet have their main grounds in Inner Hebrides, eastern Scotland, Clyde, Solway, and their big headquarters in Humber–Wash England. Few winter in Wales and fewer in Ireland. The population after productive breeding seasons in Iceland may exceed 60,000 birds.

Pl. 43.

White-fronted Goose.   Grey Lag-Goose.
Pink-footed Goose.   Bean-Goose.

Plate 11 (Thorburn's plate 44)

Family ANATIDAE, wildfowl (*continued*)

Snow Goose   B79
Anser caerulescens (Linnaeus 1758)
T3 p. 19 and pl. 44 **bottom right**
as snow-goose, *Chen hyperboreus*, Pallas

Origin doubtless nearctic; breeds along the tundra zone of
the arctic shore from easternmost Siberia (perhaps now only
Wrangel Island) through the American arctic to Hudson
Bay (including most of the Franklin Archipelago) and north-
west Greenland. Western (not north Franklin and Greenland)
population has both white and 'blue' colour phases. Normally
winters near Asian and American coasts, occasionally just
beyond nearctic region.

Rare vagrant to England, Scotland and Ireland, with a
small minority of 'blues'.

Canada Goose   B82
Branta canadensis (Linnaeus 1758)
Not illustrated

A primarily nearctic species breeding north into the tundra
zone, from the Siberian Komandorski Islands through
Mackenzie, Keewatin and Franklin to Labrador and Newfoundland, south to a California-New England line in the
United States.

Birds of the race *Branta canadensis canadensis* (Baffin Island to
New England) formed the basis of the British avicultural stock,
present from 1671 or before. The date at which a fully feral
state could be agreed is lost in history. Breeding population
of Britain-Ireland now order 3 or low order 4; national census
of 1953 showed *c* 3000 adults and young, since when there
has been a considerable increase in the main headquarters in
Norfolk, which was pushing 2000 birds in the early 1960's.
The main range of this sedentary feral is from Berkshire and
Norfolk through central England into Dumfries co., with
principal outliers, some recently established, in the Forth–Tay
area, in Wales, Devon and northern Ireland.

Barnacle Goose   B81
Branta leucopsis (Bechstein 1803)
T3 p. 21 and pl. 44 **top right**
as barnacle goose, *Bernicla leucopsis*, Bechstein

Western palearctic; breeds in east Greenland, Spitsbergen and
south Novaya Zemlya; winters in Ireland, Scotland and the
North Sea coast from Denmark to France.

Main winter haunts are on coasts of Hebrides and west
Highlands, north-west Ireland and inland in co. Wexford,
irregular in England and rare in Wales.

Red-breasted Goose   B83
Branta ruficollis (Pallas 1769)
T3 p. 20 and pl. 44 **bottom left**
as red-breasted goose, *Bernicla ruficollis*, Pallas

Central palearctic; breeds in tundra and taiga in west Siberia
from Yamal to Taimyr; normally winters on the south shore
of the Caspian Sea, occasionally in Iraq and Hungary.

Twenty records 1776–1963: England 17; Wales 1; Scotland
2; the first in London in severe frost 1776 January; all
October–March (7 in January).

Brent Goose   B80
Branta bernicla (Linnaeus 1758)
T3 p. 22 and pl. 44 **top left**
as brent goose, *Bernicla brenta*, Pallas

Holarctic; breeds on the mainland tundra coast from the
Chukotski Peninsula in Siberia east to north-east Keewatin in
Canada, on the northern coasts of Greenland, and on the
coasts of Spitsbergen and all the principal arctic islands of
Canada and Russia except (probably) Novaya Zemlya.
Winters on the Pacific and Atlantic palearctic coasts.

Winter population has declined since 1930 and is doubtless
under 10,000 birds; headquarters are the coasts of Ireland,
the Clyde, the Moray Firth and the North Sea and Channel
coast of England; the goose has been recorded from Wales.

Pl. 44.

Brent Goose.
Red-breasted Goose.

Bernacle Goose.
Snow-Goose.

Plate 12 (Thorburn's plate 46)

Family ANATIDAE, wildfowl (*continued*)

Ruddy Shelduck   B74
Tadorna ferruginea (Pallas 1764)
T3 p. 28 and pl. 46 **bottom left**
as ruddy sheld-duck, *Tadorna casarca* (Linnæus)

Origin doubtless palearctic; breeds by the waters of the drier southern palearctic regions as far east as central China and Manchuria. Western range seems to be of relict type, with limited outposts only in Tunisia, Morocco and the marismas of the Guadalquivir, Spain. Breeds otherwise in Europe now only in Greece and round Black Sea. Migrates to borders of Sahara and in Asia into oriental India and southern China; some elements wander in a dispersive way.

Rare vagrant to England, Wales, Ireland and Scotland; the records are often confused by 'escapes'.

Shelduck   B73
Tadorna tadorna (Linnaeus 1758)
T3 p. 27 and pl. 46 **bottom right**
as common sheld-duck, *Tadorna cornuta* (S. G. Gmelin)

Origin possibly the Black-Caspian-Aral Seas region; breeding distribution virtually entirely palearctic, and discontinuous, though probably *not* as the result of man's historical interference. The Asian range is fairly continuous from Iraq and Caspian through waters of drier southern palearctic Afghanistan, Persia, steppe Russia and north-west China to western Manchuria. European range fragmented: rivermouths of north and west Black Sea; one place in the Hungarian plain (the only truly inland site in Europe); the south coast of France from the Camargue west (has been reported breeding Tunisia, Algeria, Sardinia); and the coasts of Ireland, Britain, the continental North Sea from north France to beyond the arctic circle in Norway, the western Baltic and islands in the central Baltic. Most birds only have 'moult-migrations', to favoured areas; but some elements move south, just into the oriental region in India and south China, but not beyond palearctic Africa in the west.

Breeding population of Britain-Ireland order 5 (*c* 50,000 adult birds); after a nineteenth-century decrease in places, has been steadily increasing in the present century and now occupies virtually the whole coast of the four countries and has been breeding inland in many areas, decreasing only in those of habitat disturbance. Main moult-migrations in August are to Bridgwater Bay, Somerset and across the sea to the Knechtsand area of the Heligoland Bight.

Mandarin Duck
Aix galericulata (Linnaeus 1758)
Not illustrated

The native range of this sedentary duck is palearctic – Amurland and Ussuriland in far eastern Russia, Manchuria, northern China, Japan and Okinawa.

In British aviculture since 1745 or before, it first became a feral breeder to an important extent round Virginia Water, on the Surrey-Berkshire border, in 1929 or 1930. By 1950 the ducks had spread south to Bagshot Park in Surrey and west into Berkshire towards Reading, and by the New Year of 1951 the 'Virginia Water' group (the most highly feral) was *c* 400 birds. At that time about 100 were also free-winged and breeding at Woburn, Bedfordshire (where stock had been so since early in this century); an unknown number round Walcot, Shropshire, where a free-winged colony was started

in 1935, presumed elements of which had reached north Wales and Lancashire by 1944; and some free-winged at Slimbridge, Gloucestershire. A tame mandarin was encountered as far afield as Foula, Shetland 1942 June 15–16. Doubtless the British-Irish List will shortly admit this species as an established feral member of our bird fauna.

Mallard   B45
Anas platyrhynchos Linnaeus 1758
T2 pl. 37 (here pl. 27) **bottom** (♂)
as prey of gyrfalcon
T3 p. 29 and pl. 46 **top left** (♀ ♂)
as mallard, *Anas boscas*, Linnæus

Origin doubtless holarctic; virtually confined to this region, as a breeder north to the edge of the tundra zone and throughout except in parts of southern palearctic Asia and the easternmost part of North America (but breeds Greenland). Most elements do not migrate far, but some winter beyond the palearctic in México and oriental Asia.

Breeding population of Britain-Ireland order 6; nests in every county, with a population that has been generally stable for the last two decades. In winter this does not emigrate, and is strengthened by visitors (to south-east England especially) from Scandinavia.

Black Duck
Anas rubripes Brewster 1902
Not illustrated

Breeds in eastern North America from Manitoba-Newfoundland to Virginia and North Carolina.

Three records: adult male shot (from 2 birds) Listrolin, near Mullinavat, co. Kilkenny 1954 February (a few days before February 5); 1 North Slob, co. Wexford 1961 February 18–21; female shot Mayglass near Bridgetown, co. Wexford 1966 November 27.

Gadwall   B49
Anas strepera Linnaeus 1758
T3 p. 31 and pl. 46 **top right** (♂ ♀)
as gadwall, *Anas strepera*, Linnæus

An holarctic breeder, in North America largely in the prairie and areas west of it, in Eurasia mainly in drier zones, extending into the boreal zones, east to central Asia and in very scattered localities further east as far as north China and possibly Kamchatka. Its European distribution is very fragmented outside the Danubian, German, Polish and Russian plains, and apart from casuals probably confined to a few isolated populations in Iceland, Sweden, Britain, Ireland, eastern France and Austria. Northern elements are the most migratory, and birds have reached México, ethiopian Africa and the northern oriental region.

Breeding population of Britain-Ireland order 3, aided by some introductions, with a headquarters in East Anglia (especially R.S.P.B. reserve of Minsmere, Suffolk) since stock was released there over a century ago, and a smaller one at Loch Leven, Kinross co. (first nested Scotland 1906), and one in Scilly. Ireland was colonised in 1933; it breeds there rather sporadically in 4 counties. It has not been proved to breed in Wales. Except in Essex and 3 other counties outside East Anglia and in counties neighbouring Kinross co., is sporadic in England and Scotland outside the headquarters areas. Disperses in winter, when population (in Ireland especially) is increased by some migrants from Iceland.

Pl. 46.

Mallard (♂ & ♀)
Ruddy Sheld-Duck.

Gadwall. (♂ & ♀)
Common Sheld-Duck.

Plate 13 (Thorburn's plate 47)

Family ANATIDAE, wildfowl (*continued*)

Teal B46
Anas crecca Linnaeus 1758
Eurasian teal, *Anas crecca crecca*
T3 p. 34 and pl. 47 **upper mid left** (♀ ♂)
as teal, *Nettion crecca* (Linnæus)

Green-winged teal, *Anas crecca carolinensis* J. F. Gmelin 1789
T3 p. 35 and pl. 47 **mid right** (♂)
as American green-winged teal, *Nettion carolinense* (J. F. Gmelin)

Distribution very similar to that of mallard, though breeding does not extend quite so far south and not normally in Europe to the Iberian Peninsula, most of Italy and Balkans. Rather more migratory than mallard; some birds reach equator in Africa for winter.

Breeding population of Britain-Ireland order 4; has bred in present century in virtually every county, though sporadic in south Wales and parts of south England. There is some evidence of decline in parts of east-central Scotland and eastern England. The green-winged race, detectable in the field, is a casual vagrant from North America (*c* a dozen records). Winter visitors of the Eurasian race outnumber our home resident population.

Baikal Teal
Anas formosa Georgi 1775
Not illustrated

Breeds in eastern Siberia; and naturally wanders at least as far as Alaska and India.

Often kept in captivity in Europe and escapes; hence the two Scottish records (female seen Fair Isle 1954 September 29–October 7 and 1 Loch Spynie, Moray 1958 February 5) have not yet been formally admitted to the British List, though a westward wandering from Siberia is doubtless *possible*.

Pintail B52
Anas acuta Linnaeus 1758
T3 p. 33 and pl. 47 **bottom** (♀ ♂)
as pintail, *Dafila acuta* (Linnæus)

An holarctic bird whose breeding range is virtually through the boreal zone of Eurasia and western North America and extends into the tundra and temperate areas. Has outpost races on some subantarctic islands. In Europe regularly breeds in Iceland, Britain, Fenno-Scandia, the Holland-north German plain and northern Russia, with an extension into Austria and Hungary, and sporadically Spitsbergen, Faeroe, Ireland, Belgium, France and Spain. Highly migratory, wintering into the neotropical, ethiopian and oriental regions.

Breeding population of Britain-Ireland order 2; fragmented and generally sporadic, not in Wales. Headquarters have changed in Scotland in the last two decades despite general increase. In Ireland a colonisation in the last fifty years has become of a sporadic pattern and almost died out; in England colonists of the same period are now most settled in the south. Overseas birds are passengers and winter visitors in all four countries.

Shoveler B53
Anas clypeata Linnaeus 1758
T3 p. 32 and pl. 47 **top right** (♂ ♀)
as shoveler, *Spatula clypeata* (Linnæus)

Origin probably palearctic; a boreal breeding distribution with southerly extensions in virtually all Eurasia, and west and central North America where spreading south-east. Spreading in Europe where reached Iceland in 1931; and present north-west breeding limits are like those of garganey, though nests in far greater strength in Britain and Ireland; south limits western France, the north European plain and the Danubian system, beyond which breeding records are sporadic. Highly migratory, wintering into the neotropical, ethiopian and oriental regions.

Breeding population of Britain-Ireland order 4; after a great expansion in the present century, with a heartland in parts of the Lowlands and east and north England, and a headquarters in East Anglia. In the rest of England and Scotland, and in Wales and Ireland, it is rather local, with strongish groups in Shropshire and Somerset, and a tendency to increase in some areas and decrease in others, partly as a consequence of human land management. In winter our breeders tend to emigrate and to be replaced by visitors from the Low Countries, south Baltic and western Russia.

Blue-winged Teal B48
Anas discors Linnaeus 1766
T3 p. 36 and pl. 47 **lower mid left** (♀ ♂)
as American blue-winged teal, *Querquedula discors* (Linnæus)

Breeds from Canada to the southern United States.

Twenty records 1858–1966: the first Drumlanrig, Upper Nithsdale, Dumfries co.; England 7; Wales 2; Scotland 5; Ireland 6; most September–January, 2 in April.

Pl. 47.

Teal. (♂♀)   Shoveller. (♂♀)
American Blue-winged Teal. (♂♀).   American Green-winged Teal.
Pintail. (♂♀)

Plate 14 (Thorburn's plate 48)

Family ANATIDAE, wildfowl (*continued*)

Garganey   B47
Anas querquedula Linnaeus 1758
T3 p. 37 and pl. 48 **bottom right** (♂ ♀)
as garganey, *Querquedula circia* (Linnæus)

Origin doubtless palearctic, in which region breeds virtually
through the boreal zone and some distance south, extending
from Russia east to southern Kamchatka and south into
northernmost China and Persia; north-westerly limits of
regular breeding in Europe have lately been progressing and
now embrace south and west Finland, east Sweden, continental North Sea coast and south England, southerly limits
France, north Italy, Danubian system; has bred sporadically
Iceland, south Norway, Spain, south Greece, Tunisia and
some Mediterranean islands. Highly migratory; winters into
ethiopian and oriental regions.

Breeding population of Britain-Ireland order 2; centres
presently on half a dozen English counties, though has bred
in about four times as many in the present century, and
sporadically in Wales (Glamorgan 1936), Ireland (co.
Armagh 1956, co. Kerry 1959) and Scotland (Forth area
1928–29). Has tended slightly to increase in the English headquarters, aided by influxes in the late 1940's and early 1960's,
but recent drainage processes in East Anglia may have been
inhibitive. Nearly all our population winters out of Britain
and Ireland.

Wigeon   B50
Anas penelope Linnaeus 1758
T3 p. 38 and pl. 48 **top right** (♂ ♀)
as wigeon, *Mareca penelope* (Linnæus)

Origin doubtless palearctic, where breeds throughout the
boreal zone, and some distance north and south of it, from
Iceland to Anadyr. In Europe has bred sporadically in Ireland
and north France, but normally nests only in Iceland,
Faeroe, Scotland, England, Fenno-Scandia, north Germany
and north Russia. All stock migrates considerably, and
elements regularly winter to ethiopian Africa and the central
oriental region.

Breeding population of Britain (only) order 3. Before 1837
known to breed only in north Highlands, Orkney and Shetland, co. Mayo and east Norfolk; a hundred years ago had
already begun to spread and by 1950 had nested in most of
Scotland, in north Wales and in northern and North Sea
England. Though it bred formerly in Ireland in up to 5
counties it has bred only twice there in the present century,
and outside the Highland mainland and a limited Lowland
area it has, since 1950, regressed somewhat and become a
sporadic nester in the rest of Scotland, Wales and a fair
number of counties in England. A few of our birds winter
across the Channel, but most stay to be outnumbered by
winter visitors from northern Europe.

American Wigeon or **Baldpate**   B51
Anas americana J. F. Gmelin 1789
T3 p. 39 and pl. 48 **bottom left** (♀ ♂)
as American wigeon, *Mareca americana* (J. F. Gmelin)

Breeds in central and western North America from northern
Canada to California-Nebraska.

Rare vagrant to all four countries, more often Scotland
than any other, most in October–April, 1 in June.

Red-crested Pochard   B54
Netta rufina (Pallas 1773)
T3 p. 40 and pl. 48 **mid right** (♀ ♂)
as red-crested pochard, *Netta rufina* (Pallas)

Origin possibly the Black Sea-Caspian area; its main breeding
range is the wetlands of the dry central palearctic from the
Caucasus through the steppelands of Russia (and in Persia
and Afghanistan) into Chinese Turkestan. In Europe its
breeding distribution is highly fragmented and looks relict;
but it may not be so: most German, and the Dutch and
Danish breeding grounds have been colonised quite lately in
the present century (Holland *c* 1942); it also breeds in Belgium,
Czechoslovakia, Austria, some places in France and Switzerland, south Spain, south Italy, and the Danube rivermouth
system, and has bred, and may still breed on western Mediterranean islands and the north-west African coast. Winters
south within the palearctic and northern oriental regions.

This species has been in British aviculture since 1874 or
before and has bred in it since 1910. 'Wild' breeding records
in Lincolnshire in 1937 and Essex in 1958 could involve
escaped stock, though they fit the pattern of the continental
spread. An annual winter vagrant to England; rare in other
countries.

Pochard   B57
Aythya ferina (Linnaeus 1758)
T3 p. 41 and pl. 48 **top left** (♀ ♂)
as common pochard, *Fuligula ferina* (Linnæus)

Origin doubtless palearctic, breeds mainly in the boreal and
north temperate zones east to the Baikal area of central
Siberia. In Europe breeds round most of Baltic, in Britain
and sporadically Ireland, and south to eastern France and the
Danubian river system, and has bred sporadically south to
the Mediterranean, including north-west Africa. Winters to
the southern palearctic and northern oriental regions.

Breeding population of Britain-Ireland order 3, with headquarters in England-Wales, where increase marked in last
three decades (*c* 200 pairs in 17 counties 1964), particularly
Kent since 1940's. An increase in Scotland earlier in the
century seems spent; and since it was first found nesting in
co. Monaghan in 1907 the pochard's breeding has been only
sporadic in about half a dozen Irish counties. Native stock
stays for winter, when population much enhanced by European immigrants.

Pl. 48.

Pochard. (♂♀)

American Wigeon. (♂♀)

Wigeon. (♂♀)
Red-crested Pochard. (♂♀)
Garganey. (♂♀)

Plate 15 (Thorburn's plate 49)

Family ANATIDAE, wildfowl (*continued*)

Ferruginous White-eye   B58
Aythya nyroca (Güldenstädt 1769)
T3 p. 42 and pl. 49 **top right** (♂ ♀)
as ferruginous duck, *Fuligula nyroca* (Güldenstädt)

Origin probably the Mediterranean or Turkestan steppe-lands; a central palearctic bird whose breeding range extends into the boreal zone, and east to the source-basins of the great rivers of south-east Asia. In Europe it appears to have a relict distribution west of north Germany, Poland, Russia and the Danubian system, with mostly sporadic groups in west Germany, Holland, France, Italy, Spain, some Mediterranean islands and extreme north-west Africa. Winters in the southern palearctic and into ethiopian and northern oriental regions.

An annual, mostly winter vagrant to England, rather less often to Wales and least often to Ireland and Scotland. Occasionally 'irrupts', as in 1950–51.

Ring-necked Duck
Aythya collaris (Donovan 1809)
Not illustrated

Breeds from northern Canada south to a north California-New England line in the United States.

Six records 1955–66, apart from the Leadenhall Market bird of 1801 January said to have been taken in the Fens of Lincolnshire (not acceptable as to its origin) and which was the type for Donovan's description of the species. The first (a male) was seen by Peter Scott from his drawing-room window at Slimbridge, Gloucestershire 1955 March 12–14; the others are adult male Burghfield near Reading, Berkshire 1959 April 19–27; adult male Lurgan Park, co. Armagh 1960 March 20–May 1, September 25–1961 March mid and (presumed the same) 1963 October–November, 1964 October–December, 1965 November and 1966 March 13; male Stanford Battle, Norfolk 1961 April 1–22; immature male Loch Morar, Inverness co. 1963 January 2 and 27; adult male Lough Neagh, northern Ireland 1966 March 13–April 24.

Tufted Duck   B56
Aythya fuligula (Linnaeus 1758)
T3 p. 43 and pl. 49 **top left** (♂ ♀)
as tufted duck, *Fuligula cristata* (Leach)

A boreal, temperate and steppeland palearctic bird with a broad breeding distribution from Iceland to Kamchatka and northernmost Japan. In Europe breeds only sporadically in south Norway, and south of Ireland, Britain, Holland, north Germany and Poland and central Russia. Most elements migratory, some reach the ethiopian, and north and central oriental regions.

Breeding population in Britain-Ireland low order 4 (over 1000 pairs) after a marked increase and colonisation since the end of the nineteenth century, though still sporadic in Wales and west of a headquarters in eastern Somerset. Other headquarters are Loch Leven, Kinross co. and Lough Beg, co. Antrim, and yet others continue to develop in new reservoirs. In the last three decades it has spread in Ireland and through the north Highlands to Shetland. Native population winters at home and is well augmented there by continental immigrants.

Scaup or **Greater Scaup**   B55
Aythya marila (Linnaeus 1761)
T3 p. 44 and pl. 49 **bottom right** (♂ ♀)
as scaup-duck *Fuligula marila* (Linnæus)

Origin probably palearctic; breeds through the northern holarctic boreal zone, extending into the tundra, from Iceland to Anadyr and Kamchatka, and though Alaska and Canada to Hudson Bay. In Europe the main breeding headquarters, slowly moving northwards, is in highland Norway, Lapland, White Sea Russia and the northern Baltic (especially islands); it has bred sporadically in Faeroe. Most winter in the southern holarctic, some reaching México and Cuba, and India.

Breeding population in Scotland (only); sporadic – has nested in the present century in Orkney, Caithness, Sutherland, Wester Ross and Outer Hebrides. Native birds on home estuaries and coasts have wintered. Continental visitors winter in all four countries, especially in Ireland where Iceland stock has been detected.

Long-tailed Duck   B61
Clangula hyemalis (Linnaeus 1758)
T3 p. 48 and pl. 49 **bottom mid** (♀ ♂)
as long-tailed duck, *Harelda glacialis* (Linnæus)

A tundra breeder of virtually the whole holarctic region, extending a little into boreal areas and reaching most limits of the high arctic. In Europe breeds in Iceland, Spitsbergen, Bear Island, Novaya Zemlya, central Norway, Lapland and the north Russian coast including off-lying islands. Winters offshore on more northerly holarctic coasts, and in Great Lakes of North America and inland seas of Russia.

The only British breeding record of this duck (whose range is moving north) is in Orkney 1911; unconfirmed records strongly suggest it may have bred in Shetland in 1848 and 1887. Northern birds winter in some numbers on the coasts of eastern England and eastern and northern Scotland and rather irregularly round Ireland, rarely in Wales.

Goldeneye   B60
Bucephala clangula (Linnaeus 1758)
T3 p. 45 and pl. 49 **mid** (♂ ♀)
as golden-eye, *Clangula glaucion* (Linnæus)

Breeds virtually throughout the whole holarctic boreal zone, except for the gap Greenland–Iceland–Scotland; in Europe in north Russia, Fenno-Scandia (not south-west Norway, south Sweden or Denmark) and north Germany; beyond this sporadic records in England, Switzerland, Jugoslavia and near mouths of some Black Sea rivers. Winters south within holarctic and to northern oriental region.

Only British breeding records: Cheshire in 1931 and 1932. A fairly heavy passage through, and winter residence in all four countries, of continental birds.

Barrow's Goldeneye
Bucephala islandica (J. F. Gmelin 1789)
Not illustrated

Breeds discontinuously in western North America from south Alaska to California and Colorado; on the Mackenzie River; in northern Labrador and west Greenland; and in Iceland.

One record, still to be accepted by the British-Irish List Committee: 2 adult males shot Shetland 1913 March 18; backed by good photograph of one; has provedly wandered to Faeroe only *c* 200 miles from Shetland, presumably from Iceland.

Bufflehead   B59
Bucephala albeola (Linnaeus 1758)
T3 p. 47 and pl. 49 **mid left** (♀ ♂)
as buffel-headed duck, *Clangula albeola* (Linnæus)

Breeds from central and western north Canada south to Oregon and California; has lately bred North Dakota.

Six records 1830–1961: the first an adult male, Great Yarmouth, Norfolk 1830 winter; England 5; Scotland 1; all winter save 1 June.

Pl. 49.

Tufted Duck. (♂♀)   Ferruginous Duck. (♂♀)
Buffel-headed Duck. (♂♀)   Golden-eye. (♂♀)   Scaup-Duck. (♂♀)
                    Long-tailed Duck. (♂♀)

Plate 16 (Thorburn's plate 50)

Family ANATIDAE, wildfowl (*continued*)

Harlequin Duck   B65
Histrionicus histrionicus (Linnaeus 1758)
T3 p. 50 and pl. 50 **top left** (♀ ♂)
as harlequin duck, *Cosmonetta histrionica* (Linnæus)

Has curiously discontinuous holarctic breeding distribution
on swift rivers of the boreal zone, extending into the tundra
and in western North America to the temperate (savannah)
zone. Its headquarters are in (and to far up) the river systems
of the Okhotsk and Bering Seas (and over the water-parting
to the upper reaches of the Lena and more easterly Siberian
rivers), and from south Alaska and the Mackenzie River south
in the rivers of the Rocky Mountain system to California and
Colorado. The population of the Atlantic, separate but not
racially so, breeds in south-east Baffin Island, Ungava and
north-east Labrador, south Greenland and Iceland. Winters
south as conditions demand, with some tendency to wander.

Eight records 1862–1965: first, male found dead Filey,
Yorkshire 1862 autumn; England 4; Scotland 4; all December–
February save 1 April–May.

Eider   B67
Somateria mollissima (Linnaeus 1758)
T3 p. 51 and pl. 50 **right** (♂ ♀ and flock)
as eider duck, *Somateria mollissima* (Linnæus)

A breeder on the north temperate, boreal and arctic coasts
of the holarctic region, though absent from most of central
Siberia and the Canadian high arctic islands. Migrates
within holarctic on Pacific and Atlantic coasts. In Europe
breeds in Franz Josef Land, Spitsbergen, Bear Island, Jan
Mayen, Iceland, Faeroe, north Ireland and Britain, Novaya
Zemlya, Kolguev Island and on virtually all the coast
of the White Sea and Fenno-Scandia, Estonia, Latvia,
Denmark and Holland, with an outpost off the coast of
Brittany, France.

Breeding population of Britain-Ireland order 4, and
colonist; invaded Scottish mainland, from islands *c* 1850 and
first bred Ireland (co. Donegal) 1912, where reached co.
Sligo and co. Down in 1939 and also breeds co. Antrim.
Increase in Scotland gathered way, with protection, in *c* 1890;
here geographical spread south has not been great, though
Walney in Lancashire (colony now big) was invaded in 1949.
East England has ancient colonies on Farne and Coquet
Islands, Northumberland. The stock winters at sea not far
from the breeding-places; a group now occurs off the Welsh
coast in winter and some summer regularly in Glamorgan.

King Eider   B68
Somateria spectabilis (Linnaeus 1758)
T3 p. 52 and pl. 50 **bottom left** (♀ ♂)
as king-eider, *Somateria spectabilis* (Linnæus)

An holarctic duck, breeding on the mainland arctic tundra
coast of virtually the whole region except Murmansk and
Fenno-Scandia, on the Russian arctic islands except Franz
Josef and Svernaya Zemlya and on most of the Canadian
arctic archipelago and northern Greenland. Seems to winter,
normally, no further south than ice and weather insist.

A vagrant to England, Scotland and Ireland, most in
winter, and most often on the east and north.

Pl. 50.

Harlequin Duck. (♂♀)   Eider Duck. (♂♀)

King-Eider. (♂♀)

Plate 17 (Thorburn's plate 51)

Family ANATIDAE, wildfowl (*continued*)

Steller's Eider   B66
Polysticta stelleri (Pallas 1769)
T3 p. 53 and pl. 51 **top right** (♂ ♀)
as Steller's eider, *Somateria stelleri* (Pallas)

Probably of eastern Siberian origin, with a main breeding headquarters from the Lena delta to the Chukotski Peninsula, and outposts in Alaska (perhaps just into Mackenzie on north North American coast) especially in joint Yukon-Kuskokwim delta. Local outposts also west, to south Novaya Zemlya in Europe, and breeds sporadically in Varanger Fjord, Norway. Winters to south, in Europe normally to the northern Norwegian coast and the north Baltic.

Five records: nearly adult male Caister near Great Yarmouth, Norfolk 1830 February 10; young male off Filey Brigg, Yorkshire 1845 August 15; 2 (1 a male) off Gairsay, Orkney 1947 January 5–19; male seen Deerness, Orkney 1949 January 13; female or immature male Loch Fleet, Sutherland 1959 September 22.

Velvet Scoter   B62
Melanitta fusca (Linnaeus 1758)
T3 p. 55 and pl. 51 **bottom right** (♂ ♀)
as velvet-scoter, *Œdemia fusca*, Linnæus

A boreal holarctic breeder, possibly of palearctic origin, ranging through the boreal zone from Fenno-Scandia east through Siberia and Alaska to Hudson Bay, but not breeding (some sporadic cases apart) in the arc of the Canadian arctic archipelago–Labrador–Greenland–Iceland–Scotland. Winters (and wanders) south within the holarctic region.

A pair with 4 well-grown young were seen on Whiteness Voe, Shetland 1945 August 10; this is the nearest proof of breeding in Britain. Bones of this species were excavated at the Viking Dark Age horizon (*c* A.D. 800–900) of the township at Jarlshof, Shetland. There are also unconfirmed breeding reports from Orkney and Wester Ross.

Regular in winter on North Sea coast and in Irish Sea, though few records for Wales; and rather few for Ireland, where quite a spate of records in 1966.

Surf Scoter   B63
Melanitta perspicillata (Linnaeus 1758)
T3 p. 56 and pl. 51 **top mid** (♂ ♀ ♂)
as surf-scoter, *Œdemia perspicillata*, Linnæus

Breeds in Alaska and Canada to the north coast, east to central Labrador.

Annual winter vagrant to Scotland (Orkney and Shetland particularly); rare in England; a few Irish records; not known from Wales.

Common Scoter   B64
Melanitta nigra (Linnaeus 1758)
T3 p. 54 and pl. 51 **bottom left** (♂ ♀)
as common scoter, *Œdemia nigra*, Linnæus

A boreal duck, probably of palearctic origin, whose breeding range extends into the arctic tundra zone and sometimes into the temperate. Distribution, east from Ireland–Britain–Faeroe–Iceland–Spitsbergen–Bear Island, extends from Fenno-Scandia east through northernmost Russia and most of Siberia east to western Alaska. Breeding records from the rest of North America are quite sporadic and very few, and at least some need confirmation. Winters on holarctic coasts, Great Lakes and other very large inland waters.

Breeding population of Scotland-Ireland order 3. Nesting known in Scotland since 1855 (Sutherland) and Ireland since 1904 or 1905 (co. Fermanagh) and colonisation seems likely. In Scotland the duck has bred in Caithness since 1865, in the Inner Hebrides since 1889, in Shetland since 1911, in Inverness co. and Easter Ross since 1913, in Perth co. since 1921 and in Orkney since 1927. In Ireland the co. Fermanagh colony was lately over 50 pairs, and the co. Mayo colony (first proved in 1948) 20 to 30. Large non-breeding flocks summer on the coasts of Scotland and Wales; and many packs winter off the east and south coasts of England. Winterers are rare in the north-west and off Ireland.

Pl. 51.

Surf-Scoter.(♂&♀).   Steller's Eider.(♂&♀)
Common Scoter.(♂&♀).   Velvet-Scoter.(♂&♀).

Plate 18 (Thorburn's plate 52)

Family ANATIDAE, wildfowl (*continued*)

Hooded Merganser   B72
Mergus cucullatus Linnaeus 1758
T3 p. 60 and pl. 52 **top right** (♂ ♀)
as hooded merganser, *Mergus cucullatus*, Linnæus

Breeds well into boreal zone in Alaska and Canada, south to an Oregon-Tennessee line in the United States.

Five records: young male Menai Strait, north Wales 1830–31 winter; pair Cobh Harbour, co. Cork 1878 December; female Shannon estuary off Ballylongford, co. Kerry 1881 January; adult male shot Yell, Shetland 1884 July; male or immature seen Acton Lake, co. Armagh 1957 December 21.

Smew   B71
Mergus albellus Linnaeus 1758
T3 p. 59 and pl. 52 **bottom right** (♂ ♀)
as smew, *Mergus albellus*, Linnæus

Origin doubtless palearctic, in which region normally breeds in the boreal zone from Lapland and White Sea Russia through Siberia to Anadyrland and Kamchatka. In Europe has bred sporadically in Russia south to the lower Dnepr River. Winters within the palearctic and in the northerly oriental region.

Regular winter visitor to south England, where often seen on London reservoirs, irregular in Wales and virtually only a vagrant to Scotland and Ireland.

Red-breasted Merganser   B69
Mergus serrator Linnaeus 1758
T3 p. 58 and pl. 52 **top left** (♂ ♀ ♂)
as red-breasted merganser, *Mergus serrator*, Linnæus

A widespread boreal holarctic breeder, extending into the arctic tundras and north temperate zones. Breeds in Europe in Iceland, Faeroe, Britain, Ireland, all Fenno-Scandia and Baltic fringe countries and northernmost Russia, and has bred sporadically in Holland, the Ukraine and the Crimea. Winters, mainly on coasts, normally in the holarctic region.

Breeding population of Britain-Ireland order 4; has been provedly increasing since 1837, rapidly between 1866 and 1920 and more gently since from nuclei in northern and western Ireland and Scotland; now occupies all Scotland save east Lowlands and most of Ireland, and first bred England

(Cumberland) 1950, since when has spread into Westmorland, north Lancashire and north-west Yorkshire (a sporadic pair bred Lincolnshire in 1961), and has invaded Wales (Anglesey) in 1953, spreading to Merioneth in 1957 and Caernarvon co. in 1958. British stock is reinforced outside nesting season by immigrant passengers and visitors, and many birds winter off west coasts of Scotland and Ireland.

Goosander   B70
Mergus merganser Linnaeus 1758
T3 p. 57 and pl. 52 **bottom left** (♀ ♂)
as goosander, *Mergus merganser*, Linnæus

A boreal holarctic breeder, extending in places some distance into the (mainly highland) temperate zone. In Europe breeds in Iceland, Britain, Fenno-Scandia, the other Baltic fringe countries and north Russia, with outposts by the larger lakes of the Alps; and has bred sporadically in Greece and at the Danube mouth. Winters within the holarctic and to the northerly oriental region.

Breeding population of Britain (does not breed Ireland) order 3; may not have bred before 1871 (Loch Ericht, Perth co.) and had colonised all but the eastern Highland mainland, and bred in Dumfries co. by the end of the century. By 1940 it had spread into the east Highlands and to new places in the Lowlands, and since then it has colonised Galloway, and England (Northumberland 1941, Cumberland 1950) where its numbers continue to build up. Tends to winter on inland fresh waters in England and Scotland, sometimes in modest numbers in Ireland (though irregular there), often in Wales.

Ruddy Duck
Oxyura jamaicensis (J. F. Gmelin 1789)
Not illustrated

A nearctic species of Canada (high in boreal zone) and the United States, whose range extends through Central America and West Indies to Colombia.

In British aviculture since 1936: and in last decades colonists, doubtless from the free breeders in the Wildfowl Trust collection at Slimbridge, Gloucestershire have colonised the waters at Frampton in the same county and at Chew Valley Lake in Somerset; in 1965 a feral pair bred at Tring, Hertfordshire. This species may soon demand admission to the British-Irish List as an established feral bird.

Pl. 52.

Red-breasted Merganser. (♂ & ♀)   Hooded Merganser. (♂ & ♀).
Goosander. (♂ & ♀)   Smew (♂ & ♀)

Plate 19 (Thorburn's plate 35)

Order FALCONIFORMES

Family ACCIPITRIDAE, hawks and eagles

In a modern systematic order B97 (pl. 25) would follow B96 (pl. 19).

Honey Buzzard   B98
Pernis apivorus (Linnaeus 1758)
T2 p. 58 and pl. 35 **bottom** (2 colour phases)
as honey-buzzard, *Pernis apivorus* (Linnæus)

Origin probably European; breeds in the boreal and temperate zones east through the steppelands of Russia into western Siberia. In Europe breeds in England, and on the Continent north to south-east Norway, south and east Sweden, Finland (not Lapland) and north Russia, south to central Spain and south-east Portugal, the Mediterranean shore (not south Italy, south Greece or islands) and the Black Sea. Winters in tropical Africa south of the Sahara.

Breeding population of Britain (has not bred Ireland) probably order 1: is still a regular breeder in southern England, perhaps also in Wales, and probably nested in Fife in 1949. Otherwise an irregular migrant passenger in England, Wales, Scotland and Ireland, most commonly on the east coast.

Red Kite   B95
Milvus milvus (Linnaeus 1758)
T2 p. 56 and pl. 35 **top right**
as kite, *Milvus ictinus*, Savigny

Origin probably European; a palearctic species extending in breeding range outside Europe only to Asia Minor, Tunis, Algeria, Morocco, the Canaries and the Cape Verde Islands. Distributed formerly in Europe from Scotland (not Ireland), south Norway, south Sweden and south Baltic fringe countries in the north, east to the Ukraine and south to the Mediterranean including its western islands. Now exterminated, mostly in last hundred years, from (among other areas) most if not all of Greece; and Albania, north-western France, the Low Countries, Denmark (Laaland recolonised 1949), Norway, Scotland and England. It survives moderately well in south Sweden and, under intensive protection, in central Wales. The northerly elements winter to the Mediterranean; the Welsh population is resident, though young wander.

Breeding population now about 20 pairs in central Wales; at some time in the nineteenth century had bred in virtually every county in England and Wales and most of mainland Scotland (never Ireland). In present century sporadic breedings in Devon (1913, probably 1947) and Cornwall (1920). The population in the Welsh headquarters has so far survived the local rabbit crash in 1955 (myxomatosis), some human interference and even egg-collecting and produced 11 flying young in 1964, the best score for a decade. The main breeding areas are threatened by reservoir developments, but a large part has been recently purchased as a reserve by R.S.P.B.

Black Kite   B96
Milvus migrans (Boddaert 1783)
T2 p. 57 and pl. 35 **top left**
as black kite, *Milvus migrans* (Boddaert)

A species of virtually the whole continental Old World, breeding from the tropics to the boreal zone except in north-west Europe and the Sahara, and breeding also in Madagascar, Ceylon, Japan, Taiwan, Hainan, Celebes, Lesser Sunda Islands, New Guinea, New Britain and northern Australia. Absent as breeder from Finland (except south-east), Scandinavia (except one station now in Norbotten, Sweden), Low Countries, north-west France, Britain and Ireland. European breeders mostly winter in Africa south of the Sahara.

Seven records 1866–1966: earliest Alnwick, Northumberland 1866 May 11; England 4; Scotland 3; 5 May, 1 April, 1 September.

Pl. 35.

Black Kite.   Kite.

Honey Buzzard (2 varieties)

Plate 20 (Thorburn's plate 34)

Family ACCIPITRIDAE, hawks and eagles (*continued*)

Goshawk　　　　　　　　　　　　　　　　B94
Accipiter gentilis (Linnaeus 1758)
T2 p. 54 and pl. 34 **bottom** (adult and young)
as goshawk, *Astur palumbarius* (Linnæus)

Origin possibly the boreal palearctic taiga; breeds widely, though under serious persecution in developed areas, throughout the boreal and temperate forests of the palearctic and nearctic regions, though not in the North American prairie and hardwood heartland or in the steppe and dry upland area of palearctic Asia, except for an isolated population in eastern Tibet. Virtually extinct in many parts of Low Countries, France and Portugal, and well over a century ago in England.

There is no evidence that the goshawk has ever attempted to breed in Scotland, Wales or Ireland. Since 1864, when a pair attempted to breed in Lincolnshire, only 1 pair bred (Yorkshire 1893) before the recolonisation of Sussex in or before 1938. Here up to 3 pairs bred until 1951; since then there have been unconfirmed nesting records from 4 other places, and an escaped falconer's female bird nested in Shropshire in 1951. Otherwise is an annual vagrant to England, rare in Wales, Scotland and Ireland.

Sparrow Hawk　　　　　　　　　　　　　　B93
Accipiter nisus (Linnaeus 1758)
T2 p. 55 and pl. 34 **top** (♀ ♂)
as sparrow-hawk, *Accipiter nisus* (Linnæus)

Origin doubtless palearctic, in which region range very similar to that of goshawk: its ecological counterpart in North America, the sharp-shinned hawk *Accipiter striatus* is a fully different species. Range is less extensive than goshawk's in eastern Asia (it does not reach Kamchatka and breeds only in a limited area of Japan), but more extensive in the southern palearctic Asian highlands, and extends (unlike goshawk's) to Tunisia, Algeria, Morocco and the Canaries. Some elements migrate south in winter, though scarcely ever beyond the palearctic.

Breeding population of Britain-Ireland order 4; until lately, doubtless aided by absence of keepers in 1939–45, had increased and was breeding in virtually every county of the four countries; a widespread decrease began in 1955, correlated by both direct and circumstantial evidence with the wide use of chlorinated hydrocarbons, which by the early 1960's may have extinguished it over a wide area of the east Midlands and Thames counties, and heavily reduced it in parts of Scotland. It has also lately decreased in eastern Ireland. Native stock non-migratory; but a passage of continental birds takes place in spring and autumn.

Pl. 34.

A. Thorburn 1914

Sparrow-Hawk. (♂ & ♀)

Goshawk (adult & young)

Plate 21 (Thorburn's plate 31)

Family ACCIPITRIDAE, hawks and eagles (*continued*)

Rough-legged Buzzard   B92
Buteo lagopus (Pontoppidan 1763)
T2 p. 49 and pl. 31 **left**
as rough-legged buzzard, *Buteo lagopus* (J. F. Gmelin)

An holarctic bird of the low arctic boreal and tundra zones, with a virtually continuous breeding distribution north of the taiga-type forests all round the continental plains, hills and tundras of the Arctic Ocean from Norway to Labrador, including the Kuriles, Kamchatka, the Aleutians and wide inland areas of Alaska and northern Canada, and some islands near mainland arctic coasts. Winters south of breeding range, not normally outside the holarctic. In Europe the breeding range extends down to about 60°N in Norway and west Sweden, but is otherwise confined to Lapland and arctic Russia from Murmansk and the White Sea east.

Winter visitor to north and east Scotland, and to the east coast of England and inland in the English hills; is rare in Wales and Ireland.

Buzzard   B91
Buteo buteo (Linnaeus 1758)
T2 p. 48 and pl. 31 **top right** (2 birds)
as common buzzard, *Buteo vulgaris*, Leach

A palearctic bird with four very close relations, in North and Central America and the West Indies; Argentina-Chile; east Africa; and Madagascar – which could all be colonists from palearctic stock, though they are held by most authorities to be good species. In the palearctic this bird is boreal, but extends south into temperate and other zones including the Azores, Madeira, Canaries and Cape Verde Islands, and the Mediterranean (not the African side); in the east it reaches the Sea of Okhotsk and Japan but not Kamchatka and, like goshawk and sparrow hawk, has an isolated population in the central Asian palearctic highlands. In Europe it is absent as a breeder from rather few areas, notably Iceland, Faeroe, Ireland (where it was almost extirpated in the nineteenth century but has begun to breed again sporadically in the present century) and the treeless zones of extreme west and north Norway, Lapland and the White Sea region of northern Russia. Most western European buzzards are rather sedentary, but Russian elements winter in Africa south of the Sahara, and some eastern birds in the oriental region.

Breeding population of Britain order 4; bred formerly in Ireland to *c* 1915 where its last stronghold was co. Antrim, recolonised shortly *c* 1951 to *c* 1961, again (7 pairs Rathlin Island) 1966. Heavily persecuted in the nineteenth century, which doubtless cleared it from eastern England and Ulster; increased well from 1914 to *c* 1954 when the population was estimated at *c* 12,000 pairs; declined again since, probably owing to reduction of rabbit population through myxomatosis. In Scotland is still absent as a breeder from the east Lowlands and parts of the west Lowlands, but breeds through Highland mainland (rare Caithness), Inner Hebrides and Outer Hebrides (since 1930's), and first bred Orkney 1966. The British stock is resident.

Great Spotted Eagle   B90
Aquilla clanga Pallas 1811
T2 p. 49 and plate 31 **bottom**
as spotted eagle, *Aquila maculata* (J. F. Gmelin)

Origin doubtless palearctic, where breeds, largely in wet lowlands, in the boreal zone from central Europe through Russia and southern Siberia to Amurland and Manchuria. In Europe few if any breed west of south Finland or the post-war borders of Russia and Rumania. Some elements migrate and may winter into the ethiopian and oriental regions.

Fourteen records 1845–1915: first, 2 shot near Youghal, co. Cork 1845 January; England 12; Scotland 1; Ireland 1; September–January save 1 April.

Pl. 31.

Rough-legged Buzzard.   Spotted Eagle.   Common Buzzard

Plate 22 (Thorburn's plate 32)

Family ACCIPITRIDAE, hawks and eagles (*continued*)

Golden Eagle   B89
Aquila chrysaetos (Linnaeus 1758)
T2 p. 50 and pl. 32 (frontispiece)
as golden eagle, *Aquila chrysaëtus* (Linnæus)

Origin doubtless palearctic, for though the species now has a wide range in nearctic North America (and México), it is the only *Aquila* eagle in the New World. Once probably distributed virtually over the whole holarctic region to the limits of the boreal zone in mountainous and rocky country (and into its blend-zones with the neotropical and ethiopian regions in México and Mauretania) the golden eagle has been exterminated in a vast area of eastern North America and of Europe. In Europe it now breeds regularly only in Scotland, Norway, north and west Sweden, north-east Finland, northern Russia, the Carpathians, Balkans and Greece, the Alps, the backbone hills of Italy, the Massif Central of France and the Iberian Peninsula.

Breeding population of Britain (-Ireland) order 3, mainly in Scottish Highland mainland and Hebrides. Ireland, where the eagle became extinct *c* 1910 was recolonised by a pair (co. Antrim) from 1953 to 1960, and birds have lately built nests (in Cumberland) for the first time in England for well over a century, though they did not breed successfully. The population was estimated as *c* 190 breeding pairs in the early 1950's and seemed to be more or less constant for that decade. The output of the young declined drastically in the early 1960's, when largish residues of chlorinated hydrocarbons were found in birds and infertile eggs, and there is some evidence that the breeding population is now starting to drop. Outside northern England and northern Ireland the golden eagle is a rare vagrant to England, Wales and Ireland.

Pl. 32

Golden Eagle. (adult & young.)

Plate 23 (Thorburn's plate 29)

Family ACCIPITRIDAE, hawks and eagles (*continued*)

Egyptian Vulture B87
Neophron percnopterus (Linnaeus 1758)
T2 p. 44 and pl. 29 **bottom** (young and adult)
as Egyptian vulture, *Neophron percnopterus* (Linnæus)

A palearctic, ethiopian and oriental bird, with a small relict population in South Africa, populations in or near several Saharan oases, and an otherwise still fairly continuous distribution from the Cape Verde Islands and Canaries through Morocco, the Iberian Peninsula, the countries of both Mediterranean shores, Black Sea shores, all Arabia, Asia Minor, Persia, Transcaspia, Russian Turkestan and Afghanistan to India, with a salient up the Nile through the Sudan to Ethiopia, Somalia, Socotra and equatorial east Africa. Some of the population winters in Africa south of the Sahara, and elements occasionally wander north.

Two rather old English records, of immatures shot in Bridgwater Bay, Somerset 1825 October (1 of 2 birds) and at Peldon, Essex 1868 September 28.

Griffon Vulture B88
Gyps fulvus (Hablizl 1783)
T2 p. 24 and pl. 29 **top**
as griffon-vulture, *Gyps fulvus* (J. F. Gmelin)

Origin probably palearctic; range extends into oriental north India, and an isolated race (or species?) in South Africa may be descendent. Distribution is fairly continuous from Greece, Balkans and Black Sea through Asia Minor, Persia, Afghanistan to Russian Turkestan, the Pamirs, the central Asian uplands and north India. Breeds also in Morocco and along the south Mediterranean to Egypt and Israel, on the major Mediterranean islands (not Corsica) and in the Iberian Peninsula. Wandering rather than migratory in the off-season.

Three British-Irish records: immature caught near Cork Harbour, Ireland 1843 spring; 1 seen near Southampton Water, Hampshire a few years before 1889; 2 seen Ashbourne, Derbyshire 1927 June 4.

Pl.29.

Griffon-Vulture

Egyptian Vulture. (adult & young)

Plate 24 (Thorburn's plate 30)

Family ACCIPITRIDAE, hawks and eagles (*continued*)

Hen Harrier B100
Circus cyaneus (Linnaeus 1766)
T2 p. 46 and pl. 30 **top right** (♀ and ♂)
as hen-harrier, *Circus cyaneus* (Linnæus)

Origin possibly palearctic; an holarctic bird ranging towards the north limit of the boreal zone mainly on moist steppe, prairie, moor and pampas, with a probably descendent South American (neotropical) race (which may be a full species) and African (ethiopian) veldt species (which may be a well-marked race). The holarctic forms breed from Ireland, Portugal and north Spain to the Kolyma in north-east Siberia and Anadyrland, and (American 'marsh hawk') from Alaska to Québec and south to California and the central United States. In Europe the distribution reaches the Mediterranean only in north Italy and is fragmented in Ireland, Britain, the Low Countries and in Denmark and the south of Norway, Sweden and Finland. Northern European elements winter south within the palearctic, though some eastern elements reach the northern oriental region and American elements the neotropical region as far as Colombia.

Breeding population of Britain-Ireland low order 3; in nineteenth century bred in most counties of England, Wales and Scotland and several of Ireland, but progressively declined under human persecution to a relict situation in *c* 1940 when virtually confined to Orkney, the Outer Hebrides and (1 or 2 pairs) Ireland; since when there has been a considerable and steady recovery. J. L. F. Parslow estimates a present (1966) population of at least 100 pairs, with strongholds in Orkney and the Outer Hebrides and a respectable range in the rest of Scotland including the Lowlands, in Ireland (6 counties with 34 pairs in 1964—at least 35 according to R. F. Ruttledge), 8 counties by 1966, 2 counties in Wales and 1 in England. The British stock is resident, and supplemented in winter by continental birds, especially in England and Wales.

Pallid Harrier B101
Circus macrourus (S. G. Gmelin 1771)
Not illustrated

Origin possibly Turkestanian, a central palearctic dry steppe species of the temperate and boreal zones, with a normal breeding range from the Ukraine east in central Siberia to Lake Baikal and into Persia south of the Caspian. Some winter to ethiopian Africa south of the Sahara and others to the northern oriental region; some wander west and have bred sporadically in south Sweden, Czechoslovakia and Germany (west to Norderney in Frisian Islands 1952).

Four British records: male shot Fair Isle, Shetland where present 1931 April *c* 25 to May 8; adult male east Dorset 1938 April; adult male Fair Isle 1942 May 6–14; immature male shot near Driffield, Yorkshire 1952 October 2.

Montagu's Harrier B102
Circus pygargus (Linnaeus 1758)
T2 p. 47 and pl. 30 **top left** (♂ ♀)
as Montagu's harrier, *Circus cineraceus* (Montagu)

Origin probably European or Turkestanian; breeds from Atlantic Morocco, the Iberian Peninsula and England-Wales east through central Europe and the plains and steppes of Russia to the upper Yenisei, and south of the Caspian into Persia. Has extended north in the present century into Denmark and Sweden, though in western Europe has generally declined with wetland drainage. Highly migratory; winters outside the palearctic in the ethiopian veldt and oriental plains of India.

Breeding population (J. L. F. Parslow) now (1966) *c* 20 pairs scattered in England and Wales, and 1 or 2 in Ireland. Originally evidently an English-Welsh breeder only, this harrier may never have been common, and was perhaps towards its highest population (*c* 40–50 pairs) in the early 1950's when nests were proved for the first time in Scotland (1952 Perth co., 1953 Kirkcudbright st.) and Ireland (1955, though suspected 1899, 1919). The key East Anglian population, however, began to collapse in 1958, and since then the nestings have become more widely spread and sporadic, but fewer, though a main stronghold in the West Country still modestly thrives. The British stock migrates to Africa for the winter.

Marsh Harrier B99
Circus aeruginosus (Linnaeus 1758)
T2 p. 45 and pl. 30 **bottom** (♂ and young)
as marsh-harrier, *Circus æruginosus* (Linnæus)

Origin doubtless palearctic; forms in Australasia and Indian Ocean (Comoros, Madagascar, Réunion) are regarded authoritatively as descendent races. A reed-swamp breeder from the southern (not desert highland) palearctic north into boreal zone, from north-west Africa, England-Wales and western Europe to Anadyrland, Sakhalin and northern Japan. In continental Europe broadly distributed in surviving wetlands (not Alps) from Mediterranean to Denmark, the south of Sweden and Finland, and Archangel in Russia. Some northern elements winter well into the ethiopian and oriental regions.

Breeding population (now only England) order 1; the lowest for some years. In Ireland bred quite widely *c* 1840, but became extinct by *c* 1917, and in the nineteenth century ranged early through England and Wales to the Border, only to become extinct at the end. The harrier successfully recolonised Norfolk in the 1920's, and under protection spread to Suffolk in the 1940's; by 1958 about 18 pairs were nesting in East Anglia, Dorset and elsewhere, including Wales (Anglesey in and after 1945). The breeding outside East Anglia (where it no longer breeds in Norfolk) proved to be sporadic, and in the 1960's perhaps only 6 pairs have annually bred in all. British stock sometimes winters in East Anglia. The species is now really a rare vagrant in Scotland and Ireland.

Montagu's Harrier ♂ & ♀.   Marsh-Harrier (adult ♂ & young)   Hen-Harrier ♂ & ♀.

Pl. 30.

Plate 25 (Thorburn's plate 33)

Family ACCIPITRIDAE, hawks and eagles (*continued*)

White-tailed Eagle B97
Haliaeetus albicilla (Linnaeus 1758)
T2 p. 52 and pl. 33 **top** (adult and young)
as white-tailed eagle, *Haliaëtus albicilla* (Linnæus)

Origin doubtless palearctic; formerly occupied virtually the whole of the palearctic region into the continental tundra zone, with the exception of Japan, Korea and most palearctic Asian dry highlands; still has a nearctic outpost in west Greenland and formerly bred on the oriental border on the lower Yangtze in China. In western Europe, outside the south Baltic fringe countries, Russia, Hungary and the Balkans, has reduced and now fragmented populations in Iceland, Norway Sweden and Finland, breeds only sporadically or in isolated pairs in Denmark, Czechoslovakia, Austria and Sardinia, and is exterminated in Faeroe, Britain, Ireland and Corsica. The young wander considerably, within the palearctic – Greenland and Siberian birds occasionally to the holarctic mainland.

Formerly bred in most counties of Scotland and coastal Ireland, probably in the Isle of Man (to 1815) and in England in Cumberland, Devon and the Isle of Wight (to 1780). Became extinct as a breeder in Ireland in the early twentieth century, and in Scotland last bred in Shetland in 1908 and in Skye in 1816 or perhaps later.

Now no more than a vagrant to England (mostly immature birds), and a rare vagrant to Wales, Scotland and Ireland.

Family PANDIONIDAE, osprey

Osprey B103
Pandion haliaetus (Linnaeus 1758)
T2 p. 53 and pl. 33 **bottom**
as osprey, *Pandion haliaëtus* (Linnæus)

Possibly of palearctic origin, the osprey presently has a most complex and nearly cosmopolitan distribution from the tropics to some north limits of the boreal areas. The only continent it does not breed in (apart from Antarctica) is South America. From eastern Europe through most of the continental palearctic it has a fairly continuous range to Kamchatka and Japan (it is becoming rare in Japan), with a widish oriental extension in eastern China and to Assam, and a (mainly coastal) breeding distribution from Taiwan and the Philippines to Java, entering the australasian blend-zone in Celebes and the fully australasian region in the Lesser Sunda Islands, New Guinea, the Solomons and New Caledonia and round the Australian coast. This extension may be an old one, for south of Taiwan the populations have stabilised in two good races. The nearctic North American population (another race) also has a fairly continuous range south of the tundra zone, and extensions south into Lower California and México in the neotropical blend-zone, and another extension, which may be old as its population is, again, racially distinct, in the Bahamas, Cuba and Yucatán which reaches the true nearctic region. In Africa-Arabia the population is of the palearctic race and is fairly continuous round the coasts of Arabia (including the Persian Gulf) and on the African shore of the Red Sea to the Somalian coast and Socotra. Beyond, the same race has a fragmented distribution, centred on Kenya, Pemba and Zanzibar, Lake Tanganyika and isolated areas of South Africa, which may represent a relatively recent breeding colonisation of what is still part of the normal winter range of some of this race. But in western Europe and the north-west African palearctic the fragmentation doubtless represents a relict situation: the osprey still breeds in the Cape Verde Islands, but it is extinct now in the Canaries and probably in the Spanish Sahara and Morocco, breeds now in the Mediterranean only in Spain (just outside it also in south Portugal), the Balearics, Corsica, Sardinia, Sicily, Tunisia and Algeria, and has been for many years sporadic only in the rest of Europe west of the river systems of the Baltic and Dnepr, and the mouth of the Danube. It still breeds fairly widely in the Scandinavian Peninsula and Finland. A process of extinction has overtaken the western European ospreys in historical times.

Breeding population (Scotland only) order 1. Though never known to breed in Ireland or Wales, ospreys last bred in England in 1847, in Denmark in the present century, and in Scotland (Inverness co.) in 1908 (possibly till 1916). The recolonisation of Inverness co. began in 1954 (or perhaps a year or two before), since when 2 pairs have nested regularly in and near the R.S.P.B. reserve at Loch Garten, and 3 pairs attempted breeding, 2 successfully, in Scotland in 1967. Some last breeding dates before the recolonisation are Hampshire 1570, south Lakeland 1678, Devon (mainland) 1759, Dunbarton co., Stirling co. and Moray co. early nineteenth century, Lundy (Devon) 1847, Sutherland and Argyll 1850, Kirkcudbright st. 1860, Perth co. 1886 and Ross 1901.

Apart from the (sometimes detectable) comings and goings of the breeding pairs, is a regular passage migrant in England (particularly the east drainage area lakes and reservoirs, and Norfolk) and in some parts of Scotland, but no more than a vagrant in Wales and Ireland.

Pl. 33.

White-tailed or Sea Eagle.   Osprey.
(adult & young)

Family FALCONIDAE, falcons

Gyrfalcon   B106
Falco rusticolus Linnaeus 1758

Charles Vaurie's revision of 1965 shows that the widely accepted 'subspecies' are based on the relative abundance of colour phases in different regions; and he prefers not to recognise them formally. The names offered here thus may be no more than Linnean words for the most typical colour phases found in the regions cited and figured by Thorburn:

Greenland gyrfalcon, *Falco rusticolus candicans* J. F. Gmelin 1788
T2 p. 59 and pl. 36 **left** (♀)
as Greenland falcon, *Falco candicans*, J. F. Gmelin

Iceland gyrfalcon, *Falco rusticolus islandus* Brünnich 1764
T2 p. 60 and pl. 36 **right** (♂)
as Iceland falcon, *Falco islandus*, J. F. Gmelin

European gyrfalcon, *Falco rusticolus rusticolus*
See pl. 27 (Thorburn's plate 37)

An arctic species of the whole holarctic, breeding continuously through the northernmost boreal, and the tundra zones all round the continental shores of the north Polar Basin, in several islands of the Canadian arctic archipelago, in Greenland, Iceland, some off-lying Russian arctic islands including Kolguev and perhaps Wrangel, and into the Bering Sea as far as St Lawrence Island, Kamchatka and Bering Island. Has also a rather widely separated group of outpost populations (by some considered a separate, close species), which may be relicts of glacial times, in the central Asian highlands of Khangai, Tarbagatai, Ala Tau and Tian Shan and north from them some distance down the Siberian rivers. Mainly sedentary, though some elements disperse and wander in very hard winters.

An annual vagrant to Scotland and England, and a rare one in Wales and Ireland, usually in winter and spring. The Greenland type is commoner than the Iceland type; and the European type has apparently not been confirmed since 1867.

Pl. 36.

Greenland Falcon. ♀   Iceland Falcon. ♂

Plate 27 (Thorburn's plate 37)

Family FALCONIDAE, falcons (*continued*)

Gyrfalcon (*continued*)
European gyrfalcon, *Falco rusticolus rusticolus*
T2 p. 60 and pl. 37 **bottom** (♀)
as gyr-falcon, *Falco gyrfalco*, Linnæus

Peregrine   B105
Falco peregrinus Tunstall 1771
T2 p. 61 and pl. 37 **top** (young and adult ♂)
as peregrine falcon, *Falco peregrinus*, Tunstall

Cosmopolitan in all climes to the lower high arctic tundras (not in full deserts and tropical rainforests) in all regions save the antarctic. The most conspicuous gap in breeding distribution lies between the south border of the nearctic region and southern South America where an isolated race inhabits Chile, southernmost Argentina, Tierra del Fuego and the Falklands. Breeds throughout continental Europe, though local and decreasing and now virtually absent from Denmark and the Low Countries, and from a largish area of Russia north of the Black Sea. Breeds also in Ireland, Britain, Norwegian and Black Sea islands, Kolguev and south Novaya Zemlya. Northernmost elements may migrate as far as the tropics, though central populations are sedentary.

Breeding population of Britain-Ireland order 3; decrease under human persecution from the nineteenth well into the twentieth century, a stabilisation just before the Second World War, further decrease in the war years under official persecution, a rapid recovery from the late 1940's under protection, and a crash since 1955, with convincing circumstantial evidence of toxic chemicals as a major factor – as summarised by the work of Ratcliffe and Parslow. By 1961 two-fifths of the *c* 1939 British population of *c* 650 pairs had gone, and only 82 reared young; only 68 pairs reared young in 1962. In Ireland *c* 190 breeding pairs in 1950 may have fallen to under 70 in the mid-1960's. There were signs of some arresting of the decline in Britain in 1964.

Residents disperse, often inland, in winter, and there is a marked autumn passage of Scandinavian birds.

Pl. 37.

Gyr-Falcon.
♀.

Peregrine Falcon (adult & young).
♂.

Plate 28 (Thorburn's plate 38)

Family FALCONIDAE, falcons (*continued*)

Hobby   B104
Falco subbuteo (Linnaeus 1758)
T2 p. 63 and pl. 38 **top left** (♂)
as hobby, *Falco subbuteo*, Linnæus

Origin doubtless palearctic; breeding distribution extends south beyond the oriental blend-zone in China and northern Indochina and in general runs from the north Mediterranean, and southern steppe zones of Asia, into the boreal zone, and east to the Sea of Okhotsk, southern Kamchatka, the Kuriles and (very rare) Japan. In north-west Africa breeds in Morocco, Algeria and Tunisia; in Mediterranean islands breeds regularly perhaps only on Cyprus and Corsica. North limit in Europe is south England–Denmark–extreme south-east Norway, south Sweden, south Finland, and the Arch-angel district of Russia. Migratory, wintering into the ethiopian and oriental regions.

Breeding population (south England; sporadically Wales) order 2; *c* 75–100 pairs, after nineteenth-century persecu-tion, probably now stable and with Hampshire as the heartland of the nesting distribution, breeding regularly in 6 English counties, frequently in 6 more, and irregularly in 5 more and Radnor co.; has bred but not lately in 2 Welsh and 12 or 13 other English counties, as far north as Lincolnshire and Cheshire and including East Anglia. Our stock very seldom winters and normally migrates to Africa; birds visit Wales, Scotland and Ireland normally only as rare vagrants.

Merlin   B109
Falco columbarius Linnaeus 1758
T2 p. 64 and pl. 38 **bottom left** (♀ ♂ and young)
as merlin, *Falco æsalon*, Tunstall

An holarctic boreal bird which breeds in moorland of all types a little distance into the tundra, and some distance into temperate zones, round the northern world. In Europe breeds Iceland, Faeroe, Ireland, Britain, Fenno-Scandia (not Denmark, south Sweden except Gotland, south-west Finland), Estonia and north Russia. Migratory; some elements winter into the northern ethiopian and oriental regions.

Breeding population of Britain-Ireland order 3; a decrease in the present century, most marked since 1950, almost everywhere except in parts of the West Country, and possibly due to afforestation, other land-use changes and human interference. The density has changed more than the gross distribution, which still covers most of the four countries save south-east England. Our stock is normally resident, though dispersive in winter, when it is joined by winterers from northern Europe and Iceland.

Red-footed Falcon or **Red-footed Kestrel**   B108
Falco vespertinus Linnaeus 1766
T2 p. 65 and pl. 38 **top right** (♂ ♀)
as red-footed falcon, *Falco vespertinus*, Linnæus

A central and eastern palearctic species whose typical race breeds from the Danubian system, the steppe zones, extend-ing north into the boreal zones, east to just short of Lake Baikal. Beyond Baikal another race, so well marked as to be considered by some another species, occupies south-eastern Siberia and north China. All elements appear to winter in ethiopian Africa, which suggests that the species may be of western steppe, perhaps even European origin. An almost annual summer vagrant in south-east England, and a rare one in Wales, Scotland and Ireland.

Lesser Kestrel   B109
Falco naumanni Fleischer 1818
T2 p. 67 and pl. 38 **mid right** (♂)
as lesser kestrel, *Falco cenchris*, Naumann

A southern palearctic bird of the Mediterranean and steppe countries, fragmented in its eastern distribution, of which north China is the limit. Breeds in Morocco, Tangier, Algeria, Tunisia and on larger Mediterranean islands, and in rest of Europe in Iberian Peninsula, south France, south Italy, the Danubian system, Balkans and Greece and the steppes of Black Sea Russia. Winters in ethiopian Africa.

Thirteen records 1867–1934: earliest 1 shot Wilstrop, near York 1867 November; England 11; Scotland 1; Ireland 1; October–November and February–May.

Kestrel   B110
Falco tinnunculus Linnaeus 1758
T2 p. 66 and pl. 38 **bottom right** (♀ ♂)
as kestrel, *Falco tinnunculus*, Linnæus

An Old World species breeding to the edge of the tundra throughout the palearctic region east to the Sea of Okhotsk and in Japan (where rare), throughout the ethiopian region save the densest tropical forest and Madagascar and into the oriental region to south China, possibly Burma, and parts of India. Absent in Europe importantly only from Iceland and tundras of northernmost Norway and Russia. North elements migrate and some reach the ethiopian and oriental regions.

Breeding population of Britain-Ireland order 5; still breeds in every county save Shetland, where last nested in 1905. Status fluctuating but not very widely; increased generally in the 1940's but declined in areas of high agri-cultural quality (particularly in east England) quite markedly in the early 1960's, possibly with a crash in the vole population, possibly with a rise in the use of toxic chemicals – or both. There were some signs of recovery in 1964–65.

Northern elements of our stock winter south, though not normally out of Britain-Ireland, and continental elements also winter in and pass through our islands.

Pl. 38.

Hobby. ♂.

Merlin. (♂. ♀. & young).

Kestrel. ♀.

Red-footed Falcon. (♂. & ♀.)

Lesser Kestrel. ♂.

Kestrel. ♂.

Plate 29 (Thorburn's plate 56)

Order GALLIFORMES

Family TETRAONIDAE, grouse

Most standard textbooks hold this as a full family, but on anatomical grounds, and because hybridisation has been proved between some grouse and pheasants, the grouse should probably be held as no more than a subfamily, the Tetraoninae, of the following family Phasianidae.

In a modern systematic order B111 (pl. 30) would precede B112 (pl. 29).

Ptarmigan   B112
Lagopus mutus (Montin 1776)
T1 pl. 20 (pl. 79 here) (frontispiece)
as prey of raven
T3 pl. 71 and pl. 56 (♂ ♀ winter and autumn)
as ptarmigan, *Lagopus mutus* (Montin)

Origin doubtless arctic; breeding (virtually sedentary) through the tundras and alpine highlands of the holarctic, with a more or less continuous distribution round the shores of the Bering Sea and Arctic Ocean, extending deeply up the great rivers of Alaska and eastern Siberia into the high interior of their sources, and on Japan (Japanese Alps in Hondo only), the Bering-Aleutian chain of islands, the Canadian arctic archipelago, highland Newfoundland, all coasts of Greenland, Iceland, Scotland, Bear Island, Spitsbergen, Franz Josef Land and Kolguev; with separated populations in the highlands of Amurland, the European Alps and the Pyrenees.

Breeding population (Scotland only) order 6; a fluctuating (c ten-year cycle) but generally stable population on the high mainland Highland hills, with a headquarters in the Grampians, and colonies on the mountains of Skye and Mull. Ranged to southern England in Ice Age times, and survived in Lakeland mountains until the nineteenth century; presently extinct on Rhum and Outer Hebrides but possibly attempting recolonisation. Fossil bones of Ice Age to Iron Age in Ireland referred to this species may have been those of grouse. Highly resident.

Pl. 56.

A. Thorburn
1915

Ptarmigan (189). winter & autumn.

Plate 30 (Thorburn's plate 55)

Family TETRAONIDAE, grouse (*continued*)

Willow Grouse　　　　　　　　　　　　　　　BIII
Lagopus lagopus (Linnaeus 1758)
Red grouse, *Lagopus lagopus scoticus* (Latham 1787)
T3 p. 70 and pl. 55 **top** (covey, ♂ ♀)
as red grouse, *Lagopus scoticus*, Latham

Origin probably arctic: distributed (almost sedentary) through the tundra and most boreal moorland zones of virtually the whole continental holarctic region, and on some Alaskan and southern Canadian arctic islands, Newfoundland, Ireland, Britain, Norwegian islands, the New Siberian Islands and Sakhalin. In continental Europe restricted (apart from some introduced feral colonies in Belgium) to the Scandinavian Peninsula (not south Sweden), Finland and northern Russia.

The red grouse, a very marked race that does not go white in winter, and for long has been regarded as a full species, has a breeding population in Britain-Ireland of order 6, distributed over the moorlands of Scotland, Ireland and Wales, and England from the south Pennines north and in Dartmoor and Exmoor, where introduced. Has been decreasing in Britain since *c* 1940, in Ireland for rather longer, possibly with the deterioration of the heather crop under less meticulous burning and other management systems. Resident.

Black Grouse　　　　　　　　　　　　　　　BII3
Tetrao tetrix Linnaeus 1758
T3 p. 69 and pl. 55 **bottom** (♀ ♂)
as black grouse, *Tetrao tetrix*, Linnæus

A sedentary bird of forest-edge of the boreal and temperate palearctic from Britain (not Ireland), Scandinavia, the Low Countries, eastern France and alpine Italy east through the middle and upper systems of the principal Siberian rivers, including the Amur-Ussuri, nearly to the Sea of Okhotsk, in Europe not extending far into Lapland and ranging in the south-east into the hills of the Balkans and Carpathians but not into the Black Sea plains.

Breeding population of Britain order 5; not recorded from Ireland, even as a fossil. Was probably distributed throughout England, Wales and Scotland in Ice Age times and after; its bones were found fossil in a Shetland dig of Viking times, and it held on in most of southern England and the Isle of Man until the nineteenth century, in Cornwall, Wiltshire, Dorset and Hampshire to *c* 1920. After a marked decrease, probably due to habitat destruction, breeds now in England in very small numbers on Exmoor and the Quantocks and otherwise perhaps only from the south Pennines north, in most Welsh counties and through mainland Scotland and some inner isles of the west.

Pl. 55.

Red Grouse. (♂ & ♀.)
Black Grouse. (♂ & ♀.)

Plate 31 (Thorburn's plate 54)

Family TETRAONIDAE, grouse (*continued*)

Capercaillie   B114
Tetrao urogallus Linnaeus 1758
T3 p. 67 and pl. 54 (♂ ♀)
as capercaillie, *Tetrao urogallus*, Linnæus

A palearctic sedentary species, mainly boreal but extending into temperate hill country, distributed almost continuously in the forest belt where conifers are common or dominant, from the Scandinavian Peninsula and north Poland through Finland and north Russia and through Siberia to reach Lake Baikal and the upper Lena in places. In continental Europe has a discontinuous distribution south of this, which may be partly natural and partly due to forest felling and extermination by man, in two groups: the hills of southern Germany, Czechoslovakia and Poland extending through the Carpathians and the Alps to the Dinaric Alps of Jugoslavia; and the Pyrenees, and Cantabrian Mountains of northern Spain. From fossil evidence it probably survived in England and Wales until after the Ice Age, and inhabited Ireland and Scotland where it was exterminated by about 1790 and 1762 respectively.

Reintroduced, from Swedish stock, at Taymouth, Perth co. in 1837–38 and has now recolonised most of the mainland Highlands, with a headquarters in the east, breeding in order 5. The population fell around both world wars with forest clearance. Resident.

Pl. 54.

Capercaillie (♂♀)

Plate 32 (Thorburn's plate 58)

Family PHASIANIDAE, pheasants, fowl, partridges and quail

Red-legged Partridge   B115
Alectoris rufa (Linnaeus 1758)
T3 p. 76 and pl. 58 **bottom left** (♂ ♀)
as red-legged partridge, *Caccabis rufa* (Linnæus)

Origin probably Mediterranean; a sedentary bird confined to Europe, where it has withdrawn from the Channel Islands, Brittany, Rhineland Germany and Switzerland in historical times. Its natural range is now limited to the Iberian Peninsula, central and southern France, north-west Italy, Elba and Corsica; but it has been successfully introduced into the Azores, Madeira, Canaries and Balearic Isles, in north-west Europe, and to England in *c* 1770 (after unsuccessful attempts from 1673), thence colonising Wales.

Breeding population (almost entirely England) order 6; its hold on Wales is now tenuous, and its headquarters remains in the drier side of England, particularly East Anglia; its northern limit is Staffordshire, Derbyshire and Yorkshire. Resident.

Partridge   B116
Perdix perdix (Linnaeus 1758)
T4 p. 75 and pl. 58 **top** (♂ ♀)
as common partridge, *Perdix cinerea*, Latham

A sedentary palearctic of boreal and temperate Europe and the Russian plains and steppelands east to Chinese Turkestan and the upper Yenisei, extending into northern Turkey and north-west Persia. Extends in continental Europe north to south-east Norway, south and east Sweden, south Finland and Archangel, and south to the Massif Central of France, Italy, Jugoslavia, Albania and northern Greece, and has an isolated population in the Pyrenees and Spanish Cantabrian Mountains. It has been successfully introduced into North America.

Breeding population of Britain-Ireland order 6; virtually breeds everywhere save the Outer Hebrides, Orkney and Shetland, though almost everywhere decreasing (since the 1930's) except in Ireland where an earlier decrease has been reversed under conservation measures at least in the grain-growing areas. The British decrease may be linked with wet summers and farming changes. Resident.

Quail   B117
Coturnix coturnix (Linnaeus 1758)
T3 p. 77 and pl. 58 **bottom right** (♂ ♀)
as quail, *Coturnix communis*, Bonnaterre

Possibly of ethiopian origin, though its widest distribution is palearctic, through which region it is continuously distributed well into the boreal zone east to Amurland and northern Japan (the race east of Lake Baikal is held by some as a separate species), extending as breeder into the oriental region in north India. In palearctic Africa it breeds on the Cape Verdes, Canaries, Madeira and the Azores, and in Morocco, Algeria, Tunisia and Egypt (probably not normally in Arabia); in ethiopian Africa from Kenya through southern Africa outside the main forest belt, and in Madagascar. In Europe it breeds from the Mediterranean (including islands) north sporadically to Faeroe, southernmost Norway and Sweden and south Finland, normally to Denmark, the south Baltic and the Ladoga-Onega latitudes of north Russia. All elements are migratory; those of Europe winter into Africa north of the equator and have been heavily cropped on passage in the eastern Mediterranean from Italy to Egypt, for many centuries.

Breeding population of Britain-Ireland order 3, with signs of recovery in the last two decades after a marked decrease when its nesting became everywhere sporadic. Now after good immigrations in 1947, 1953 and 1964 breeds regularly in parts of southern England and Ireland; and is beginning to be less sporadic as a nester in Wales and in Scotland where it has bred to Shetland.

Pl. 58.

Common Partridge. (♂ & ♀)

Red-legged Partridge. (♂ & ♀)   Quail. (♂ & ♀)

Plate 33 (Thorburn's plate 57)

Family PHASIANIDAE, pheasants, fowl, partridges and quail (*continued*)

Pheasant   B118
Phasianus colchicus Linnaeus 1758
T3 p. 73 and pl. 57
as pheasant, *Phasianus colchicus* (Linnæus)

The feral stock shows the pattern of several wild races which have been used to refresh it; the birds figured by Thorburn resemble the following:

Black-necked pheasant, *Phasianus colchicus colchicus* and races in its group **mid** (♂) and **bottom right** (♀)
as pheasant

Mongolian pheasant, *Phasianus colchicus mongolicus* Brandt 1845 and races in its group **top left** (♀ ♂)
as Mongolian pheasant

Grey-rumped pheasant, *Phasianus colchicus torquatus* J. F. Gmelin 1789 and races in its group **bottom left** (♂)
as Chinese ring-necked pheasant

Japanese, or green pheasant, *Phasianus versicolor* Vieillot 1825. Held a full species by Vaurie in 1965, as a race by other authorities; birds of this type in Britain and Ireland hybridise readily with the others: **mid right** (♂)
as Japanese pheasant:

The *natural* range of this palearctic sedentary species runs from the Volga delta and Caucasus east through the steppes of Russia and Chinese Turkestan to Mongolia and Amurland (or Japan if the Japanese pheasant be included), and south in eastern Asia into the oriental region as far as north Burma and Indochina. Stock from different races has been widely introduced to, and become feral in many parts of the world, including Ireland, Britain, Corsica and every country of continental Europe except Portugal, to limits in southern Fenno-Scandia, north-east Spain, north and central Italy and northern Greece.

On fossil evidence the pheasant was brought to Britain by the Romans, but appears not to have remained feral after their departure. The date of the reintroduction cannot be proved to be earlier than 1059, or just pre-Norman. Besides the original black-necked stock birds of the grey-rumped race-groups were introduced before, and of the Japanese race-group (or species) in, 1741; Mongolian pheasants arrived in the nineteenth century. The present breeding population of Britain-Ireland is order 6; it has bred in every county save Shetland, and has been increasing lately almost everywhere (possibly not Wales) with the help of improved management, stocking and rearing. Resident.

Pl. 57.

Mongolian Pheasant. (♂♀).   Pheasant. (♂♀).   Japanese Pheasant.(♂)
Chinese Ring-necked Pheasant. (♂).

Plate 34 (Thorburn's plate 59)

Order GRUIFORMES

A modern systematic order of the British-Irish families is Gruidae, Rallidae, Otididae.

Family RALLIDAE, rails

Water Rail   B120
Rallus aquaticus Linnaeus 1758
T3 p. 83 and pl. 59 **mid**
as water-rail, *Rallus aquaticus*, Linnæus

A palearctic species breeding from the south of the region into the boreal zone, with a very fragmented distribution in Asia as far east as the upper Lena and the Amur river systems, Sakhalin and Japan. In North Africa breeds in Algeria, Tunis and Egypt. It breeds virtually throughout Europe, including most Mediterranean islands, north to Iceland, south Norway and Sweden, southernmost Finland, and Leningrad in Russia. Northern European elements winter to the Mediterranean.

Breeding population of Britain-Ireland order 4; may be fairly stable, with headquarters in Ireland. Scarce in the north-west Highlands and apparently Wales. Continental birds winter in Britain, and our own stock has weather movements.

Spotted Crake   B121
Porzana porzana (Linnaeus 1766)
T3 p. 79 and pl. 59 **mid right**
as spotted crake, *Porzana maruetta* (Leach)

A western palearctic bird that breeds north into the boreal zone rather further than the water rail; its eastern limit appears to be the headwaters of the Yenisei west of Lake Baikal. From the Mediterranean (where it may breed on the western islands) it ranges north (not Portugal, or, since *c* 1851, Ireland) to Britain, south-west Norway, south Sweden, Finland and Archangel in Russia. In recent times has become rare through much of Europe, doubtless with marsh drainage. The European birds winter in Africa north of the equator.

Has been sporadic as a breeder in England, Wales and Scotland since the nineteenth-century drainage of the principal marshes, though may still breed somewhere almost every year. In 1966 bred in Sutherland, not having previously been found nesting north of the Lowlands. Somerset seems to be the headquarters county. Known only from Ireland now, and many parts of Britain, as a passage migrant.

Sora   B122
Porzana carolina (Linnaeus 1758)
T3 p. 80 and pl. 59 **mid right left**
as Carolina crake, *Porzana carolina* (Linnæus)

A North American species breeding from boreal Canada south to Lower California, the southern Rockies and a line Colorado-Pennsylvania, migrating to northern South America.

Five records: 1 on the River Kennet, near Newbury, Berkshire 1865 October 4; 1 near Cardiff, Glamorgan 1888; female Tiree, Inner Hebrides 1901 October 25; immature male Lewis, Outer Hebrides 1913 November 12; adult male Slyne Head, co. Galway 1920 April 11.

Little Crake   B124
Porzana parva (Scopoli 1769)
T3 p. 81 and pl. 59 **bottom mid**
as little crake, *Porzana parva* (Scopoli)

A western palearctic bird whose breeding range extends into the southern boreal zone and east to round Lake Balkhash in Kazakhstan. In Europe its distribution is fairly continuous in the marshes of the river systems of the Elbe, the south Baltic and the Black Sea; but elsewhere offers a highly relict appearance – indeed, apart from a breeding group in the Po valley, north Italy, nestings reported from Estonia, south Sweden, Holland, Switzerland, France and Spain must be regarded as sporadic, as probably are nestings in Morocco and Egypt. European birds winter in Africa north of the equator.

A rare vagrant to England, more rarely Wales, Scotland and Ireland, most often in spring, occasionally June–November.

Baillon's Crake   B123
Porzana pusilla (Pallas 1776)
T3 p. 82 and pl. 59 **bottom left**
as Baillon's crake, *Porzana bailloni* (Vieillot)

All regions of Old World; breeds Morocco, Portugal, Spain, France, Po valley in Italy and sporadically in England (to 1889), Holland, Sweden, Germany, Czechoslovakia, Austria, Hungary and Jugoslavia; also in systems of Russian inland seas and upper Siberian rivers, Japan, east China, north India, Australia, New Zealand, ethiopian Africa and Madagascar. European birds winter to the Mediterranean.

Bred in Cambridgeshire in 1858 and Norfolk possibly in 1866, certainly in 1889. May never have been more than sporadic; is now a rare vagrant at passage time, most often to England, very rarely to Wales, Scotland and Ireland.

Corncrake   B125
Crex crex (Linnaeus 1758)
T3 p. 78 and pl. 59 **bottom right**
as land-rail, *Crex pratensis*, Bechstein

Western palearctic; breeds east in Asia to upper Lena, south to Lake Balkhash system, in north Persia and Asia Minor; in Europe south to France, northern Italy and Greece, north to Faeroe (sporadic), Scotland, southern Fenno-Scandia and Archangel. European birds winter in ethiopian Africa to south.

Breeding population of Britain-Ireland order 4, after about a century of progressive decrease, possibly correlated with early mowing, other agricultural changes and the proliferation of pylons and wires. Once breeding in every county, has strongholds now mainly in the Outer Isles and western Ireland, and is virtually extinct in all lowland areas of better farmland. Continental birds visit on passage.

Moorhen   B126
Gallinula chloropus (Linnaeus 1758)
T3 p. 84 and pl. 59 **mid left**
as moor-hen, *Gallinula chloropus* (Linnaeus)

Cosmopolitan; occupies virtually the whole world, including a few oceanic archipelagos, from tropical to temperate climes (not deserts) and some low boreal areas, except Australasia where a close species may be descendent. European birds breed north to south Fenno-Scandia and Leningrad; some migrate to the Mediterranean.

Breeding population of Britain-Ireland order 6; successful and stable, and perhaps generally increasing in the north. Breeds in every county; resident except in the north; some continental birds winter with us.

American Purple Gallinule
Porphyrula martinica (Linnaeus 1766)
Not illustrated

Breeds from the southern United States to northern Argentina, the northern elements migratory and wandering.

One record: an immature female Hugh Town, St Mary's, Scilly 1958 November 7–9.

Coot   B127
Fulica atra Linnaeus 1758
T3 p. 85 and pl. 59 **top**
as coot, *Fulica atra*, Linnæus

Origin possibly palearctic, in which region breeds north into the boreal zone and east to Japan; and breeds through most of the continental oriental region and in Papua and Australia. Some elements migrate, some European birds to Africa north of the equator. Breeds in Europe to southern Fenno-Scandia.

Breeding population of Britain-Ireland order 5; has nested in present century in every county and on the whole stable, though has lately withdrawn as regular breeder from some northern Scottish isles. The British-Irish population is generally resident.

Pl.59.

Coot.

Moor-hen.   Water-Rail.   Carolina Crake. Spotted Crake.
Baillon's Crake.   Little Crake.   Land-Rail.

Plate 35 (Thorburn's plate 60)

Family OTIDIDAE, bustards

Great Bustard B128
Otis tarda Linnaeus 1758
T3 p. 86 and pl. 60 (frontispiece) (♂ ♂ displaying and ♀ ♀)
as great bustard, *Otis tarda*, Linnæus

A palearctic bird with a clearly relict distribution in Spain and south Portugal, perhaps still nearby Morocco; the Danubian system; the north German plain and parts of Poland and Czechoslovakia; and (by no means continuous) through the Russian and central Asian steppes to Manchuria and Ussuriland. Now extinct in north-west Europe, including Scotland and England; reported to have bred Scotland (Berwick co.) before 1526; last indigenous birds died in Norfolk in 1845.

A very rare vagrant now to England; has been recorded in Wales, Scotland and Ireland.

Pl. 60.

Great Bustard. (♂ & ♀)

Plate 36 (Thorburn's plate 61)

Family OTIDIDAE, bustards (*continued*)

Little Bustard
B129

Otis tetrax Linnaeus 1758
T4 p. 1 and pl. 61 **top left** (♀ ♂)
as *Otis tetrax*, Linnæus

A palearctic bird with a distribution, now fragmented, from Portugal and south Spain and the opposite African shore east through central and southern France, Sardinia, south Italy, the Balkans and the Danubian system to the steppes of the north Caspian, the uppermost Ob and to the Lake Balkhash area of central Asia.

A rare vagrant, mostly in autumn to eastern England; has been recorded from Wales, Scotland and Ireland.

Houbara
B130

Chlamydotis undulata (Jacquin 1784)
T4 p. 2 and pl. 61 **mid right**
as *Otis macqueeni*, J. E. Gray

A southern palearctic bird of the semi-desert, breeding from the Canaries through North Africa, Asia Minor and the Russian, Persian and Chinese steppes and deserts to Outer Mongolia; a considerable wanderer.

Five records (the four based on specimens were all of the eastern race not breeding west of Sinai): 1 Kirton-in-Lindsay, Lincolnshire 1847 October 7; adult male Marske, near Redcar, Yorkshire 1892 October 5; young male Easington, Holderness, Yorkshire 1896 October 17; female Pitfour, St Fergus, Aberdeen co. 1898 October 24; young male seen Hinton, Westleton, Suffolk 1962 November 21–December 29.

Family GRUIDAE, cranes

Crane
B119

Girus grus (Linnaeus 1758)
T4 p. 3 and pl. 61 **bottom**
as crane, *Grus communis*, Bechstein

A palearctic bird formerly breeding throughout most of the region north far into the boreal zone, and east to about the headwaters of the Indigirka in Siberia. In recent historical times its breeding distribution has become much fragmented, in Asia Minor and Europe with the claiming of wetlands and human predation, and is most continuous from central south-east Norway, south and east Sweden, Finnish Lapland and Archangel south to north Germany, north Poland and the Ukraine. Elsewhere it has been virtually exterminated, though there are apparently still relict populations in the Danube mouth, Jugoslavia and the marismas of the Guadalquivir, and it recolonised Denmark in 1952. It is now extinct as a breeder in Ireland (perhaps since the fourteenth century), Britain (last England *c* 1600), France, Italy, Austria, Hungary (*c* 1910), Albania and Greece, and from fossil evidence probably bred in other European countries in and after the Ice Age. The European population winters into ethiopian Africa north of the equator.

After its extinction in Britain-Ireland (once bred in all four countries), became a progressively sporadic visitor into first half of the present century, but lately has become fairly regular on passage in England and has occasionally over-wintered. Welsh and Scottish records are rarer, and Irish records very few.

Order CHARADRIIFORMES

A modern systematic order of the British-Irish families is Haematopodidae, Charadriidae, Scolopacidae, Recurvirostridae, Phalaropodidae, Burhinidae, Glareolidae, Stercorariidae, Laridae, Alcidae.

Family BURHINIDAE, thick-knees

Stone Curlew
B189

Burhinus oedicnemus (Linnaeus 1758)
T4 p. 5 and pl. 61 **top right**
as stone-curlew, *Œdicnemus scolopax* (S. G. Gmelin)

Origin probably the Mediterranean area or the dry steppes and semi-deserts of Turkestan; from the Canaries and western Europe through the Mediterranean zone, the north Sahara, Arabia and the steppes and deserts to the Lake Balkhash area, and through India to Burma. Breeds north in Europe, rather discontinuously, to the south Baltic. European birds mostly winter to Africa north of the equator.

Breeding population (England only) order 3, perhaps 200–400 breeding pairs. Became much reduced in nineteenth century, and again in twentieth-century wartime, through cultivation of habitat, and is declining even in heartland of Suffolk and Norfolk heaths and brecks; some fairly stable populations in Berkshire and Hampshire. Most British birds migrate, though a few have wintered in southernmost England; a vagrant only to Wales, Scotland and Ireland.

Pl. 61.

Little Bustard. ♂♀.
Crane.

Stone. Curlew.
Macqeen's Bustard.

Plate 37 (Thorburn's plate 64)

Family HAEMATOPODIDAE, oyster-catchers

Oystercatcher   BI31
Haematopus ostralegus Linnaeus 1758
T4 p. 20 and pl. 64 **top right** (summer and winter)
as oyster-catcher, *Hæmatopus ostralegus*, Linnæus

A palearctic or cosmopolitan bird – depending on systematic opinion. The palearctic group is fragmented, with a main coastal race inhabiting nearly all Europe; an inland race occupying the systems of the Ob in the west Siberian plain and of the northern Black Sea, the Caspian, Aral and Balkhash rivers; and an east Asian race with a curious relict distribution on the shores of Korea and the Sea of Okhotsk and in Amurland. Other forms in the Americas, Canaries, west and southern Africa, Australia and New Zealand may be conspecific. Most elements are migratory.

Breeding population of Britain-Ireland order 5 (20,000–40,000 pairs); has recovered and lately expanded from a decrease in the nineteenth century; breeds on virtually all our coasts and increasingly inland in north England, Scotland and western Ireland. Many passengers and winter visitors (probably at least as many as our breeding population) come to Britain-Ireland from Iceland, Faeroe and the Continent.

Family RECURVIROSTRIDAE, stilts and avocets

Black-winged Stilt   BI86
Himantopus himantopus (Linnaeus 1758)
T4 p. 22 and pl. 64 **bottom left**
as black-winged stilt, *Himantopus candidus*, Bonnaterre

A cosmopolitan species with a somewhat fragmented distribution that includes large parts of the Americas (including the West Indies), the Mediterranean and the Black Sea, Caspian, Aral and Balkhash river systems, the continental oriental region, the central and eastern ethiopian region including Madagascar, and Australia, New Zealand and Hawaii. In Europe normally breeds north to south-west France, but has bred sporadically further north to Holland (1935, 1949, 1958).

Normally a rare vagrant to south-east England, recorded also in west England, Scotland and Ireland. In 1945 an abnormal irruption took place and a small colony (2 or 3 successful nests) bred on Nottingham sewage farm.

Avocet   BI85
Recurvirostra avosetta Linnaeus 1758
T4 p. 21 and pl. 64 **mid right**
as avocet, *Recurvirostra avocetta*, Linnæus

A palearctic bird, probably of central steppe origin, with small isolated populations (possibly recent colonists) in the central and southern ethiopian regions, and a headquarters from the Black Sea to beyond (south of) Lake Baikal. In western Europe breeds discontinuously in the Iberian Peninsula, south France, the Low Countries, Denmark and northwest Germany, and in England (has bred once Ireland). Has very close relations in the Americas and Australia. The European stock migrates to ethiopian Africa.

Breeding population (England now) high order 2 or low order 3. Having become extinct in England with wetland drainage for about a century avocets recolonised in the 1940's (a sporadic pair having bred in co. Wexford, Ireland, in 1938), presumably from Holland, where a stock was flourishing under protection. After a nest in Essex in 1944 and another in Norfolk in 1946 a colony settled at Havergate, Suffolk (now R.S.P.B. and National Nature Reserve) in 1947. Birds also bred at Minsmere in Suffolk in 1947–48 and have again from 1963, and in Essex in 1954 and Kent in 1958. The Havergate colony became the headquarters, and stabilised *c* 1952, reaching a total of nearly 100 breeding pairs in 1957, and normally rearing up to 60 young from about the same number of nests.

No less than *c* 145 young were reared in England 1966. Outside south-east England the avocet is a rarish passage and summer migrant to the rest of England, Wales and Ireland and has been recorded in Scotland.

Family PHALAROPODIDAE, phalaropes

Grey Phalarope   BI87
Phalaropus fulicarius (Linnaeus 1758)
T4 p. 23 and pl. 64 **top left** (summer and winter)
as grey phalarope, *Phalaropus fulicarius* (Linnæus)

A tundra breeder extending into the high arctic zone round the northern Bering Sea and Polar Basin and on many arctic islands, wintering at sea in the southern hemisphere.

Travels on passage by many European inland waters and coasts, and is regular in southern England, particularly in autumn, fairly often recorded on the coasts of Wales, the Lowlands and Ireland, and rare elsewhere.

Red-necked Phalarope   BI88
Phalaropus lobatus (Linnaeus 1758)
T4 p. 24 and pl. 64 **bottom right** (winter and summer)
as red-necked phalarope, *Phalaropus hyperboreus* (Linnæus)

A circumpolar low arctic and boreal zone breeder, reaching few major arctic islands apart from south Greenland, ranging as a breeder south to a limit in Scotland and Ireland.

Breeding population of Britain-Ireland order 2; decreased in the nineteenth century as the result of egg-collection, from which recovered with protection; present decrease may be due to increased warmth and humidity of summer climate at the south end of its range. Has stabilised at *c* 30 pairs in Shetland, but has decreased to a very low population in Orkney and co. Mayo; breeds also Outer Hebrides and Tiree in Inner Hebrides, and has bred co. Donegal. Otherwise a passage migrant in south-east England, and rare in Wales, and away from breeding grounds in Scotland and Ireland.

Wilson's Phalarope
Phalaropus tricolor (Vieillot 1819)
Not illustrated

Breeds from boreal Canada south in the western mountains and uplands to California, Colorado and the Middle West, wintering normally to Chile and Argentina.

Twenty records 1954–66; first, 1 seen Rosyth, Fife 1954 September 11–October 5; England 13; Wales 3; Scotland 3; Ireland 1; May–November, half August–September.

Family CHARADRIIDAE, plovers and turnstones

A modern systematic order is BI34, 135 (pl. 39), 137 (pl. 38), 136, 138, 142 (pl. 39), 140, 141, 139, 132, 133 (pl. 38), 143 (pl. 37).

Turnstone   BI43
Arenaria interpres (Linnaeus 1758)
T4 p. 19 and pl. 64 **mid left** (winter and summer)
as turnstone, *Strepsilas interpres* (Linnæus)

An holarctic bird, breeding principally in the arctic and into the highest arctic in northern Greenland and on most of the principal islands of the Arctic Ocean, and on coasts into the boreal and temperate zones in the north Bering Sea, virtually all Scandinavia and the Estonian and Russian Baltic. A globe-spanning migrant; some elements winter in high southern latitudes in South America, South Africa and the New Zealand Archipelago.

A regular passage migrant and winter visitor to the whole of Britain-Ireland; non-breeding birds often summer in northern Scotland. Chiefly on coast, but inland also on passage.

Grey Phalarope. (winter & summer).   Oyster.catcher. (summer & winter).
Turnstone. (summer & winter).   Avocet.
Black winged Stilt.   Red.necked Phalarope. (summer & winter).

Plate 38 (Thorburn's plate 63)

Family CHARADRIIDAE, plovers and turnstones (*continued*)

Golden Plover BI40
Pluvialis apricaria (Linnaeus 1758)
T4 p. 15 and pl. 63 **mid left** (winter and summer)
as golden plover, *Charadrius pluvialis*, Linnæus

Origin probably European; breeds in Iceland, Faeroe, Ireland, Britain, north Denmark, Norway, western Sweden and the Baltic islands of Öland and Gotland, northern Finland, a broad strip of the Russian coastal tundras from Murmansk east to the lower Yenisei, and from Leningrad to Lithuania. Winters to the African Mediterranean and north India.

Breeding population of Britain-Ireland order 5; decreasing (causes not identified) except in the main hills of Highland mainland; still breeds in England to the south Pennines and in the West Country survives now only on Dartmoor; has withdrawn in Wales and in Ireland to the north and north-west. Icelandic and other passengers visit Ireland and Britain.

Lesser Golden Plover BI41
Pluvialis dominica (P. L. S. Müller 1776)
T4 p. 16 and pl. 63 **mid right** (winter)
as Asiatic golden plover, *Charadrius dominicus*, P. L. S. Müller

Origin palearctic or nearctic; breeds from Yamal and Yenisei in Siberia (where overlaps with golden plover) east via the Arctic Ocean coastal tundras and the coasts of the Bering Sea through Alaska into Canadian arctic Franklin. Winters in the oriental region and on Pacific lands to New Zealand and in eastern South America to Argentina.

Eleven British-Irish records 1870–1966; those identified to race equally divided between the palearctic and nearctic forms; the first 1 Epsom, Surrey 1870 November 12; England 3; Scotland 3; Ireland 5; all September–November.

Grey Plover BI39
Pluvialis squatarola (Linnaeus 1758)
T4 p. 14 and pl. 63 **bottom left** (winter and summer)
as grey plover, *Squatarola helvetica* (Linnæus)

An holarctic breeder, but scarcely breeds Europe; nests in the wide tundra strip of the Arctic Ocean coast from Kanin and Kolguev in northern European Russia east more or less continuously to Franklin in Canada, on the west coast of the north Bering Sea, and on a few islands of the Polar Basin (not Greenland), mostly in the Canadian arctic. A globe-spanning migrant to most temperate southern hemisphere coasts.

Passage migrant and winter visitor to Britain-Ireland, on all coasts (vagrant only inland) but specially those of south-east England.

Sociable Lapwing BI32
Vanellus gregarius (Pallas 1771)
T4 p. 18 and pl. 63 **top left** (young and adult)
as sociable plover, *Vanellus gregarius* (Pallas)

A bird confined to the Turkestanian steppes (formerly eastern Ukraine, has declined) of Russia from the lower Volga to the upper Ob and Lake Balkhash. Normally migrates to the eastern ethiopian and western oriental regions north of the equator; wanders, and has done so to several western European countries.

Eight British-Irish records *c* 1860–1963: England 5; Scotland 1; Ireland 2; the earliest 1 near St Michaels-on-Wyre, Lancashire *c* 1860 autumn; August–December, 1 April.

Lapwing BI33
Vanellus vanellus (Linnaeus 1758)
T3 pl. 60 (2 flying, here pl. 35), and
T4 p. 19 and pl. 63 **bottom right**
as lapwing, *Vanellus vulgaris*, Bechstein

A palearctic bird, breeding from the drier plains north into the boreal zone, east to Ussuriland; in Europe breeds locally in Portugal and Spain (also in 1 place in north-west Morocco), *not* in the Mediterranean islands, Italy (except breeds Po valley), high Alps, Carpathians, or south Greece, but otherwise north to Ireland, Britain, Faeroe and Iceland where sporadic, south Scandinavia and Russia to Lake Onega. Northern European elements migrate to the Mediterranean.

Breeding population of Britain-Ireland order 6; may still breed in every country, though has been *generally* decreasing for about a century. Decrease was probably temporarily arrested in some areas by a special protection Act of 1926, and has been reversed in northern Scotland (where it still slowly increases) in the present century, but since *c* 1940 has become marked in most other areas, including Ireland and Wales, probably as a consequence of changes in farming methods. Migratory movements in Britain-Ireland involve departing northern breeders in autumn and an influx of continental winter visitors.

Killdeer BI37
Charadrius vociferus Linnaeus 1758
T4 p. 14 and pl. 63 **top right**
as killdeer, *Ægialitis vocifera* (Linnæus)

A nearctic species breeding from boreal Canada to northern México and the Gulf Coast, normally to northern South America and the West Indies.

Fourteen British-Irish records 1859–1964; first, Knapp Mills, near Christchurch, Hampshire 1859 April; England 8; Scotland 1; Ireland 5; all November–April.

Pl. 63.

Sociable Plover (adult & young).   Killdeer Plover.
Golden Plover (summer & winter).   Asiatic Golden Plover.
Grey Plover (summer & winter).   Lapwing

Plate 39 (Thorburn's plate 62)

Family CHARADRIIDAE, plovers and turnstones (continued)

Ringed Plover   B134
Charadrius hiaticula Linnaeus 1758
T4 p. 11 and pl. 62 **lower mid right**
as ringed plover, *Ægialitis hiaticola* (Linnæus)

Origin doubtless palearctic; basically an arctic bird of the northern boreal and tundra zones of northern Asia west from the Chukotski Peninsula into northern Europe, with outposts on some arctic islands, reaching the nearctic in Greenland and eastern Baffin Island. Outside Fenno-Scandia, Iceland, Faeroe and northern Scotland breeds on the *coasts* of the Baltic, Denmark, the Low Countries, northern France and Britain-Ireland, and has bred sporadically in Italy and Germany. Western European elements winter to southern African coasts.

Breeding population of Britain-Ireland order 4; still breeds in virtually every coastal county and some inland ones notably in Scotland, Ireland and the Norfolk–Suffolk breckland; but since the 1930's, and progressively since the Second World War has become fragmented in distribution and often seriously reduced in population owing to human disturbance, coastal building and agricultural changes inland; has maintained its status best in Highlands and Ireland.

Little Ringed Plover   B135
Charadrius dubius Scopoli 1786
T4 p. 12 and pl. 62 **bottom mid**
as little ringed plover, *Ægialitis curonica* (J. F. Gmelin)

Origin probably palearctic, in which breeds from semi-desert well into the boreal zone, east in Asia to the Okhotsk Sea, Sakhalin and Japan; extends through the oriental region from India through most of continental Asia and Ceylon to Hainan, Taiwan and the Philippines; has an outpost in New Guinea and New Ireland. Northern European elements migrate to equatorial Africa. In Europe breeds from Mediterranean to extreme south-east Norway, south and Baltic Sweden, south Finland and the White Sea in Russia.

Breeding population (England so far) order 3; *c* 170–200 pairs; invaded England from the Continent first in 1938 when bred at Tring, Hertfordshire; since subsequent breeding (2 pairs Tring and 1 Ashford, Middlesex 1944) has bred every year in increasing numbers and now nests or has lately nested in every English county west to Hampshire, Gloucestershire and Cheshire and north to Yorkshire. By 1947 12 to 15 pairs summered in 11 places in 6 counties; by 1950 29 in 21 in 11; by 1956 74 in 47 in 20; by 1962 157 in 87 in 23; the increase continued after this. The successful invasion may be due partly to climate change, partly to the proliferation of gravel pits. Previously was a very rare passage migrant, as such virtually confined to south-east England. Recorded from Scotland (Outer Hebrides) and Wales, and once from Ireland.

Kentish Plover   B136
Charadrius alexandrinus Linnaeus 1758
T4 p. 13 and pl. 62 **bottom right**
as Kentish plover *Ægialitis cantiana* (Latham)

Cosmopolitan; breeds coastally in Gulf and western United States, Lower California, West Indies, Peru, Chile, Europe from south Sweden to Portugal, Mediterranean and Black Seas, Azores, Madeira, Canaries, Cape Verdes, virtually all Africa, Madagascar, Arabia, Persian Gulf to Kathiawar, Ceylon, Japan to Indochina, Java, Australia and Tasmania; and inland mainly in central Asia, southern Australia, east Africa, parts of United States and the middle Danube. Partially migratory.

Formerly nested in England, from which banished lately by seaside interference and development and perhaps collectors: in the early years of the present century survived well in Kent, where between 30 and 44 pairs in 1906–08, and occasionally bred in neighbouring east Sussex; last bred in Kent 1937 or rather later, in Sussex 1956 (last record) in Suffolk (sporadic) 1952. Now only a rare passenger, more often in spring than autumn, in southern and eastern England; has been recorded in Wales, Scotland and Ireland.

Caspian Plover   B138
Charadrius asiaticus Pallas 1773
T4 p. 10 and pl. 62 **mid left** (young and adult)
as Caspian plover, *Ægialitis asiatica* (Pallas)

Palearctic; breeds from north of the Caucasus to the Kirghiz steppes and Lake Balkhash; winters south of the Sahara.

One record: adult male shot, and another bird seen North Denes, near Great Yarmouth, Norfolk 1890 May 22.

Dotterel   B142
Eudromias morinellus (Linnaeus 1758)
T4 p. 9 and pl. 62 **bottom left**
as dotterel, *Eudromias morinellus* (Linnæus)

Origin possibly arctic; with a highly fragmented distribution in north Britain; the Scandinavian mountain backbone, Lapland, the Kola Peninsula of north Russia; the Urals; Sudeten Czechoslovakia; the Carpathians; the easternmost Alps; the Abruzzi in Italy; in Asia and Taimyr, two areas further east in Siberia; and between Lakes Balkhash and Baikal. A breeding pair has been collected at Barrow, Alaska. European elements winter to the south Mediterranean.

Breeding population (Britain only) order 2; *c* 60–80 pairs, after a century of decrease probably under shooting and collecting pressures. Headquarters is now in the Cairngorms and Monadhliaths; other populations survive in Easter Ross, but the bird has probably nested only sporadically in England (Cumberland-Westmorland) since *c* 1927 and in Kirkcudbright st. since 1945, and has been extinct in Sutherland since the last century. A regular spring and rarer autumn passage migrant through England and the Lowlands, occasional in Wales, rare in north Scotland and Ireland.

Family GLAREOLIDAE, coursers and pratincoles

Cream-coloured Courser   B192
Cursorius cursor (Latham 1787)
T4 p. 7 and pl. 62 **upper mid right**
as cream-coloured courser, *Cursorius gallicus* (J. F. Gmelin)

A semi-desert bird breeding in northern Africa, Arabia, Iraq, Persia, Russian Transcaspia, Afghanistan and Baluchistan, perhaps more wandering than migratory.

Rare (October–December) vagrant to eastern and southern England; recorded from Wales, Scotland and Ireland.

Pratincole   B190
Glareola pratincola (Linnaeus 1766)
T4 p. 6 and pl. 62 **top right** (2 birds)
as pratincole, *Glareola pratincola* (Linnæus)

Origin possibly oriental: breeds in dry country in the southern Iberian Peninsula, north-west Africa, Sicily, the Rhône delta in France, the Po delta in Italy, and from Greece and the Balkans east through the Black Sea area and Asia Minor to beyond Lake Balkhash in the steppes, and south-east through Persia and Afghanistan to India and most of the continental oriental region and on Hainan, Taiwan, Japan (rare) and the Philippines. Also breeds south of the Sahara in semi-desert zone to southern Africa. Migratory and dispersive.

Rare but almost annual vagrant to eastern and southern England, more rarely to Scotland; has been recorded in Wales and Ireland.

Black-winged Pratincole   B191
Glareola nordmanni Nordmann 1842
T4 p. 7 and pl. 62 **top left** (2 birds)
as black-winged pratincole, *Glareola melanoptera*, Nordmann

A dry country bird, breeding from the Danube delta in Rumania through Russian steppes from the Ukraine to the Aral Sea area; has bred in Hungary and may have in Iraq. Migrates to Africa south of the equator; and dispersive.

Six British-Irish records 1909–60; first 1 near Northallerton, Yorkshire 1909 August 17; England 4; Scotland 1; Ireland 1; May, June and 4 August.

Pl. 62.

Black-winged Pratincole.   Pratincole.
Caspian Plover. (adult & young).   Cream-coloured Courser.
                                     Ringed Plover.
    Dotterel.   Little Ringed Plover.   Kentish Plover.

Plate 40 (Thorburn's plate 65)

Family SCOLOPACIDAE, sandpipers, snipe, etc.

A modern systematic order is B180 (pl. 42), western sandpiper (pl. 40), 171, 173, 172 (pl. 41), 174 (pl. 40), 175 (pl. 41), 176, sharp-tailed sandpiper (pl. 40), 170, 178, 179, 169, 181 (pl. 41), 184 (pl. 42), 183 (pl. 40), 149, 182 (pl. 42), long-billed dowitcher, 144, 162, 163, 161 (pl. 43), 164 (pl. 81), 166, 165, 156, 158 (pl. 43), 157, 167, 159, 160 (pl. 42), 168 (pl. 40), stilt sandpiper, 154, 155, 150, 153, 151, 152 (pl. 44), 148, 145, 146, 147 (pl. 40).

Woodcock   B148
Scolopax rusticola Linnaeus 1758
T4 p. 25 and pl. 65 **top right**
as woodcock, *Scolopax rusticula*, Linnæus

A palearctic bird with a wide range through temperate, boreal and wooded highland zones from the Azores, Madeira and Canaries, and western Europe across central Eurasia to Amurland, Sakhalin and Japan; and has a separated population in the Himalayas which extends a little into the oriental region. Some European elements migrate to the Mediterranean.

Breeding population of Britain-Ireland order 5; has lately increased in some new plantations, decreased in (fewer) areas where woodland has been felled. Breeds in all counties save Cornwall, Pembroke co. and Anglesey – through Scotland after a surge north in the late nineteenth century; though sporadic in Shetland, Orkney, the Outer Hebrides (and co. Donegal). Some of our stock migrates to south Europe; continental birds pass and winter, especially in Ireland.

Snipe   B145
Gallinago gallinago (Linnaeus 1758)
T4 p. 27 and pl. 65 **top left** (2 birds)
as common snipe, *Gallinago cœlestis* (Frenzel)

Cosmopolitan: breeds in most of South America and continental ethiopian Africa, with outposts in oriental India. The holarctic range reaches the edge of the tundra in continental Eurasia, Alaska and Canada, and includes Iceland, Faeroe, Ireland and Britain. In Europe has an outpost in north Portugal; otherwise its south limit is central France, the Alps and the Danube valley. Some European birds migrate to Africa north of the equator.

Breeding population of Britain-Ireland order 6; spread around the turn of the present century after a decrease in early nineteenth, though has declined in parts of England in the last two decades; now probably extinct in old Middlesex, sporadic in Isle of Wight, but otherwise may breed in every county. Has a migratory pattern similar to the woodcock's.

Great Snipe   B146
Gallinago media (Latham 1787)
T4 p. 26 and pl. 65 **mid right**
as great snipe, *Gallinago major* (J. F. Gmelin)

A boreal bird of the western palearctic, breeding continuously from south Finland to Lithuania and east in Russia to virtually the whole system of the Ob and the upper systems of the Dnepr, Don, Volga and Ural Rivers. Has an outpost population virtually the length of the Norway-Sweden mountain backbone. Winters to Africa well south of the Sahara.

A scarce passage visitor to eastern and southern England; no more than a vagrant in Wales, Scotland and Ireland.

Jack Snipe   B147
Lymnocryptes minimus (Brünnich 1764)
T4 p. 28 and pl. 65 **mid left**
as jack snipe, *Gallinago gallinula*, Linnæus

A boreal Siberian species, breeding in Lapland and north Finland but otherwise in Russia from Murmansk and Latvia east through the middle systems of the arctic-flowing rivers to the Kolyma, reaching to the edge of the tundra. Some European elements winter to Africa south of the equator.

A regular passage migrant and winter visitor in smallish numbers to England, Wales, Scotland and Ireland.

Broad-billed Sandpiper   B183
Limicola falcinellus (Pontoppidan 1763)
T4 p. 29 and pl. 65 **bottom left**
as broad-billed sandpiper, *Limicola platyrhyncha* (Temminck)

A 'Siberian'-type bird whose nest has never been found in Siberia, though a race seems to live east of the Yenisei which migrates as far as Australia. The European race breeds in the mountain backbone of Norway-Sweden to Lapland, north Finland and the Kola Peninsula of Russia, and migrates to the Mediterranean, Red Sea and as far as India and Ceylon.

A rare vagrant, mostly to eastern and southern England at autumn passage time; also in spring, and rarely in Scotland and Ireland; has been recorded from Wales.

Terek Sandpiper   B168
Xenus cinerus (Güldenstädt 1775)
T4 p. 30 and pl. 65 **mid left bottom**
as Terek sandpiper, *Terekia cinerea* (Güldenstädt)

Another Siberian wader; breeds in the boreal palearctic, to the edge of the tundra, in a wide band in Russia from Estonia south to the upper systems of the Volga and most Siberian rivers; has bred sporadically in Finland. Migrates through the oriental region to Australia, straggling even to New Zealand.

Five English sight records: 1 Midrips, Sussex 1951 May 30; 1 Southwold, Suffolk 1951 June 2–6 (same bird?); 1 Teesmouth, Durham 1952 September 27–28; 1 Melancoose Reservoir near Newquay, Cornwall 1961 June 13; 1 Pennington Marshes, Hampshire 1963 May 25–31.

Baird's Sandpiper   B174
Calidris bairdii (Coues 1861)
T4 p. 31 and pl. 65 **bottom right**
as Baird's sandpiper, *Tringa bairdi* (Coues)

A nearctic arctic breeder, reaching the high arctic in the tundra zone, and extending into the palearctic in the Chukotski Peninsula of Siberia. Nests from Alaska east through the Canadian arctic to north-west Greenland. Normally winters into the neotropical region as far as Chile and Argentina.

Sixteen records 1903–66: the earliest 1 Hunstanton, Norfolk 1903 September 16; England 13; Scotland 1; Ireland 2; June–October, mostly September.

Pectoral Sandpiper   B176
Calidris melanotos (Vieillot 1819)
T4 p. 31 and pl. 65 **mid right bottom**
as pectoral sandpiper, *Tringa maculata*, Vieillot

Holarctic; breeds in Siberia east from Taimyr in the tundra and north boreal zones through Alaska and the Canadian arctic to south Hudson Bay. Winters south in the neotropical region to Chile and Patagonia; has reached Samoa, Australia and New Zealand.

Lately an annual passage vagrant, mainly in autumn to south and east England, quite often inland at reservoirs and sewage farms; has been recorded from other parts of the four countries.

Sharp-tailed Sandpiper
Calidris acuminata (Horsfield 1821)
Not illustrated

An eastern Siberian species whose breeding range may centre on the Indigirka-Kolyma delta systems. Normally migrates via Pacific shores and islands, often to Australia and New Zealand.

Seven British records 1848–1963: England 6; Scotland 1; the first, Yarmouth, Norfolk 1848 September; 6 August–October; 1 January.

Western Sandpiper
Calidris mauri (Cabanis 1857)
Not illustrated

Breeds in tundras of coastal west and north Alaska, wintering to western South America from the region of the equator.

Three records: 1 seen and trapped Fair Isle, Shetland 1956 May 28–June 3; 1 Kilcoole, co. Wicklow 1960 October 14; 1 Akeagh Lough, co. Kerry 1961 September 17–23.

Pl. 65.

Common Snipe.   Woodcock.

Jack Snipe.   Great Snipe.

Broad-billed Sandpiper. Terek Sandpiper. Pectoral Sandpiper. Baird's Sandpiper.

Plate 41 (Thorburn's plate 66)

Family SCOLOPACIDAE, sandpipers, snipe, etc. (*continued*)

Little Stint BI71
Calidris minuta (Leisler 1812)
T4 p. 34 and pl. 66 **upper mid right** (autumn and summer)
as little stint, *Tringa minuta*, Leisler

An arctic palearctic bird, breeding on the coastal tundras from northernmost Norway and the Kola Peninsula east to the Yana delta, and on Kolguev, Vaigach, south Novaya Zemlya and the New Siberian Islands. Winters normally to southern Africa, India, and Indian Ocean islands.

A passage migrant, not uncommonly in autumn on the east and Irish Sea coasts of England, Wales, Scotland and Ireland, scarce in spring and rare in winter.

Temminck's Stint BI73
Calidris temminckii (Leisler 1812)
T4 p. 35 and pl. 66 **lower mid right**
as Temminck's stint, *Tringa temmincki*, Leisler

An arctic palearctic breeder of the tundra and northern boreal zones, ranging in Russia from the Kola Peninsula east to the Bering Sea in the Chukotski Peninsula, and the Anadyr. In Norway breeds in Lapland and off-lying islands and south on isolated highlands; in Sweden and Finland breeds in Lapland and on both coasts of the Gulf of Bothnia. European birds migrate to Africa just south of the equator.

A scarce passage visitor, mainly to south and east England, rarer in Scotland, and a vagrant to Wales and Ireland; but has bred (unsuccessfully) in the Cairngorms in 1934, 1936 and 1956 and in central Yorkshire in 1951.

Least Sandpiper BI72
Calidris minutilla (Vieillot 1819)
T4 p. 34 and pl. 66 **bottom mid**
as American stint, *Tringa minutilla*, Vieillot

A boreal nearctic species breeding to the edge of the tundra from Alaska to Labrador and south in Canada to James Bay, islands in the Gulf of St Lawrence, Newfoundland and Sable Island. Winters to beyond the equator in South America.

Twelve records 1853–1966: the earliest 1 Marazion Marsh, Mount's Bay, Cornwall 1853 October 10; England 7; Scotland 1; Ireland 4; August–October.

White-rumped Sandpiper BI75
Calidris fuscicollis (Vieillot 1819)
T4 p. 32 and pl. 66 **mid left**
as Bonaparte's sandpiper, *Tringa fuscicollis*, Vieillot

A nearctic tundra breeder, ranging from north Alaska to Melville, and nesting on Baffin and Southampton Islands. Winters into South America as far as Tierra del Fuego.

A rare vagrant, mostly in autumn to Channel England and the West Country, also to Ireland, and recorded in Scotland (not Wales); a few spring and winter records.

Purple Sandpiper BI70
Calidris maritima (Brünnich 1764)
T4 p. 36 and pl. 66 **bottom left** (summer and winter)
as purple sandpiper, *Tringa striata*, Linnæus

A tundra breeder of the holarctic, reaching the high arctic, with a fragmented breeding distribution. The population of the Bering Sea coasts and islands differs enough to be held a full species by some modern authorities. The main groups, possibly of palearctic origin, breed in Canadian Franklin, Hudson Bay and Keewatin; in Greenland, Iceland, Faeroe, Norway, central Sweden and the Murmansk coast; on Bear Island, Spitsbergen, Franz Josef Land, Novaya Zemlya, Taimyr and south Svernaya Zemlya, possibly the New Siberian Islands. The European population appears to winter mostly in Britain-Ireland and west France and Spain.

In Britain-Ireland present on virtually all rocky coasts except in high summer, and in places common.

Dunlin BI78
Calidris alpina (Linnaeus)
T4 p. 33 and pl. 66 **top right** (winter and summer)
as dunlin, *Tringa alpina*, Linnæus

An arctic breeder of the holarctic, mostly on the tundra but with extensions, particularly in Europe, into the boreal zone. Apart from our own breeding race, breeds from high arctic east Greenland and Spitsbergen through Norway and adjoining parts of western Sweden round the northern coastal tundras of Russia (including south Novaya Zemlya) to the north Bering Sea coasts, Alaska and north-western Mackenzie, with a group in Keewatin, Southampton Island and Hudson Bay. Our race breeds from low arctic east Greenland, Iceland, Faeroe, Ireland and Britain to Holland (sporadic), Denmark, south-east Sweden, the Baltic islands, the south Baltic coast from north Germany to Leningrad and western Finland; and winters to the African coasts, generally north of the equator.

Breeding population of Britain-Ireland order 4; stable, with some signs of decrease in coastal and southern areas; is now extinct in Norfolk and Lincolnshire, and indeed in England south of Derbyshire save for relict populations on Dartmoor, Devon and perhaps Bodmin Moor, Cornwall. Breeds now only in 4 counties of central and north Wales and is becoming rare in Cardigan co. The Irish status (has bred in at least 15 counties) needs re-examination. Still breeds in virtually every Scottish county. In winter our own race is replaced by the northern European race in our countries.

Curlew Sandpiper BI79
Calidris ferruginea (Pontoppidan 1763)
T4 p. 36 and pl. 66 **bottom right** (autumn and summer)
as curlew-sandpiper, *Tringa subarquata* (Güldenstädt)

An east-central Siberian tundra breeder, with a headquarters on the Taimyr Peninsula between the Yenisei and Khatanga, and scattered nesting places further east to the New Siberian Islands and the Kolyma area. Winters to South Africa and through oriental region to Australia and New Zealand.

A regular passage migrant through all four countries, largely in autumn along the east coast or across the Border country and down the Irish Sea coasts, in spring (less common) mostly up east coast.

Knot BI69
Calidris canutus (Linnaeus 1758)
T4 p. 37 and pl. 66 **mid** (summer and winter)
as knot, *Tringa canutus*, Linnæus

An arctic (virtually high arctic) breeder with a fragmented distribution in the holarctic: in the palearctic in east Greenland, Spitsbergen, north Taimyr, the New Siberian Islands and Wrangel Island; in the nearctic in scattered localities in Alaska, the Franklin Archipelago, Melville, Southampton Island, and north-west Greenland. Winters to the coasts of Africa beyond the equator and through the oriental region to Australia and New Zealand.

Passage migrant and winter visitor in large flocks mainly on the sandflats of east coast Scotland and England, and in the northern Irish Sea and round the north of Ireland.

Sanderling BI81
Calidris alba (Pallas 1764)
T4 p. 38 and pl. 66 **top left** (summer and winter)
as sanderling, *Calidris arenaria*, Linnæus

An holarctic breeder with a distribution resembling the knot's, mainly high arctic; in the palearctic from east Greenland and Spitsbergen to Taimyr, Svernaya Zemlya, the Lena delta and New Siberian Islands; in the nearctic in scattered localities from north Mackenzie and Keewatin, and Franklin to extreme north-west Greenland. Winters to South Africa, Indian Ocean islands and through oriental region to Australia, on Pacific islands and to South America.

Passenger and winter visitor, with autumn flyways by sandflats from Shetland down east Scotland to east England and Irish Sea, and down Hebrides to north and west Ireland.

Pl. 66.

Sanderling *(winter & summer)*.   Dunlin. *(winter & summer.)*
Bonaparte's Sandpiper.   Little Stint *(summer & autumn)*
                    Knot. *(winter & summer)*
Purple Sandpiper *(winter & summer)*   American Stint.
                    American Stint.
                    Temminck's Stint.
                    Curlew Sandpiper *(summer & autumn)*

Plate 42 (Thorburn's plate 67)

Family SCOLOPACIDAE, sandpipers, snipe, etc. (*continued*)

Semipalmated Sandpiper B180
Calidris pusillus (Linnaeus 1766)
T4 p. 39 and pl. 67 **mid left**
as semi-palmated sandpiper, *Tringa pusilla*, Linnæus

A nearctic low arctic breeder ranging from Alaska to Labrador, and south to northern Manitoba and Québec, and normally wintering to southern South America.

Seven records 1953–1966: the earliest 1 seen Cley, Norfolk 1953 July 19; England 3; Wales 1; Scotland 1; Ireland 2; July–October.

Ruff B184
Philomachus pugnax (Linnaeus 1758)
T4 p. 39 and pl. 67 **bottom** (3 ruffs and reeve)
as ruff, *Machetes pugnax*, Linnæus

A palearctic bird of the boreal zone, breeding into temperate and tundra areas from western Europe through the upper Volga and lower Siberian river systems to the Chukotski Peninsula and Anadyr. In Europe has isolated breeding groups in the Hungarian plain and western France, and breeds from the Low Countries, north Germany, Poland and White Russia to the Arctic Ocean, with a sporadic range in southern Finland, and a gap in south-east Norway and south-central Sweden. Winters to South Africa and the oriental region.

In England, as in neighbouring western Europe, the ruff's range became endangered early by the claiming of wetlands. In the early nineteenth century it nested in Somerset, Essex, Suffolk, Norfolk, Lincolnshire, Yorkshire, Lancashire, Cumberland and Northumberland, towards the end of the nineteenth century only in Norfolk and Lincolnshire and already sporadically. The 6 or 7 recorded nests of the present century were all sporadic and led to no colonisations. Recent wetland restorations have brought us back some species, but not (yet) the ruff. Meanwhile, the bird has settled down as a fairly common autumn passage migrant, and an occasional winterer, non-breeding summer visitor and spring passenger, rather scarce in north Scotland, west England and Wales but regular elsewhere, including parts of Ireland.

Upland Sandpiper or **'Upland Plover'** B149
Bartramia longicauda (Bechstein 1812)
T4 p. 41 and pl. 67 **mid right**
as Bartram's sandpiper, *Bartramia longicauda* (Bechstein)

A declining species that breeds from Alaska and Canada to the south-central United States, and normally winters on the pampas of southern South America.

Fifteen records 1851–1964: the earliest 1 near Warwick 1851 October 31; England 9; Wales 2; Scotland 1; Ireland 3; September–December.

Buff-breasted Sandpiper B182
Tryngites subruficollis (Vieillot 1819)
T4 p. 40 and pl. 67 **mid**
as buff-breasted sandpiper, *Tringites rufescens* (Vieillot)

A nearctic arctic breeder, nesting in northern Alaska, Yukon and Mackenzie and the southern Canadian arctic archipelago, and wintering in central Argentina, with a considerable record of accidental wandering.

Was a very rare vagrant until *c* 1950, since when has become of virtually annual occurrence, usually in autumn in England; there are records from Scotland, Wales and Ireland

Wood Sandpiper B157
Tringa glareola Linnaeus 1758
T4 p. 43 and pl. 67 **top right**
as wood-sandpiper, *Totanus glareola* (J. F. Gmelin)

A boreal palearctic bird, ranging as a breeder also into the temperate and tundra zones, virtually occupying the whole of Eurasia north of latitude 52°N to the arctic shore in Europe and almost so in eastern Siberia (though barely as far as the Gulf of Ob and not to Taimyr in western Siberia) and ranging east to Kamchatka. Breeds in Europe from Denmark, north Germany and Poland and the northern Ukraine continuously north on the mainland, though not near the south Swedish coast. Has bred in Holland, but became extinct there in 1936. Winters to South Africa and through the oriental region to Australia.

Bred in Northumberland in 1853 (clearly sporadic); but the Highlands may have been truly colonised when a pair bred in Sutherland in 1959, 1960 and in some years to 1965. In 1960 also bred west Inverness co.; in 1961 probably and 1962 certainly in another place in Sutherland; and in 1960 probably in north Perth co. Other breeding records are unpublished. While Scotland may be receiving a full western extension of range, the wood sandpiper remains mainly a passenger (especially in east England) and an occasional non-breeding summer visitor, with records also from Wales, Scotland and Ireland.

[Grey-rumped Sandpiper B167
Tringa brevipes (Vieillot 1816)
T4 p. 41, **not figured**, as *Totanus brevipes*, Vieillot

Eastern palearctic; breeds in Siberia from Yenisei eastwards; migrates to oriental and australasian regions. Listed by Thorburn in all good faith but now rejected from the List: an adult pair said to have been shot Rye Harbour, Sussex, 1914 September are 'Hastings Rarities'.]

Common Sandpiper B159
Tringa hypoleucos Linnaeus 1758
T4 p. 42 and pl. 67 **top left**
as common sandpiper, *Totanus hypoleucus* (Linnæus)

A palearctic bird with a very close nearctic relative, the spotted sandpiper (next) which some believe no more than a race of the common sandpiper and many consider descendent from it. A small outpost breeding population in ethiopian Africa may have been colonised by palearctic migrants. Breeds north to about the limits of the boreal zone, ranging over a very wide band east to Kamchatka, the Kuriles and Japan. In Europe it breeds on the Continent from the Mediterranean shore to the edge of the Kola and Kanin tundras and the North Cape and is absent virtually from only south Spain and Portugal and the continental North Sea coast (though it may breed in one place in Denmark). Winters to South Africa and through the oriental region to Australia.

Breeding population Britain-Ireland order 5; there has been a slight but progressive decrease in the last three or four decades. Still breeds, however, in very nearly every British-Irish county north-west of the Severn–Humber line, and is only sporadic south-east of it. British migrants tend to use west coast routes, continental passage migrants east.

Spotted Sandpiper B160
Tringa macularia Linnaeus 1766
T4 p. 42 and pl. 67 **top mid**
as spotted sandpiper, *Totanus macularius*, Linnæus.

The nearctic counterpart of the common sandpiper; breeds from beyond the boreal zone of Alaska and northern mainland Canada south approximately to the southern tier of the United States; winters normally to southern Brazil, occasionally Argentina.

Ten records 1866–1965; England 8; Wales 1; Ireland 1; the first pair shot at the Crumbles, Eastbourne, Sussex 1866 October early; 6 September–November; 1 February; 3 May–June.

Pl. 67.

Common Sandpiper   Spotted Sandpiper   Wood Sandpiper
        Buff-breasted Sandpiper   Bartram's Sandpiper
Semipalmated Sandpiper
            Ruff Sandpiper, & Reeve

Plate 43 (Thorburn's plate 68)

Family SCOLOPACIDAE, sandpipers, snipe, etc. (*continued*)

Spotted Redshank B162
Tringa erythropus (Pallas 1764)
T4 p. 47 and pl. 68 **upper right** (winter and summer)
as spotted redshank, *Totanus fuscus* (Linnæus)

A palearctic species breeding from Lapland to the upper Anadyr in eastern Siberia, in the northern boreal zone verging to the tundra; winters to the ethiopian and oriental regions mostly north of the equator. In Europe breeds almost to the Murmansk coast in Kola, and round the White Sea.

Almost strictly a passage migrant, with regular flyways on English south-east coast and from Lowlands through inland western England; rarer in Wales, and in Ireland though it occasionally winters there, and very rare in the Highlands.

Greater Yellowlegs B163
Tringa melanoleuca (J. F. Gmelin 1789)
T4 p. 45 and pl. 68 **bottom right**
as greater yellowshank, *Totanus melanoleucus* (Gmelin)

A nearctic species, breeding typically in muskeg country from south Alaska and central British Columbia east through Alberta to Québec and Newfoundland. Winters normally to Tierra del Fuego in southernmost South America.

Seventeen records 1906–64; England 8; Wales 1; Scotland 2; Ireland 6; first 1 shot Tresco, Scilly 1906 September 16; most July–October; 2 January; 3 April–May.

Redshank B161
Tringa totanus (Linnaeus 1758)
T4 p. 46 and pl. 68 **upper mid left**
as redshank, *Totanus calidris* (Linnæus)

A palearctic species breeding north into the boreal zone, from Russia between the Black Sea and Leningrad through the steppes and Chinese-Mongolian uplands to Ussuriland. In Europe breeds Iceland, Faeroe, Ireland, Britain, only now sporadically south of the Low Countries, the Danubian system and northern Greece, and north to Lapland, though in central Sweden and south Finland may breed only near the coast of the Gulf of Bothnia. Migrates generally to Africa north of the equator and the oriental region (mainly continental), though most European birds go no further than the Mediterranean, and British birds are mostly sedentary.

Breeding population Britain-Ireland order 5; decreased in early nineteenth century with the claiming of wetlands; began increasing *c* 1865 and spread almost dynamically 1893–1915 when 26 counties of England and Wales first colonised; slight regress in south England since 1940, perhaps because of harder winters, and in places sharp depopulation after severe winter of 1962–63 from which recovery rather slow. Scottish and Irish populations are generally stable. Has bred in every county but Cornwall and 3 in Ireland. A fairly heavy passage on all main flyways of Iceland and continental birds.

Lesser Yellowlegs B164
Tringa flavipes (J. F. Gmelin 1789)
See plate 81; (pl. 80B of Thorburn)

Marsh Sandpiper B166
Tringa stagnatilis (Bechstein 1803)
T4 p. 49 and pl. 68 **upper mid right**
as marsh-sandpiper, *Totanus stagnatilis*, Bechstein

A palearctic bird of the steppes and south boreal zone, with a fragmented distribution and a western outpost in Austria and Hungary round the Neusiedlersee, since 1914, perhaps sporadic. Main breeding areas are from Bulgaria and the Rumanian Danube delta through the Ukraine to the Kirghiz steppes and the upper Irtysh; and from Transbaicalia through the upper Amur system, Mongolia and Manchuria possibly to Ussuriland. Normally winters to South Africa and through the oriental region to Australia.

Fifteen English records 1887–1964; first 1 shot Tring Reservoirs, Hertfordshire 1887 October; all April–October.

Greenshank B165
Tringa nebularia (Gunnerus 1767)
T4 p. 48 and pl. 68 **lower mid left**
as greenshank, *Totanus canescens* (J. F. Gmelin)

A palearctic bird breeding from Scotland and northern Fenno-Scandia through central Siberia to the upper Anadyr and Kamchatka. Winters to South Africa and through the oriental region to Australia and New Zealand.

Breeding population (Scotland only) order 3: *c* 300–500 pairs; increase started a hundred years ago but this has lately reversed in southern part of range in central Highlands: further north the Outer Hebrides have been stably colonised in the last three decades, and sporadic breeding has been recorded in other North Isles and in one place in the Lowlands. In autumn continental birds join British stock on flyways on both east and west coasts and cross-country. A few winter in England, Wales and Ireland.

Green Sandpiper B156
Tringa ochropus Linnaeus 1758
T4 p. 44 and pl. 68 **top left**
as green sandpiper, *Totanus ochropus* (Linnæus)

A boreal palearctic breeder, ranging from the Baltic and Norway over a broad belt east through Siberia to the upper Kolyma and Amurland, with a big scatter of sporadic records outside. The stable European range is from the north Black Sea through central Ukraine to north Poland and Germany, Bornholm and south-east Norway, north to central Norway, east Sweden, central Finland and the White Sea. Winters to south-central Africa and through oriental region to Borneo.

Britain's share of the sporadic breedings are: pair with young Westmorland 1917, and a successful breeding in Inverness co. 1959. Normally a passage migrant (coastal and cross-country) and occasional winterer and non-breeding summer visitor. Ireland has few spring visitors.

Solitary Sandpiper B158
Tringa solitaria Wilson 1813
T4 p. 45 and pl. 68 **bottom left**
as solitary sandpiper, *Totanus solitarius* (Wilson)

The nearctic counterpart of the green sandpiper; breeding in boreal North America through Canada to central Québec and Labrador, and normally wintering south to Argentina.

Nine British records 1870 (or before)–1966; England 8; Scotland 1; first 1 banks of Clyde, Lanark co. some years before 1870; all July–October.

Long-billed Dowitcher
Limnodromus scolopaceus (Say 1823)
Not illustrated

A western nearctic bird of the tundra zone, with a palearctic eastern Siberian distribution in the Chukotski Peninsula and the Anadyr system, and a North American breeding range from north-west coastal Alaska into Mackenzie on the Anderson River and Franklin Bay; winters to Central America.

Short-billed Dowitcher B144
Limnodromus griseus (J. F. Gmelin)
T4 p. 49 and pl. 68 **lower mid right**
as red-breasted snipe, *Macrorhamphus griseus* (J. F. Gmelin)

A western and central nearctic boreal bird breeding from south Alaska through southern Mackenzie, through northern Alberta and Saskatchewan to north-eastern Manitoba, probably to northern Ontario and Québec; winters to Peru and central Brazil beyond the equator.

The field distinctions between the two dowitchers have only been fully worked out lately, and 42 of the 69 records *c* 1801–1966 are indeterminable. Seventeen identified longbills are first, male (first winter) Devon probably 1801 October; England 10; Wales 1; Scotland 1; Ireland 5; 1 May, rest September–December: 10 shortbills are first, 1 shot on Brent, Stone Bridge, Middlesex 1862 autumn; England 7; Ireland 3; 1 February–March, rest September–November. It is interesting that the more westerly and arctic species is the more frequent.

Pl. 68.

Green Sandpiper.   Spotted Redshank. (Summer & winter).

Redshank.

                    Greenshank.   Red-breasted Snipe.   Marsh Sandpiper.

Solitary Sandpiper.   Greater Yellowshank.

Plate 44 (Thorburn's plate 69)

Family SCOLOPACIDAE, sandpipers, snipe, etc. (*continued*)

Stilt Sandpiper
Micropalama himantopus (Bonaparte 1826)
Not illustrated

A nearctic species breeding in the north boreal and tundra zones from north-eastern Alaska through Mackenzie and Keewatin, and on southern Victoria Island, to northern Manitoba and Ontario and south to the tree-line; winters to northern Argentina.

Five English records: 1 seen Spurn, Yorkshire 1954 August 31–September 4; 1 Chichester Gravel Pits, Sussex 1962 September 1–7; 1 adult trapped Wisbech sewage farm, Lincolnshire–Norfolk–Cambridgeshire 1963 July 19–August 7; 1 adult Manhood End, Chichester Harbour, Sussex 1963 August 7–13; 1 Wisbech sewage farm 1965 August 12–26.

Black-tailed Godwit   B154
Limosa limosa (Linnaeus 1758)
T4 p. 51 and pl. 69 **top right** (winter and summer)
as black-tailed godwit, *Limosa belgica* (J. F. Gmelin)

A palearctic breeder, with a fairly continuous band of nesting distribution from the Low Countries (increasing since 1920) and Denmark through the river systems of the south Baltic, north Black Sea, north Caspian, upper Ob tributaries, upper Yenisei, Lake Baikal and upper Lena to Amurland and Ussuriland and Kamchatka. Outside this the distribution in western Europe is much fragmented, with a stable colony in west Iceland, increasing since *c* 1920, and nestings in Faeroe (sporadic), Scotland (sporadic), England (now established), three areas of France, one in Spain, south Norway (sporadic), north Norway (once, 69°N, 1955), southern Sweden, south-east Finland (sporadic 1955, 1956) and Hungary (fluctuating). This is clearly a relict distribution, though there are signs of recolonisation especially in Britain, where the birds involved may prove to be of the Icelandic race. Doubtless the situation derives from the draining of wetlands.

The British breeding population became extinct (last in England) in about 1830, but since a sporadic nesting of a pair in southern England in 1937 has gradually re-established itself, and in 1966 may have been of the order of 40 pairs. In 1941 and 1942 birds nested in Lincolnshire, in 1946 in Caithness, in 1947 probably in west Suffolk, from 1948 or 1949 on in Shetland (1 or 2 pairs), in 1949 probably again in west Suffolk, from 1952 on in an area of one-time fen in East Anglia which now harbours over 30 pairs, in 1956 in Orkney and in 1963 in Somerset: even if most of these areas have sporadic breeders the black-tailed godwit is back in our fauna after over a century of absence. Apart from the new colonists, all four countries enjoy a strong passage of continental birds, many of which now winter and some of which are non-breeding summer visitors. Autumn passage is perhaps strongest in south England, East Anglia, Lincolnshire and Mersey. The Irish passage is chiefly of Icelandic birds.

Bar-tailed Godwit   B155
Limosa lapponica (Linnaeus 1758)
T4 p. 50 and pl. 69 **top left** (winter and summer)
as bar-tailed godwit, *Limosa lapponica* (Linnæus)

A palearctic bird of the north boreal and tundra zone, breeding on most of the coastal and apron (i.e. inland from the coast) tundras of the Lapland and Russian arctic east through Siberia to the Chukotski Peninsula and across the Bering Strait in the (nearctic) Alaskan deltas of the Kuskokwim and Yukon and north to Barrow. European birds migrate to the Mediterranean and Africa but the main population winters through the oriental region to Australia and New Zealand.

In Britain-Ireland a regular passage migrant and winter visitor; the main autumn routes are Moray–Aberdeen co. and south down east coast; Shetland–Hebrides–Ireland; Lowlands–across land–Irish Sea and its Irish, Welsh and English coasts. Spring migrants use the east coast mostly, and non-breeders stay for the summer.

Curlew   B150
Numenius arquata (Linnaeus 1758)
T4 p. 51 and pl. 69 **mid**
as common curlew, *Numenius arquata* (Linnæus)

A palearctic bird, breeding from western Europe through the systems and source-hills of the Baltic and north Black Sea rivers, the Onega, the Ob, the upper Yenisei and its tributaries, Lake Baikal and the upper Lena to the upper Amur. In west breeds in Faeroe, Ireland, Britain and from the Low Countries south through the Rhineland to the upper Rhône, and in Brittany; and north to Fenno-Scandia and Archangel. Some elements migrate to Africa and into the oriental region.

Breeding population of Britain-Ireland order 5; after an almost continuous increase during the present century, slowing up a little in the last decade; has spread into lowland pastures widely over England, and in Wales, Scotland and Ireland; now breeds, according to John Parslow's analysis, in every county except Outer Hebrides (a biological county) and 7 counties in south-east England, in 1 of which (Cambridge) it bred until driven out by drainage and disturbance. Some of our stock emigrates but is replaced in winter by northern European birds, which also pass in large numbers.

[Slender-billed Curlew   B153
Numenius tenuirostris Vieillot 1817
T4 p. 54 and pl. 69 **mid right**
as slender-billed curlew, *Numenius tenuirostris*, Vieillot

A Siberian species now rejected from the List, though figured by Thorburn in all good faith. Six specimens, said to be obtained in Kent and Sussex 1910 are 'Hastings Rarities'.]

Whimbrel   B151
Numenius phaeopus (Linnaeus 1758)
T4 p. 52 and pl. 69 **bottom left**
as whimbrel, *Numenius phaeopus* (Linnæus)

An holarctic boreal and tundra breeder with a fragmented distribution; with populations in eastern Siberia east of the Lena and north of the Sea of Okhotsk; in north-western Alaska and Mackenzie; on the west coasts of Hudson Bay; and in Europe in Iceland (a stronghold), Faeroe, northern Scotland, western Norway and Lapland south through most of Finland to northern Latvia and east through northern Russia into Asia to the Yenisei. Migrates and winters to southern Africa, Indian and Pacific Ocean islands to New Zealand.

British breeding population (Scotland only) order 2; under 100 pairs, fluctuating but lately recovering. Became extinct in Orkney in the late nineteenth century, and decreased in its Shetland headquarters until *c* 1930. Recovery since then has been positive but not rapid; it now breeds in at least 6 separate places in Shetland, and since 1957 has had a very small but perhaps stable outpost in Lewis, Outer Hebrides; has bred sporadically also in Sutherland and on St Kilda in the 1960's. A regular passage migrant on all British-Irish coasts and to some extent inland, perhaps more common in spring.

Eskimo Curlew   B152
Numenius borealis (J. R. Forster 1772)
T4 p. 53 and pl. 69 **mid left**
as Eskimo curlew, *Numenius borealis* (J. R. Forster)

A nearctic bird; the rarest living wader. Its nests have been found only between 1822 and 1865 in Mackenzie, Canada. In the nineteenth century it migrated from mysterious Canadian and probably Alaskan breeding grounds usually down the eastern North American coastal flyway to winter in Patagonia, returning north usually up the central Mississippi flyway. On these routes hunters had virtually exterminated it by the early years of the present century. No bird has provedly been seen in South America since 1939, and no spring migrant has been seen anywhere but on the Texas coast since 1926. Here one or two have been recorded in every year since 1959, on their way to some unknown last breeding ground which may possible be in Franklin.

Seven British-Irish records, all shot 1852–87; the first two near Woodbridge, Suffolk 1852 November; England 2; Scotland 4; Ireland 1; all September–November.

Pl. 69.

Bar-tailed Godwit. (summer & winter)   Black-tailed Godwit. (summer & winter)
Eskimo Curlew.   Slender-billed Curlew.
Whimbrel.   Common Curlew.

Plate 45 (Thorburn's plate 75)

Family STERCORARIIDAE, skuas

Great Skua
Stercorarius skua (Brünnich 1764)
T4 p. 73 and pl. 75 **top right** (2 birds)
as great skua, *Megalestris catarrhactes* (Linnæus)

B194

A bipolar breeder, possibly of northern origin, though the present North Atlantic population may well have been colonised from the South Atlantic. Breeds on the Antarctic Continent, on most antarctic and subantarctic islands north to southern New Zealand, Chile, Tierra del Fuego, the Falklands and the Tristan-Gough Archipelago, with an outpost race breeding in northern Scotland, Faeroe and south Iceland. Has a dispersive winter movement into the broad Atlantic.

Breeding population (Scotland only) order 4; now probably rather over 1500 pairs, and of the whole North Atlantic race under 10,000 pairs. Since discovered breeding at Saxavord, Unst, Shetland in 1774 has fluctuated, and was much persecuted by farmers in its Shetland headquarters into the present century. Population was probably lowest in early 1880's when just *c* 60 pairs Foula, *c* 5 Unst. Since the Second World War has spread and multiplied under protection; spread from Shetland, still the present headquarters with perhaps 90 per cent of the British population, dates from 1908 when birds prospected Hoy in Orkney, where they first bred in *c* 1915; there are now at least 16 breeding stations in Shetland and 6 in Orkney; and the 'bonxie' colonised Caithness in 1949, the Outer Hebrides in 1959, and in the 1960's St Kilda, North Rona and Handa in Sutherland.

Pomarine Skua
Stercorarius pomarinus (Temminck 1815)
T4 p. 74 and pl. 75 **bottom left** (dark and light phases)
as pomatorhine skua, *Stercorarius pomatorhinus* (Temminck)

B195

An holarctic tundra breeder, nesting fairly continuously round all the tundra aprons and coasts of the Polar Basin except in western Europe, from the Kanin Peninsula to the Chukotski Peninsula (and on some Siberian islands) and from the Alaskan coast of the north Bering Sea to the southerly islands of the Canadian arctic and part of west Greenland. Winters at sea off many tropical and subtropical coasts of the world.

A passage migrant, most common on the North Sea and Channel coasts in autumn, on the west coasts and particularly the Hebrides in spring.

Arctic Skua
Stercorarius parasiticus (Linnaeus 1758)
T4 p. 74 and pl. 75 **top left** (dark and light phases)
as Richardson's skua, *Stercorarius crepidatus* (J. F. Gmelin)

B193

An holarctic breeder, nesting within wider limits than the previous bird – into the high arctic tundra on some Canadian and European islands, extending most southerly to the Aleutian Islands and Kamchatka and in western Europe where it reaches the boreal-temperate zone boundary. In Europe breeds north to Franz Josef Land and south to the coasts of north Russia, Norway and Scotland, with outposts in the Gulf of Bothnia and on the Kattegat coast of Sweden. Winters at sea in the southern oceans.

Breeding population (Scotland only) order 3 or low order 4; a marked decrease, mainly due to human persecution, in nineteenth and early twentieth centuries, and a mid-twentieth-century recovery. Headquarters since early records Shetland, but eighteenth-century records Inner and Outer Hebrides. Is now generally increasing in Shetland, though stable or slightly decreasing on some islands; Orkney headquarters is on Hoy with about a dozen small groups on other islands; fluctuating colonies continue in Outer and a few Inner Hebrides, and in Caithness; but in the present century sporadic breeding only has been recorded from Sutherland, Inverness co. and Argyll. Our breeding stock, and birds from northern Europe, passes south (in much greater numbers than in spring) mainly along North Sea and Channel coasts, and by the Hebrides and north-west Ireland.

Long-tailed Skua
Stercorarius longicaudus Vieillot 1819
T4 p. 75 and pl. 75 **bottom right**
as long-tailed or Buffon's skua, *Stercorarius parasiticus* (Linnæus)

B196

An holarctic high boreal and tundra breeder, nesting on the coastal apron-land of virtually the whole Polar Basin and some of its islands especially in the Canadian arctic, including all sides of Greenland, and of the north Bering Sea (not the Aleutians) and Kamchatka. In Europe nests only on Jan Mayen, Spitsbergen (sporadically), Bear Island and in Norway, Lapland and northernmost Russia, including Novaya Zemlya. Winters in the southern oceans.

A fairly regular autumn (very rare spring) passage visitor to the east and south British coasts and (fewer) to the Hebrides and north-west Ireland; very rare in Wales.

Pl. 75.

Richardson's Skua.
Pomatorine Skua.

Great Skua.
Long-tailed or Buffon's Skua.

Plate 46 (Thorburn's plate 72)

Family LARIDAE, gulls and terns

A modern systematic order is B204, laughing gull (pl. 47), 205, 206, 207, 208 (pl. 46), slender-billed gull, 199, 200, 203 (pl. 47), 202, 198 (pl. 48), 201, 209 (pl. 46), 211 (pl. 48), 210 (pl. 46), 197 (pl. 48), 212, 213, 214, 215, 216 (pl. 49), 223, royal tern, 217, 218, 219 (pl. 50), 220 (pl. 49), 221, 222 (pl. 50).

Ross's Gull   B210
Rhodostethia rosea MacGillivray 1824
T4 p. 62 and pl. 72 **top left** (winter and summer)
as Ross's gull, *Rhodostethia rosea*, Macgillivray

Breeds in the alder-scrub in the deltas and lower reaches of the Indigirka, Alazeya, Kolyma and other neighbouring rivers of eastern Siberia, and appears normally to winter in the Polar Basin itself, though wanderers appear at that time in the more northerly Pacific and Atlantic countries.

Four British records: 1 near Tadcaster, Yorkshire 1846 December 22 or 1847 February; immature caught between Whalsay and the Skerries, Shetland 1936 April 28; adult male freshly dead (had been shot) Holywell Ponds, Northumberland 1960 April 30; 1 seen Bridlington, Yorkshire 1962 February 17–22.

Mediterranean Gull   B205
Larus melanocephalus Temminck 1820
T4 p. 65 and pl. 72 **lower mid left**
as Mediterranean black-headed gull, *Larus melanocephalus*, Natterer

Origin doubtless in the eastern Mediterranean-inland sea area of central Eurasia, with a seemingly relict distribution, nesting now normally only in Turkey-in-Asia, Greece, and the Danube delta and Crimean areas of the Black Sea. Normally winters to the central Mediterranean, but some elements move further west and north-west in Europe; there are fairly recent sporadic breeding records from Hungary and Holland.

Since c 1950 this gull has become a regular annual vagrant (most often in autumn) to Channel and North Sea coastal England; it is still a rare vagrant to Wales, Scotland and Ireland.

Bonaparte's Gull   B206
Larus philadelphia (Ord 1815)
T4 p. 64 and pl. 72 **mid right**
as Bonaparte's gull, *Larus philadelphia* (Ord)

A nearctic bird with a mainly boreal breeding distribution, typically in muskeg forest, in central Alaska and Canada east to west-central Ontario. Winters from the United States south into northern México and larger islands of the West Indies.

Seventeen British-Irish records 1848–1966; the first 1 on River Lagan, near Belfast, cos. Antrim–Down 1848 February 1; England 15; Scotland 1; Ireland 1; all months save March, May, December, most frequent 7 October–November.

Little Gull   B207
Larus minutus Pallas 1776
T4 p. 64 and pl. 72 **bottom left**
as little gull, *Larus minutus*, Pallas

A palearctic species with a fragmented range; has an Asian headquarters from the upper Lena to Lake Baikal and the uppermost Amur tributaries; a central Russian headquarters in the Ob system and that of the upper Ural River; and a possibly colonist distribution in Europe and Asia Minor, with outposts or sporadic groups in Armenia and Turkey, the Danube delta and the Crimea, Poland, Germany, Holland, Denmark and south Sweden, and a main group from the Baltic islands, east Baltic south to Danzig and north to the head of the Gulf of Bothnia, east into Russia's upper Volga system. Erratically dispersive in winter, in Europe annually reaching Britain – and occasionally crossing the Atlantic to eastern North America where it founded a small nesting colony at Oshawa, Ontario in 1962.

A regular autumn and winter visitor to east and south England and south-east Scotland; irregular in Ireland and scarce in Wales.

Black-headed Gull   B208
Larus ridibundus Linnaeus 1766
T4 p. 65 and pl. 72 **bottom right** (summer and winter)
as black-headed gull, *Larus ridibundus*, Linnæus

Breeds far into the boreal zone over a wide area of the palearctic, south to the steppes, east to Amurland, Sakhalin and the Kolyma River, with an outpost on Kamchatka. In Europe breeds south to the Danube and the Alps, with an outpost in the Po valley, Italy and a south-westerly limit in central France and down the Rhône; and north nearly to Archangel, to south Finland and Sweden (where it has multiplied exceedingly since 1900), south-west Norway (colonised c 1880), Faeroe, and Iceland (colonised in 1911). Some European birds migrate to Africa north of the equator, others disperse, some west; numbers have reached eastern North America recently.

Breeding population Britain-Ireland low order 6; after a widespread decrease during nineteenth century, recovery has been on the whole progressive in the twentieth century and continues: in England-Wales breeding pairs have increased from c 35,000–40,000 in 1938 to c 51,000–56,000 in 1958 though the evidence from Scotland for the same period suggests an upward trend with certainty only in Sutherland. The Irish population appears stable or lately increasing and is certainly high, especially in the Shannon system. Has nested in the present century in all counties of Wales, all but 2 of Ireland, all but 3 of Scotland and all but 12 of England; not in the Isle of Man.

Common Gull   B201
Larus canus Linnaeus 1758
T4 p. 66 and pl. 72 **upper mid left** (young and adult)
as common gull, *Larus canus*, Linnæus

Origin doubtless palearctic; breeds in a broadish band from the north temperate to some high boreal zones from north-west Europe east to Anadyrland, Kamchatka, the Komandorski Islands, Kuriles and Sakhalin, and in north-western North America from south and central Alaska into Mackenzie, Yukon, Saskatchewan (extreme north-west) and western British Columbia. Breeding range in western Europe extends to Iceland and Faeroe, south to Holland, north Germany, the south Baltic and Russia from Latvia to the upper Volga; north to the Arctic Ocean. The European population does not normally winter south of the Mediterranean and much of it is more or less resident.

Breeding population of Britain-Ireland order 5; has been increasing gradually for over a century, and in the twentieth century extended its breeding range from its headquarters in the Highlands, west Lowlands and north-west Ireland into England and other parts of Ireland, though not Wales. In Ireland it spread into co. Down in 1934 and co. Antrim in 1940, and has bred in other counties, and for some time in co. Kerry. The English invasions have produced only sporadic breeding in Cumberland and the Farne Islands off Northumberland; but in 1919 the Dungeness area of Kent was colonised, possibly from the Continent, and in 1932 the colony spread over the Sussex border, though its status has become rather precarious lately. There is a considerable passage of continental birds through Britain, and some passage through Ireland.

Sabine's Gull   B209
Larus sabini Sabine 1819
T4 p. 62 and pl. 72 **top right**
as Sabine's gull, *Xema sabinii* (Joseph Sabine)

A tundra breeder of the holarctic region, extending from the high arctic into the low, though nesting in the European sector only sporadically, in Spitsbergen and perhaps Franz Josef Land. Its main belt of breeding is in the tundra apron of coastal Siberia from the Taimyr to Chukotski Peninsulas, and from the Kuskokwim-Yukon delta tundras of Alaska along the arctic American coast to north-east Keewatin; it breeds also in the Canadian arctic archipelago and in west and east Greenland, mostly in the high arctic. Winters south, at sea, into Atlantic and Pacific, including North Sea and Bay of Biscay.

A scarce passage and winter visitor to all four countries, most frequently England and Wales; has been also so lately in Ireland where formerly only a vagrant.

Pl. 72.

Ross's Gull. (summer & winter).   Sabine's Gull.
        Common Gull. (adult & young).   Bonaparte's Gull.
    Mediterranean Black-headed Gull.
        Little Gull (adult & young).   Black-headed Gull. (summer & winter).

Plate 47 (Thorburn's plate 73)

Family LARIDAE, gulls and terns
(continued)

Great Black-headed Gull   B204
Larus ichthyaetus Pallas 1773
T4 p. 66 and pl. 73 **bottom right**
as great black-headed gull, *Larus ichthyaëtus*, Pallas

A breeding bird of the central steppes and deserts of the palearctic, with a fragmented and apparently relict distribution except perhaps from the Aral Sea to beyond Lake Balkhash; the easternmost colonies are in Mongolia and high-plateau China. In Europe breeds by the Caspian shores and in one place in the Crimea. It winters into the oriental region, but some elements wander into western Europe occasionally.

Five English records: adult off Exmouth, Devon 1859 end May or early June; 1 seen Telscombe Cliffs, Sussex 1910 January 4; 1 seen Bournemouth, Hampshire 1924 November–December; 1 seen Cromer, Norfolk 1932 March 2–9; 1 seen Hove, Sussex 1932 August 9.

Laughing Gull
Larus atricilla Linnaeus 1758
Not illustrated

A nearctic species breeding on the Atlantic coast of North America from southernmost Canada (Halifax co., Nova Scotia) to Florida, the Bahamas and West Indies; along the coast of the Gulf of México and on islands off northern Venezuela; and in the Salton Sea in southern California and the Gulf of California, México. Winters normally south, some elements reaching the equatorial coasts of South America.

One record: an adult seen at Lade gravel pits near Dungeness, Kent 1966 May 11.

Slender-billed Gull
Larus genei, Brême 1839
Not illustrated

Origin doubtless south palearctic; has an apparently relict breeding range of which the main part embraces the coasts of the Black Sea and easternmost Mediterranean, and runs from the Tigris-Euphrates system along the coasts of the Persian Gulf to West Pakistan; also breeds in the Caspian and its lower river systems, and between the Aral Sea and the Ob. Otherwise nesting is only known from Mauretania off westernmost Africa, in the marismas of the Guadalquivir in Spain, and sporadically in the Camargue (River Rhône delta) in France, and perhaps Sardinia. Is more dispersive than migratory.

Two English (Sussex) records; an immature seen at Langney Point 1960 June 19–July 10 and an immature (first summer) seen at Rye Harbour 1963 April 28.

Lesser Black-backed Gull   B199
Larus fuscus Linnaeus 1758
T4 p. 68 and pl. 73 **mid right**
as lesser black-backed gull, *Larus fuscus*, Linnæus

A palearctic species very closely related to the herring gull, with which, though linked by a chain of races round the northern world, it overlaps in Europe where the two are distinct species, separated in form, behaviour and ecology. Breeds from the north temperate zone into the coastal arctic tundra apron from the Taimyr Peninsula coast to Britain, Ireland, Faeroe and south Iceland (where a recent colonist), in Europe south to Brittany, the Low Countries and the Baltic, not far inland in the Scandinavian Peninsula, wintering into tropical Africa.

British-Irish breeding population order 5; has been increasing in mid-present century (after a decrease in the first third) in all four countries except northernmost Scotland, and inland in Scotland, Ireland and north England; virtually absent as a breeder from south-east England. An important element has lately begun to winter in the south of Britain.

Herring Gull   B200
Larus argentatus Pontoppidan 1763
T4 p. 67 and pl. 73 **top** (young and adult)
as herring-gull, *Larus argentatus*, J. F. Gmelin

An holarctic bird with a chain of yellow-legged races breeding from the Azores, Madeira, the Canaries, north-west Africa and the Iberian Peninsula east through the Mediterranean–Black Sea–Caspian–Aral Sea and steppelands to Lake Baikal and the upper Amur, connected to the lesser black-back group by racial links through the Yenisei system and breeding east from Taimyr along the northern tundra apron to the Chukotski Peninsula and on the New Siberian and Wrangel Islands; another race, doubtless the ancestor of our north-west European population, breeds widely from south-east Alaska through Canada well into the tundra zone and south into the United States in the Great Lakes area and New England. The north-western European populations breed on all coasts east to Murmansk and the Baltic, Lakes Ladoga and Onega, north to Bear Island, west and south to Iceland, Faeroe, Ireland, Brittany and the North Sea coast. The species is more or less sedentary and wandering.

British-Irish population order 6; has fluctuated in numbers with the fortunes and redistributions of the fishing industry, on which it is more or less parasitic; but has widely increased since the Second World War and breeds now in nearly all the coastal counties save those of south-east England, with a general tendency towards continued expansion and the colonisation of inland sites and even buildings.

Iceland Gull   B203
Larus glaucoides Meyer 1822
T4 p. 70 and pl. 73 **bottom left**
as Iceland gull, *Larus leucopterus*, Faber

A member of the chain of closely related gulls that includes the herring gull and the lesser blackback. Breeds in south Greenland, south Baffin Island and the northern Ungava Peninsula of Québec; winters to New England, Iceland, Faeroe, north-west Ireland, Britain, Norway, occasionally reaching the southern North Sea and Channel.

Quite regular in Shetland in winter; beyond it scarce on the east coast and outer west coast migration flyways.

Pl. 73.

Herring Gull. (adult & young).

Lesser Black-backed Gull.

Iceland Gull.   Great Black-headed Gull.

Plate 48 (Thorburn's plate 74)

Family LARIDAE, gulls and terns
(*continued*)

Glaucous Gull   B202
Larus hyperboreus Gunnerus 1767
T4 p. 69 and pl. 74 **bottom right**
as glaucous gull, *Larus glaucus*, O. Fabricius

An holarctic bird of the coastal tundra aprons, extending far into the high arctic, where has been moving north during the climatic amelioration of the present century, and has withdrawn from its former southern range in boreal Newfoundland and some other places. Nests on virtually all islands of the Polar Basin and Canadian arctic south to Ungava and Labrador, and into the northern Bering Sea; in the European sector only in Iceland (decreasing), Jan Mayen, Bear Island, Spitsbergen, Franz Josef Land, Novaya Zemlya and the Russian coast east of Murmansk. The Atlantic-Arctic elements normally winter to New England and north-west Europe.

A regular winterer on the Scottish coasts (particularly in the north) and down the east coast to Norfolk and west coast to north-west Ireland; scarce elsewhere.

Great Black-backed Gull   B198
Larus marinus Linnaeus 1758
T4 p. 69 and pl. 74 **top left** (young and adult)
as great black-backed gull, *Larus marinus*, Linnæus

An Atlantic species, breeding in North America from Long Island (the eastern United States was colonised in 1916) north along the coast through the Gulf of St Lawrence and Newfoundland to Labrador and Ungava, in south-west Greenland, probably the Angmagssalik area of east Greenland; and in Europe in Iceland, Faeroe, Britain, Ireland and Brittany, on Bear Island and south Spitsbergen, on virtually all coasts of the Scandinavian and Murmansk Peninsulas, on the west coast of Finland, and Estonia, on the main Baltic islands and on Danish islands in the Kattegat. Some elements of the European population winter south to the Mediterranean.

Breeding population of Britain-Ireland order 5; was decreasing until *c* 1880, since when a recovery and a continuous increase during the present century mainly as a consequence of the increase of human coastal refuse; over 1000 pairs bred in England, Wales and the Isle of Man in *c* 1930, where it was virtually extinct in 1900, and since then there has been a further important increase (over 1600 in 1956, with a trebling in the island areas, and a further increase

since) and increases too in Scotland and Ireland, though the gull breeds nowhere (except sporadically) on the east and Channel coast between Kincardine co. and the Isle of Wight. In winter many elements wander with the fishing movements.

Kittiwake   B211
Rissa tridactyla (Linnaeus 1758)
T4 p. 71 and pl. 74 **top right** (adult and young)
as Kittiwake gull, *Rissa tridactyla* (Linnæus)

An holarctic bird breeding from temperate coasts into the high arctic; in Asia on Svernaya Zemlya, Cape Chelyuskin, the Khatanga River mouth, the New Siberian, Bennett and Wrangel Islands, the east Siberian coast from the Kolyma round the Chukotski Peninsula to Kamchatka, the Komandorski Islands, the northern Sea of Okhotsk, the Kuriles and islands off Sakhalin; on the western coast of Alaska, most Bering Sea islands and the Aleutians; on Bering Island and adjacent islands; in Newfoundland and the Labrador coast and islands of the Gulf of St Lawrence; in west and east Greenland; and in the European sector on Jan Mayen, Bear Island, Spitsbergen, Franz Josef Land, Novaya Zemlya and Vaigach; in Iceland, Faeroe, Ireland, Britain, Brittany and the western and northern coast of Norway and the Murmansk coast. Has bred sporadically on Heligoland and in Denmark. Has a full-ocean dispersal in winter.

Breeding population of Britain-Ireland order 6; increasing rapidly since the relaxation of human predation in the nineteenth century, especially in England and Wales, where *c* 37,000 pairs in 1959 (about the same number in Ireland), but also in Scotland. Breeding has been only sporadic in south-east England between Flamborough Head, Yorkshire and Dorset.

Ivory Gull   B197
Pagophila eburnea (Phipps 1774)
T4 p. 72 and pl. 74 **bottom left**
as ivory gull, *Pagophila eburnea* (Phipps)

A high arctic breeder and a pack-ice bird of the Canadian arctic (Prince Patrick, Melville, north Baffin and Ellesmere Islands), north-west and north-east Greenland, Spitsbergen, Franz Josef Land, northern Novaya Zemlya, Uedineniya Island, Svernaya Zemlya and perhaps other Siberian islands. Normally winters in the Arctic Ocean but may wander into the North Atlantic and Pacific.

A vagrant, most often in winter, to Shetland and Orkney, rarer further south in Scotland and England, and recorded a few times in Wales and Ireland.

Pl. 74.

Kittiwake Gull (adult & young).
Great Black-backed Gull (adult & young).
Ivory Gull.   Glaucous Gull.

Plate 49 (Thorburn's plate 70)

Family LARIDAE, gulls and terns
(continued)

Black Tern   B212
Chlidonias niger (Linnaeus 1758)
T4 p. 55 and pl. 70 **upper mid right**
as black tern, *Hydrochelidon nigra* (Linnæus)

An holarctic bird probably of palearctic origin, with two races.
The palearctic race breeds east to the Aral-Balkhash systems
and the upper tributaries of the Ob, just reaching the upper
Yenisei in the central Russian plain. In western Europe it has
populations in Portugal, southern Spain and the Po valley,
north Italy; its main range runs south to France (not Brittany),
the German plain, and the Danubian system, and north to the
Low Countries, Denmark, the south Baltic, Baltic islands,
south Sweden, Leningrad and the upper Volga, formerly to
England. The nearctic race breeds from south Canada, south
to California and the central United States, east to the Great
Lakes and upper St Lawrence. Both races are migratory,
palearctic birds wintering to tropical Africa.

English breeding population disappeared with the eighteenth–nineteenth-century wetland draining; last breedings,
some of the later ones sporadic, appear to be Lincolnshire
(abundant in eighteenth century) 1832, Yorkshire (East
Riding) c 1840, Cambridgeshire 1843 or 1844, Cumberland
1855?, Oxfordshire c 1854–60?, Norfolk 1853 after a flood and
1858, when breeding pair shot, Suffolk 1875? and Kent 1824
and c 1884. In the twentieth century a recolonisation was
reported at Pett Level in Sussex during a temporary wartime flooding, 1941–42, but failed when drainage was re-
stored in 1943; and another sporadic breeding occurred in
England.

Passage migrant, rare in Highland Scotland, irregular in
Wales, scarce but regular in Ireland, most regular along
coasts and through inland waters in Lowlands and England.

White-winged Black Tern   B213
Chlidonias leucopterus (Temminck 1815)
T4 p. 55 and pl. 70 **top right** (young and adult)
as white-winged black tern, *Hydrochelidon leucoptera* (Schinz)

A palearctic bird, breeding from the Danubian system east
through the systems of the other Black Sea rivers, and the
western and northern Caspian rivers, to the plains of the upper
Ob, sporadically in the Baikal system, but regularly in Amurland south of the river, south Sakhalin, Mongolia and Manchuria. Migrates to Australia and New Zealand through the
oriental region, and to the southern ethiopian region. Has
bred sporadically west of main range in Germany (1936),
Belgium (1937), France, Portugal and possibly in seven other
countries of Europe, and Algeria – and (doubtless birds
halted on passage) in Kenya and northern Tanganyika, and
possibly (though not provedly) even in New Zealand.

An annual vagrant to England, rare in Wales, Scotland and
Ireland, mainly on passage, most often in East Anglia.

Whiskered Tern   B214
Chlidonias hybrida (Pallas 1811)
T4 p. 56 and pl. 70 **top left** (young and adult)
as whiskered tern, *Hydrochelidon hybrida* (Pallas)

Origin possibly palearctic, with a broken breeding range in
the Old World, where very local in Europe. Main nesting
areas are the Danube, north Black Sea, Caspian, Aral and
Mesopotamian systems; the Indian subcontinent and Manchuria and Ussuriland south into China; and south-east and
southern Africa, the Celebes, Moluccas and New Guinea,
southern Australia and the South Island of New Zealand. The
western European and north-west African breeding populations are local in Tunisia, Algeria, Morocco, south-west
Portugal, southern Spain, France (Landes and Loire-Rhône
systems only), Po valley of north Italy (since 1939), Albania,
and Hungary; and sporadic in Czechoslovakia, Switzerland
(1931) and Holland (1938, 1945, 1958). Western birds winter
in Africa to around the equator.

A rare vagrant to south-east England, usually in late
summer; recorded elsewhere in all four countries.

Gull-billed Tern   B215
Gelochelidon nilotica (J. F. Gmelin 1789)
T4 p. 56 and pl. 70 **lower mid right** (adult and young)
as gull-billed tern, *Sterna Anglica* (Montagu)

Perhaps once cosmopolitan; in the Americas (3 races) breeds
from south California into north-west México; from Texas and
Maryland through Florida into the West Indies; and in South
America. Another race has a fragmented distribution in
Australia; another breeds on the coast of south-east China.
The palearctic race, which extends from the north shore of the
Persian Gulf along the Makran coast into the oriental region
up the Indus, has its main range from the Black Sea and
Turkey through the Caspian and Aral systems and steppes to
beyond Lake Balkhash. In western Europe it is local and often
sporadic, declining with wetland drainage, and breeds (or
has bred) in Denmark (a minor headquarters), the Camargue
of south France, Portugal, south Spain, the Po valley in north
Italy, Austria, Hungary, Greece, central Germany (to 1934)
and Holland (1931–49): also breeds or has bred in north-west
Africa in Tunisia and Mauretania. European birds may winter
to the Mediterranean and western Africa north of the equator.

Has bred once in England, at Abberton Reservoir in Essex,
where a territorial pair was present in 1949 and a pair produced at least 1 young (later found dead) in 1950. Otherwise
an annual vagrant to south-east England, mostly on spring
passage; has been recorded (though very rare) elsewhere in
England, and in Wales, Scotland and Ireland.

Caspian Tern   B216
Sterna caspia Pallas
T4 p. 57 and pl. 70 **bottom**
as Caspian tern, *Sterna caspia*, Pallas

Like the preceding terns, has the remains of an apparently
cosmopolitan breeding distribution. In North America about
a score of isolated groups range north to the Great Slave Lake
in Mackenzie, east to southern Labrador and formerly to
Newfoundland, south to Texas and north-west México, west
to California and Oregon. In Africa there are 10 or more
breeding groups, nearly all on isolated coastal marshes and
deltas, from the Mediterranean to South Africa. In New
Zealand it breeds on most coasts of the main islands, and in
Australia rather discontinuously from the east coast to the
west. Palearctic groups extend into the oriental region from
Lake Khanka in Manchuria-Ussuriland along the Chinese
coast to the borders of Indochina, and from the coasts of the
Persian Gulf along the Makran coast to the Indus delta; and
there is an outpost colony in northern Ceylon. It breeds from
the Danube-Dnestr deltas and the west coast of the Sea
of Azov, and from the Volga delta and Russian shore of the
Caspian Sea east through the steppes and Aral-Balkhash
systems to the upper Irtysh. The stable population of north-
west Europe is confined to the Baltic and the Gulf of Bothnia,
in east Sweden (where local), west Finland, Estonia and on
some Baltic islands; but it has bred in the past in the Frisian
Islands of Germany (to c 1916) and Denmark (to 1919) and
sporadically on the Baltic coast of Germany, on the south
coast of Jugoslavia, and on Sardinian islands. The European
population winters to Africa north of the equator.

A rare vagrant to eastern England, mainly in spring and
summer; has been recorded from other parts of England,
Wales and Ireland.

Sooty Tern   B220
Sterna fuscata Linnaeus 1766
T4 p. 58 and pl. 70 **mid left**
as sooty tern, *Sterna fuliginosa*, J. F. Gmelin

A tropical tern breeding widely on the islands of the Pacific
and Indian Oceans, and in the Atlantic from St Helena,
Martin Vas, Ascension and Fernando Noronha to the West
Indies, Bahamas, Florida, Louisiana and reefs of Yucatán,
México. Disperses widely over warm seas.

At least seventeen British records 1852–1961; the first 1
shot Tutbury, near Burton-on-Trent, Staffordshire 1852
October; England 14; Wales 1; Scotland 2; all March–
October, most 9 April–June.

Pl. 70.

Whiskered Tern. (adult & young).   White-winged Black Tern. (adult & young).

Black Tern.

Sooty Tern.   Gull-billed Tern (adult & young).

Caspian Tern.

Plate 50 (Thorburn's plate 71)

Family LARIDAE, gulls and terns
(*continued*)

Sandwich Tern   B223
Sterna sandvicensis Latham 1787
T4 p. 58 and pl. 71 (frontispiece) **bottom left** (young and adult)
as Sandwich tern, *Sterna cantiaca*, J. F. Gmelin

Another tern with a relict distribution: breeds from the southern United States to tropical South America, if the elegant and Cayenne terns be included as races, and from Europe and Caspian shores to the Mediterranean. The palearctic race breeds on the east and south Caspian, possibly still in Tunisia, and in Europe now stably only in the Black Sea, the Camargue and Brittany in France, Ireland, Britain, Holland, the German Frisian Islands, Denmark and south Sweden; and sporadically in Spain, Portugal, Italy, Sicily, Sardinia, the Dieppe coast of France, Channel Islands, north Germany and Danzig; winters to South Africa, some perhaps to north-west India.

Breeding population of Britain-Ireland order 4; J. F. Parslow estimates *c* 6000 pairs 1962; decreased with persecution in the nineteenth century, recovered under protection in the twentieth, with a colonisation of the Norfolk coast in 1914–23, where numbers, though fluctuating, reached record *c* 2754 occupied nests in 1965. Other headquarters are Farne Islands (known since 1802), Northumberland, *c* 1500 pairs 1964; Firth of Forth since 1921, over 1120 1962; and (under 1000) Cumberland–north Lancashire since *c* 1843, co. Down since 1906; (200 or less) Suffolk since 1951, Anglesey since 1915, Nairn co. since 1881, the Clyde since 1910, co. Wexford since *c* 1934, cos. Sligo–Mayo–Galway since 1857, co. Donegal since *c* 1861; (small) Hampshire since 1954, Angus, Aberdeen co., Caithness, Orkney since 1893, co. Kerry since 1955. Has bred formerly or sporadically in present century in 9 other counties.

Baltic and North Sea birds swell the passage movements, especially on the east and the south coast of England.

Royal Tern
Sterna maxima Boddaert 1783
Not illustrated

Has 2 races: one breeding coastally in south-east United States, Bahamas, West Indies, México and Venezuela; the other on the Arguin Bank off Mauretania, north-west Africa, which migrates north to Tangier and sometimes Gibraltar.

One Irish record: the remains of a bird long dead were found at the North Bull, co. Dublin 1954 March 24.

Common Tern   B217
Sterna hirundo Linnaeus 1758
T4 p. 59 and pl. 71 (frontispiece) **mid right** (adult and young)
as common tern, *Sterna fluviatilis*, Naumann

Breeds through the holarctic region, except in western North America and easternmost Siberia, to about the north limit of the boreal zone, nesting south on the Atlantic coasts to Venezuela in the neotropical and western Nigeria in the ethiopian regions. In the western palearctic breeds coastally in Mauretania, Azores, Madeira, Canaries, Tunisia, the north Mediterranean including Sardinia, Portugal, Spain, France, the North Sea and Baltic, Norway, Faeroe, Britain and Ireland; and inland in most river systems from Finland and south Sweden to France, north Italy, Jugoslavia and Greece; and winters normally to Africa as far as the Cape.

Breeding population of Britain-Ireland order 5; recovered in mid-present century after 100 years of disturbance and habitat destruction. In England *c* 5500–6000 pairs 1965, East Anglia having over half British population, and strongholds also in 8 other coastal counties, inland breedings increasing; a Welsh stronghold in Anglesey. In Scotland also increasing inland, and in North Isles perhaps with climate change. In Ireland decreasing inland, but many coastal strongholds, especially Strangford Lough, co. Down. Migrant transit is by coastal routes; a very few may winter.

Arctic Tern   B218
Sterna paradisaea Pontoppidan 1763
T4 p. 60 and pl. 71 (frontispiece) **top right** (adult and young) as arctic tern, *Sterna macrura*, Naumann

An holarctic bird breeding virtually throughout the island and apron tundras of the Polar Basin, extending south on coasts to England, New England and the Sea of Okhotsk. In Europe breeds inland in Lapland and Iceland, and on most Baltic and open sea coasts south to the Low Countries, Norfolk, Wales and Ireland, perhaps still Scilly and Brittany. A formidable migrant; some winter to Antarctica and Australia.

Breeding population of Britain-Ireland order 5; has been shifting north since late nineteenth century. In Isle of Man, Anglesey and England (Norfolk, Lancashire, Cumberland) in a minority to common terns except in Farne Islands, Northumberland. In Scotland breeds in virtually every county, in some inland, and strongly in the North Isles. It is decreasing in Ireland and has become lately extinct in many inland lake sites. Native and European birds pass by coastal routes.

Roseate Tern   B219
Sterna dougallii Montagu 1813
T4 p. 59 and pl. 71 (frontispiece) **upper left** (young and adult) as roseate tern, *Sterna dougalli*, Montagu

Cosmopolitan, with a scattered, relict breeding distribution mostly on islands in australasian, oriental ethiopian, northern neotropical and Atlantic regions in tropical to temperate climes. In the palearctic nests in Azores, Rio de Oro and Tunisia, sporadically in Denmark, the German Frisian Islands and the Camargue of France, and regularly only in Brittany; and in Britain-Ireland, its European headquarters. European birds winter from west Africa to the Cape.

Breeding population of Britain-Ireland order 4; may have been *c* 3500 pairs in 1962, with headquarters presently concentrated on the Irish Sea coasts (a few Scilly, most Anglesey, cos. Wexford, Dublin and Down), the Farne Islands in Northumberland, and the Firth of Forth, outside which has bred sporadically in 4 other English, 4 other Scottish and at least 7 other Irish counties, some on west coast. Decreased with nineteenth-century persecution and collection, since when has increased, and since 1940's flourished, under protection. Migrates coastally.

Bridled Tern   B221
Sterna anaethetus Scopoli 1786
Not illustrated

Breeds on tropical coasts and islands of Caribbean, west Africa, Red Sea, Persian Gulf, Indian Ocean, west Pacific, East Indies and Australia. Disperses widely in off-season.

Four records, all of single birds found dead: Dungeness, Kent 1931 November 19; North Bull, co. Dublin 1953 November 29; Gower, Glamorgan 1954 September 11; near Weston-super-Mare, Somerset 1958 October 17.

Little Tern   B222
Sterna albifrons Pallas 1764
T4 p. 61 and pl. 71 (frontispiece) **bottom right** (adult and young)
as little tern, *Sterna minuta*, Linnæus

Cosmopolitan, breeding on sandy coasts and up alluvial rivers far inland, extending from tropical to some boreal climes; in the south holarctic, Caribbean nearctic, tropical ethiopian and oriental regions and Australia. European birds breed on coasts north to Ireland, Britain, Denmark, Estonia and south Sweden; and up the Danubian system and some French rivers; winter to Indian Ocean and north-west Africa.

Breeding population of Britain-Ireland order 4; J. F. Parslow estimates *c* 800 pairs England-Wales *c* 1963–65, probably fewer Scotland-Ireland. Up to 150 small scattered coastal colonies, and a few over 100 pairs in north Norfolk, Flint and Fife, have survived the work of holidaymakers, caravanners, bungalow builders, service installations and gravel-dealers since the Second World War. Scottish northern limits are Moray or Nairn and southern Outer Hebrides: in Ireland a very local breeder in co. Cork, and from co. Galway round north and east to co. Wexford. Migrates coastally.

Pl. 71.

Roseate Tern.   Arctic Tern.

                        Common Tern.

   Sandwich Tern.   Little Tern.

        (Adults & young.)

Plate 51 (Thorburn's plate 76)

Family ALCIDAE, auks

Little Auk   B226
Plotus alle (Linnaeus 1758)
T4 p. 79 and pl. 76 **bottom right** (summer and winter)
as little auk, *Mergulus alle* (Linnæus)

Breeds in the Atlantic arctic in Greenland, Jan Mayen, Bear Island, Spitsbergen, Franz Josef Land, north Novaya Zemlya, Svernaya Zemlya and Iceland (small numbers Grímsey, formerly Langanes). Normally winters to the convergence of Atlantic and polar water, but after long cyclones may be forced south in numbers at irregular intervals.

Reaches Shetland in varying numbers every winter, but 7 big cyclones in last hundred years, last in 1949–50, have grounded birds coastally and inland in almost every county, most in eastern England, Scotland and northernmost Ireland.

Razorbill   B234
Alca torda Linnaeus 1758
T4 p. 76 and pl. 76 **mid left** (winter and summer)
as razorbill, *Alca torda*, Linnæus

An Atlantic sea bird, breeding from Greenland to New Brunswick, formerly Maine from Bear Island (? sporadic), Murmansk Russia, Norway, Iceland, Faeroe, Britain and Ireland to Channel Isles and Brittany (formerly Normandy); also on Heligoland (a few), Græsholm in Denmark, in the Baltic in Sweden and Finland, and on Lake Ladoga. Some English and Irish birds winter to the Mediterranean.

Breeding population Britain-Ireland order 6; breeds in scattered colonies, some large in the west and north, round most coasts, though now only on Flamborough Head, Yorkshire between Isle of Wight and Farne Islands, Northumberland. A decrease in south Wales and England since 1940's has been connected with oil-fouling of the sea.

Great Auk   B225
Pinguinus impennis (Linnaeus 1758)
T4 p. 76 and pl. 76 **mid bottom**
as great auk, *Alca impennis*, Linnæus

A flightless North Atlantic sea bird finally exterminated on Eldey, Iceland 1844 June 4; became extinct through human hunting and collecting. Formerly bred in at least 3 and possibly 8 colonies in Maine–St Lawrence–Newfoundland (last Funk Island 1785), 1 in East Greenland (*c* 1586–96), at least 3 and possibly 5 in Iceland, possibly 2 in Faeroe, and in Britain. Migrated south to Florida and the Mediterranean.

Breeding population of Britain (-Ireland) extinct since 1812; bred St Kilda (to some years before 1697), Papa Westray, Orkney 1812, possibly Calf of Man 1692. Last records of birds co. Waterford 1834, St Kilda *c* 1840.

Common Guillemot   B227
Uria aalge (Pontoppidan 1763)
T4 p. 77 and pl. 76 **top mid** (plain and bridled)
as common guillemot, *Uria troile* (Linnæus)

Origin probably in the Bering Sea: breeds in north Pacific and Atlantic with a population of *c* 10–20 million birds (Leslie Tuck), from Hokkaido, Japan through Okhotsk and Bering Seas to Farallon Islands in California: from Gulf of St Lawrence through Newfoundland, Labrador, west Greenland (1 station), Iceland, Faeroe, Bear Island, south Novaya Zemlya, Murmansk Russia, Norway, Britain, Ireland, Channel Islands, Brittany and north-west Spain to the Berlenga Islands, Portugal; also on Græsholm, Stora Karlsö and other islands in the Fenno-Scandian Baltic. Disperses in winter on or near continental shelf.

Breeding population of Britain-Ireland order 6; perhaps between 300,000 and 500,000 pairs after decrease nineteenth century (human persecution), increase early twentieth (protection) and decrease mid twentieth ascribed to oil-fouling. Breeds in virtually all coastal cliffy counties except between Isle of Wight and Bempton, Yorkshire where now extinct (last Kent *c* 1910). About 9 stations each over 10,000 pairs exist in North Isles, Sutherland and south-west Ireland.

Arctic Guillemot or Brünnich's Guillemot   B228
Uria lomvia (Linnaeus 1758)
T4 p. 78 and pl. 76 **mid right** (winter)
as Brünnich's guillemot, *Uria bruennichi*, E. Sabine

An holarctic-arctic bird possibly of Bering Sea origin. The Pacific breeding arc is from Kuriles and Sea of Okhotsk to Bering Sea islands; Polar Basin circle on most major arctic islands and a few mainland cliffs; Atlantic arc from Iceland and Greenland to Newfoundland and the Gulf of St Lawrence. Eleven English, Scottish and Irish records 1884–1960 (first 1 shot near Farne Islands, Northumberland 1883–84 winter) appear to be fully acceptable, though the species has doubtless occurred over 20 times (i.e. rare vagrant) in nearly all months.

Black Guillemot or Tystie   B229
Cepphus grylle (Linnaeus 1758)
T4 p. 78 and pl. 76 **top left** (summer and winter)
as black guillemot, *Uria grylle* (Linnæus)

An holarctic coastal breeder, nesting from temperate to high arctic climes. Birds of Pacific arc (separated by some as a full species, the pigeon guillemot) breed from the Chukotski Peninsula and Kamchatka through the Bering Sea to California. The Atlantic races breed from Maine through eastern Canada north to Baffin Bay, and Greenland, round the palearctic Polar Basin to the Chukotski Peninsula and perhaps north Alaska, and in Iceland, Faeroe, Ireland, Britain, Fenno-Scandia, the Kattegat, the Baltic and perhaps Lake Ladoga. Sedentary, wintering in the Polar Basin and dispersing coastally short distances in Europe.

Breeding population of Britain-Ireland order 5; formerly bred in 5 counties of east coast; but only records in last hundred years sporadic. Last breeding record Wales was *c* 1874 until recolonisation of Anglesey *c* 1962; in Irish Sea also colonised Kirkcudbright st. 1920, Cumberland 1940 (only station now in England), co. Wexford 1953 and is increasing elsewhere. Breeds on most Scottish and Irish Atlantic coasts from Shetland to co. Waterford with strongholds in North Isles, north-west Highlands and co. Kerry.

Puffin   B230
Fratercula arctica (Linnaeus 1758)
T4 p. 81 and pl. 76 **top right** (winter and summer)
as puffin, *Fratercula arctica* (Linnæus)

A North Atlantic species breeding on the west side from Nova Scotia and New Brunswick (formerly Maine) to the Gulf of St Lawrence, Newfoundland and Labrador; in Greenland; and on the European side in Jan Mayen, Iceland, Faeroe, Ireland, Britain, Channel Islands, Norwegian and Swedish islands in the Skagerrak, the Norwegian coast and Russian Murmansk coast, Bear Island, Spitsbergen and Novaya Zemlya. Bred on Heligoland to the 1830's. Disperses in winter, western European birds normally reaching Portugal and into the Mediterranean.

Breeding population of Britain-Ireland order 7; may be one to two million pairs, probably over half St Kilda; the most abundant of our sea birds despite long decrease ascribed to gull predation, rat infestation of islands, turf erosion by puffins themselves, sea oiling and human interference. Breeders just survive in Dorset and Isle of Wight and may survive in south Devon; population from Scilly, Cornwall and Lundy (Devon) to south Wales (now probably extinct Glamorgan and Cardigan co.) may now be no more than a tenth of that in 1939, though the Skokholm and Skomer colonies (Pembroke co.) are still fairly strong; all Irish Sea colonies are reduced, as is that on Ailsa Craig in the Clyde. In east the largish Farne Islands station, Northumberland has increased; the 9 other regular stations south of Caithness are low. Among rest of *c* 130 main colonies are signs of decrease in well over a dozen, though *some* in Shetland are increasing: stations with at least 10,000 burrows are now found only in Shetland, possibly Orkney, the Outer Hebrides (vast colony on St Kilda) and Sutherland, and decreases have been marked in west Sutherland, Ross, some Outer Hebrides and co. Kerry. Stations with over 1000 burrows survive in Yorkshire and cos. Kerry, Wexford, Mayo, Donegal and Rathlin, co. Antrim.

Pl. 76.

Black Guillemot. (summer & winter).
Common Guillemot.
Razorbill (summer & winter).
Great Auk.

Puffin. (summer & winter).
Brünnich's Guillemot.
Little Auk. (summer & winter.)

Plate 52 (Thorburn's plate 53)

Order COLUMBIFORMES

Family PTEROCLIDAE, sand grouse

Pallas's Sand Grouse   B231
Syrrhaptes paradoxus (Pallas 1773)
T3 p. 66 and pl. 53 **bottom**
as Pallas's sand-grouse, *Syrrhaptes paradoxus*, Pallas

A palearctic bird of the steppes and Asian highlands breeding from the Kirghiz steppes east to Manchuria and into the deserts of Mongolia and highland China. Mostly sedentary but subject to irregular migrations; invasions or 'irruptions' into Europe have occurred at least 20 years between 1848 and 1944 and have reached Britain in the major ones to 1909; first record male shot Walpole St Peters, Norfolk 1859 July early; last, flock of 9 seen West Coatham, Yorkshire 1909 May 17. Recorded from England and Scotland only; in 1888 bred near Beverley, Yorkshire, and in 1888 and 1889 on the Culbin Sands in Moray co.

Family COLUMBIDAE, pigeons

Woodpigeon   B234
Columba palumbus Linnaeus 1758
T3 p. 61 and pl. 53 **top left**
as wood pigeon, *Columba palumbus*, Linnæus

A palearctic bird possibly of Russian steppe woodland origin, breeding into the oriental region in northern India and east to the central Asian highlands between the Himalayas and Lake Balkhash, north to northern Russia, southern Finland, Sweden and Norway, Britain and Ireland, south to the Azores, Madeira, Africa from Morocco to Tunisia, the Mediterranean (including islands), Mesopotamia, north Persia, Afghanistan and the Indian subcontinent. Migrates relatively short distances in most areas.

Breeding population Britain-Ireland order 7; R. K. Murton's analysis, for Britain only, suggests over three million breeding pairs for Britain-Ireland. Increased in Scotland since the eighteenth-century revival of woodland and has increased generally since the nineteenth with the improvement of arable agriculture; also spreading into suburbs and parks. Breeds in every county since the colonisation of Shetland in *c* 1940. Movements are complex; a varying continental immigrant element winters in England, as do some Scottish birds; some English West Country birds may winter in Ireland.

Stock Dove   B232
Columba oenas Linnaeus 1758
T3 p. 63 and pl. 53 **top right**
as stock-dove, *Columba oenas*, Linnæus

A palearctic bird possibly of European steppe origin, breeding east to the plainslands of the upper Ob system in Russia, and to the Caspian Sea and north Persia, with an outpost in Russian and Chinese Turkestan, south to Morocco and the north Mediterranean, north to southern Fenno-Scandia and the upper Volga system in Russia. Largely sedentary.

Breeding population of Britain-Ireland order 5; in early nineteenth century was virtually confined to central and south-east England; by the end of the century had spread throughout England and Wales, into Lowland Scotland and the east Highlands, to the Isle of Man and into Ulster. Now breeds in most Irish counties and breeds or has bred in all mainland Scottish counties (not Wester Ross or western Inverness co.). A marked decrease noted in east Scotland and many parts of England *c* 1957–63 may now have ended, and has been linked with the use of agricultural toxic chemicals.

Rock Dove   B233
Columba livia J. F. Gmelin 1789
T3 p. 64 and pl. 53 **mid right** (2 birds)
as rock-dove, *Columba livia*, J. F. Gmelin

Probably of palearctic Mediterranean or steppe origin, with a primary distribution as a wild species (ancestor of the domestic pigeon) from the Mediterranean and steppe zones into the dry subtropics, and even tropics, from the Iberian and Mediterranean countries and the central steppes of Russia and China into the Sahara, to west Africa, the Sudan, Arabia, India and Ceylon; also in the Cape Verdes, Canaries, Madeira and the Azores (though perhaps introduced except in Canaries) and with an outpost range on the coasts of western France, Britain, Ireland and Faeroe. Sedentary.

Breeding population Britain-Ireland probably order 5, though true wild stock has decreased so markedly in last hundred years that it is doubtful whether 100 pairs survive on the cliffs of England and Wales, or many in south-east Scotland; only on the coasts of the north and west Highlands, the North Isles and Ireland does a stable population survive.

Collared Dove
Streptopelia decaocto (Frivaldszky 1838)
Not illustrated

Probably of Indian origin, with a basic range from India and north Ceylon into Russian and Chinese Turkestan and east to Mongolia, north-eastern China and Korea; introduced in Japan. Had spread through Persia to Constantinople by 1547, possibly (not provedly) by introduction, and before 1912 was established in Albania, the Balkans and Rumania. In 1912 an explosive north-westerly spread started with the colonisation of Belgrade; and the species reached Hungary in *c* 1928; Czechoslovakia in 1935, Austria in 1938, Poland in 1940, Germany and Italy in 1944, Holland in 1947, Denmark and Russia in 1948, Sweden and Switzerland in 1949, France in 1950, England and Belgium in 1952, Finland in 1953, Norway and Luxemburg in 1954, Scotland and Estonia in 1957, Wales and Ireland in 1959; and a bird was seen in Iceland in 1964.

Breeding population Britain-Ireland order 4; *c* 3000 breeding pairs (*c* 19,000 *birds*) 1964 (Robert Hudson). First record Manton, Lincolnshire 1952 July 24; first breeding record near Cromer, Norfolk 1955. By the end of 1964 it had been recorded from all but Rutland of the 40 counties of England and had bred in 34; from all but 3 of the 13 counties of Wales and had bred in 8; from the Isle of Man though had not bred there; from half of the 32 counties of Ireland and had bred in 12 (and by 1966 had been recorded from another and had bred in 16). Sedentary; young have a dispensive tendency and are probably mainly responsible for colonisation.

Turtle Dove   B235
Streptopelia turtur (Linnaeus 1758)
T3 p. 65 and pl. 53 **mid left** (2 birds)
as turtle-dove, *Turtur communis*, Selby

A palearctic bird possibly of steppe origin, breeding from the Canaries, Madeira and Sahara north to Denmark and the south Baltic and east through the full Black, Caspian and Aral Sea river systems to those of Lake Balkhash, and into Mesopotamia, Persia and Afghanistan. European elements migrate to Africa north of the equator.

Breeding population Britain-Ireland order 4; from 1800, when virtually confined to central-south and east England, increased to colonise Wales and northern England by 1865, northernmost England and Lowland Scotland by 1946; has now reached the south-west Highlands and Ireland, where has bred intermittently in co. Dublin since 1939, co. Down possibly in 1953, and in co. Wicklow in 1962. May have decreased locally in last decade in Wales and the Welsh border counties of England.

Rufous Turtle Dove   B236
Streptopelia orientalis (Latham 1790)
T3 p. 65, **not figured**
as rufous turtle-dove, *Turtur orientalis*

An Asian palearctic species breeding from the Urals east to Sakhalin, the Kuriles and Japan, south to Taiwan, northern Siam, Burma, India, Afghanistan and Turkestan; normally winters mainly in the oriental region.

Three English records: immature near Scarborough, Yorkshire 1889 October 23; immature female shot Castle Rising, Norfolk 1946 January 29; 1 seen St Agnes, Scilly 1960 May 2–6.

Pl. 53.

Wood Pigeon.   Stock Dove.
                         Rock Dove.
Turtle Dove, Pallas's Sand Grouse. (♂ & ♀)

Plate 53 (Thorburn's plate 26)

Remaining Orders

A modern systematic order is Cuculiformes, Strigiformes, Caprimulgiformes, Apodiformes, Coraciiformes, Piciformes, Passeriformes. The order following differs from this owing to the necessity of fitting the sequence to Thorburn's plates.

Order STRIGIFORMES

Family TYTONIDAE, barn owls

Most standard textbooks hold this as a full family; but on anatomical grounds it should probably be held as no more than a subfamily, the Tytoninae, of the following family Strigidae.

Barn Owl   B241
Tyto alba (Scopoli 1769)
T2 p. 34 and pl. 26 **bottom left**
as barn-owl, *Strix flammea*, Linnæus

A cosmopolitan species breeding in the Americas from southernmost Canada to Argentina, including the West Indies and the Galápagos Islands; in virtually all ethiopian Africa save the Congo forests, in Arabia, from India to Malaya and Indochina, and from Java to Papua, Australia and islands of the south-west Pacific. Breeds in the palearctic region only in Arabia, north-west Africa and Europe, where extends north to Ireland, Britain, Denmark, southernmost Sweden, the south Baltic and the Ukraine.

Breeding population of Britain-Ireland order 5; has been generally decreasing since nineteenth century and particularly in the last decade, due early to human persecution, more lately partly through rodent poisons and other agricultural changes; has bred in every county except the North Isles and only sporadically in the Inner Hebrides, and is presently still decreasing in Scotland, England (all but north-east), south Wales, north-east Ireland and the Isle of Man.

Family STRIGIDAE, typical owls

A modern systematic order is B244 (pl. 55), 243 (pl. 54), 248, 249 (pl. 53), 242, 250, 246, 245 (pl. 55), 247 (pl. 53).

Long-eared Owl   B248
Asio otus (Linnaeus 1758)
T2 p. 35 and pl. 26 **top left**
as long-eared owl, *Asio otus* (Linnæus)

An holarctic species breeding in North America from southern Alaska, south-west Mackenzie and provincial Canada (not Newfoundland) south to Lower California and the United States (not the south-east States), and in the palearctic from the Azores, Canaries and north-west Africa north through Europe into the boreal forests of south Fenno-Scandia and east through Siberia, north China and Mongolia to Amurland and Japan. Northern European elements winter to the Mediterranean.

Breeding population Britain-Ireland probably low order 5; has bred in virtually every county, though once only in Shetland (1935). Has decreased markedly in present century in Wales and southern England, and since the 1930's in northern England and the Lowlands, partly through interference and habitat destruction; but is increasing or stable in Highland Scotland and other areas of conifer afforestation and remains stably the commonest (though local) owl of Ireland.

Short-eared Owl   B249
Asio flammeus (Pontoppidan 1763)
T2 p. 36 and pl. 26 **bottom right**
as short-eared owl, *Asio accipitrinus* (Pallas)

A palearctic and neotropical bird with Pacific outposts in the Marianas, Carolines and Hawaiian Islands. Breeds in North America from California and the central and north-eastern United States to the continental arctic tundra shore; in the West Indies, the northern Andes, Galápagos Islands, southern South America and the Falklands, and in Eurasia from France, the Danubian system, the steppes, Amurland, Sakhalin and Kamchatka north to the arctic shores (except in central Siberia) and Iceland (since 1920's, not Faeroe). Northern European elements winter to North Africa.

Breeding population of Britain-Ireland probably order 4; very fluctuating with the numbers of vole prey, but some increase in present century in north-central and eastern England and new forests in Wales and Scotland; sporadic in other parts of southern England, south Wales – and Shetland (where no voles); in Ireland an irregular passenger and winter visitor, and has only attempted to nest in co. Mayo (1923), once successfully nested in co. Galway (1959), and possibly (unconfirmed) has nested in cos. Tipperary and Kilkenny.

Tawny Owl   B247
Strix aluco Linnaeus 1758
T2 p. 37 and pl. 26 **top right**
as tawny owl, *Syrnium aluco* (Linnæus)

Origin probably palearctic, where breeds from north-west Africa and the Mediterranean, Asia Minor and north Persia north to Britain, southern Fenno-Scandia and the Volga system, east to the plains of the upper Ob system and from Turkestan and north Afghanistan through the Himalayas to central and southern China, Korea and Taiwan, thus reaching the oriental region. Resident.

Breeding population of Britain order 5; is quite unknown in Ireland, the Isle of Man, Orkney and Shetland and breeds only at Stornoway in the Outer Hebrides; breeds in every other British county. Decreased with human persecution in nineteenth century; decrease was arrested and generally reversed in twentieth century though has lately continued in Yorkshire; in southern Scotland has stabilised after the earlier twentieth-century increase: in general has stabilised everywhere since the 1950's.

Pl. 26.

Long-eared Owl.   Tawny Owl.
Barn Owl   Short-eared Owl.

Plate 54 (Thorburn's plate 28)

Family STRIGIDAE, typical owls
(*continued*)

Eagle Owl   B243
Bubo bubo (Linnaeus 1758)
T2 p. 43 and pl. 28 (♀)
as eagle-owl, *Bubo ignavus*, T. Forster

A palearctic and oriental species breeding south to the Sahara, Asia Minor, the Persian Gulf, India and south China, east to the Pacific coast and Sakhalin, and north to about the boreal tree-line, in Europe north to Lapland and the White Sea, though not in western France, the Low Countries, Denmark and south-west Sweden. Generally resident with a tendency to wander.

A very rare vagrant to England and Scotland, October–May.

Pl. 28.

Eagle-Owl ♀.

Plate 55 (Thorburn's plate 27)

Family STRIGIDAE, typical owls
(*continued*)

Snowy Owl   B244
Nyctea scandiaca (Linnaeus 1758)
T2 p. 40 and pl. 27 **bottom**
as snowy owl, *Nyctea scandiaca* (Linnæus)

An holarctic bird of the high boreal and tundra zones, extending into the high arctic, breeding in central Iceland, from the Norwegian mountains and round the tundra apron of the Polar Basin's coast from Murmansk through Siberia to Alaska and Canada, on Novaya Zemlya, Wrangel Island, the Canadian arctic archipelago and north and north-east Greenland. Generally resident, with a tendency to invade southwards after seasons of vole and lemming shortage.

Bred Fetlar, Shetland 1967; otherwise a rare vagrant to England, Wales, Scotland and Ireland, mostly November–April; in nineteenth century almost annual North Isles but rarer since until a few began to summer Shetland 1963.

Scops Owl   B242
Otus scops (Linnaeus 1758)
T2 p. 42 and pl. 27 **top right**
as scops-owl, *Scops giu* (Scopoli)

An Old World species breeding in most of the ethiopian region save the Congo forests and Madagascar, and from north-west Africa, the Iberian Peninsula and Mediterranean Europe east through the Black, Caspian and Aral Sea systems nearly to Lake Baikal, and through Persia and Afghanistan to India, Malaya, Indochina, China, Japan, the Philippines and the central East Indies. The European birds winter to Africa north of the equator.

A rare vagrant to England and Scotland; has been recorded in Wales and Ireland; mostly April–June, a number November.

Tengmalm's Owl   B250
Aegolius funereus (Linnaeus 1758)
T2 p. 38 and pl. 27 **top mid**
as Tengmalm's owl, *Nyctala tengmalmi* (J. F. Gmelin)

An holarctic species of the boreal forest zone of Alaska and Canada, and of northern and highland Europe through the upper Siberian river systems to Amurland, Sakhalin, Kamchatka and the Anadyr, with some isolated outposts to the south in highland Asia. In Europe does not breed west of the lower Rhône, Switzerland and the Rhine or in the Low Countries, south-west Sweden and northernmost Germany. Resident with a tendency to wander.

A rare vagrant to eastern England, recorded also from other parts of England and from Scotland; most October–January and March–May.

Little Owl   B246
Athene noctua (Scopoli 1769)
T2 p. 39 and pl. 27 **mid right**
as little owl, *Athene noctua* (Scopoli)

Origin possibly the Turkestanian steppes; a palearctic species extending into Red Sea Africa as far as Ethiopia and into the Sahara, breeding north in Europe to Britain, Denmark and the south Baltic and through the Black, Caspian and Aral river systems to the Amur and the borders of Korea, south to the borders of the oriental region (entering Kashmir) and Arabia. Resident with a tendency to wander.

Breeding population of Britain (does not breed Ireland) order 4; known from Pleistocene fossil in Devon, but now present by introduction, successfully in Northamptonshire in 1889, since when has spread to every English county (last Cumberland 1950), every Welsh county and Berwick co. in Scotland (1958), perhaps now also Dumfries co. and East Lothian. Decreased markedly in some areas after the severe winters of 1947, 1956 and 1963, and may have been affected by pesticides in some parts of England since *c* 1955.

Hawk Owl   B245
Surnia ulula (Linnaeus 1758)
T2 p. 41 and pl. 27 **top left**
as hawk-owl, *Surnia funerea* (Linnæus)

An holarctic bird with a boreal distribution almost the same as that described for Tengmalm's owl, save that it extends in Europe nowhere south of Fenno-Scandia and Russia's upper Volga. Resident but invasive.

Ten British records 1830–1966 of both American and European races: the first 1 off Cornwall 1830 March; England 6; Scotland 4; most August–December, 2 March–April.

Pl. 27.

A. Thorburn. 1919

Hawk-Owl.

Tengmalm's Owl (with Dusky Warbler)
Little Owl.

Scops Owl.

Snowy Owl. ♂

Plate 56 (Thorburn's plate 23)

Order CAPRIMULGIFORMES

Family CAPRIMULGIDAE, nightjars

Common Nighthawk   B251
Chordeiles minor (J. R. Forster 1771)
Not illustrated

Breeds from southern Yukon and Mackenzie through provincial Canada to central Québec and southern Labrador south to California, northern México, the Bahamas, Jamaica and Puerto Rico. Normally winters south to central Argentina.

   Two English records: female Tresco, Scilly 1927 September 17; 2 seen St Agnes, Scilly 1957 September 28, 1 until October 5.

Nightjar   B252
Caprimulgus europaeus Linnaeus 1758
T2 p. 17 and pl. 23 **mid right**
as nightjar, *Caprimulgus europæus*, Linnæus

A palearctic bird breeding through virtually the whole region north to Ireland, Britain, southern Fenno-Scandia, and in Russia nearly to Archangel, and to the upper Ob and Yenisei (Tunguska) systems, east to near Lake Baikal and into western upland China, and into north-western India (not Arabia or Africa east of the Morocco-Tunis palearctic zone). Migrates to Africa, some wintering to the south.

   Breeding population of Britain-Ireland order 4; has decreased in and deserted old nesting areas since *c* 1930, especially in most of eastern England and the Midlands, most parts of Wales, north-west England, parts of the east Highlands and northern Ireland; never common in and now breeds but sporadically in the Lowlands, western Highlands and parts of central and south-west Ireland; has never been more than a vagrant to the North Isles. Is still fairly common in southern England, and survives quite well in the larger Inner Hebrides, Arran and Bute, and the Isle of Man, from J. Stafford's analysis; the decrease seems largely due to recreational disturbance and the spread of housing estates, military and other enterprises on to the poor agricultural land which is its favoured habitat.

Red-necked Nightjar   B253
Caprimulgus ruficollis Temminck 1820
T2 p. 19 and pl. 23 **bottom left**
as red-necked nightjar, *Caprimulgus ruficollis*, Temminck

Breeds only (provedly) in Portugal, central and southern Spain, Morocco, Algeria and Tunisia, migrating to Africa, where recorded in the Sahara; its winter quarters are unknown.

   One English record: a bird shot at Killingworth near Newcastle, Northumberland 1856 October 5.

Egyptian Nightjar   B254
Caprimulgus aegyptius Lichtenstein 1823
T2 p. 20 and pl. 23 **bottom right**
as *Caprimulgus ægyptius*, Lichtenstein

A southern palearctic species; breeds in the northern Sahara from Algeria and Tunisia east to Egypt, and through Mesopotamia and Persia into the steppes of Russian Turkestan as far as the Aral Sea system; the western elements at least winter to the northern Sudan and may wander north.

   One English record: a bird at Rainworth near Mansfield, Nottinghamshire 1883 June 23.

Order APODIFORMES

Family APODIDAE, swifts

(White-throated) Needle-tailed Swift   B257
Hirundapus caudacutus (Latham 1801)
T2 p. 16 and pl. 23 **top left**
as needle-tailed swift, *Acanthyllis caudacuta* (Latham)

An eastern palearctic and northern oriental breeder, nesting from the Tomsk area of the upper Ob and the Himalayas east to Sakhalin, the Kuriles, Japan and Taiwan, south into Assam and perhaps northern Burma; some elements may normally migrate through the oriental region to Australia.

   Four records: 1 Great Horkesley near Colchester, Essex 1846 July 8; 2 seen (1 shot) Ringwood, Hampshire 1879 July 26 or 27; 1 seen Fair Isle, Shetland 1931 August 6; 1 seen Cape Clear Island, co. Cork 1964 June 20.

White-rumped (or **Little** or **House**) **Swift**
Apus affinis (J. E. Gray 1830)
Not illustrated

Old World; breeds in most of ethiopian Africa and the oriental region east to Borneo and Java, and in the palearctic in the drylands from Afghanistan, Transcaspia and Persia through Iraq, Jordan, Syria, Palestine and parts of Arabia to the northern Sahara (and Mauretania), where spread from Tunis and Algeria to Morocco in 1925, Tangier in early 1950's and Sierra de la Plata in southernmost Spain, where present 1962, breeding proved 1966–67. Generally resident, but western palearctic birds, including those of Spain, migrate to Africa, and may reach Nigeria.

   One Irish record, of a bird seen at Cape Clear Bird Observatory, co. Cork 1967 June 12.

Swift   B255
Apus apus (Linnaeus 1758)
T2 p. 13 and pl. 23 **mid left**
as swift, *Cypselus apus* (Linnæus)

A palearctic species breeding from the Mediterranean shores and islands, Turkey and Persia (not Arabia), extreme north-west India and northern China east not quite to the Pacific in China and to Lake Baikal, north through the boreal zone to the central systems of the Siberian rivers, Archangel, northern Finland and Sweden and central Norway. Migrates to southern Africa.

   Breeding population of Britain-Ireland order 6; nests stably in every county save the Inner Hebrides (where a sporadic breeder) and the North Isles (where only wanderer and passenger). May have increased in western Ireland since 1900, certainly since 1932.

Alpine Swift   B256
Apus melba (Linnaeus 1758)
T2 p. 15 and pl. 23 **top right**
as *Cypselus melba* (Linnæus)

A palearctic, ethiopian and oriental species breeding in India and Ceylon; in eastern tropical and southern Africa and Madagascar; in southern Russian Turkestan, Persia and Asia Minor, and in the Mediterranean islands, Portugal, Mediterranean zones of the Mediterranean countries and Switzerland. The European birds migrate to tropical Africa.

   An annual vagrant to southern England, mostly April–October; has been recorded in northern England, Wales, southern Scotland and Ireland.

Pl. 23.

Swift.   Needle-tailed Swift.   Nightjar.   Alpine Swift.
      Red-necked Nightjar.   Egyptian Nightjar.

Plate 57 (Thorburn's plate 25)

Order CUCULIFORMES

Family CUCULIDAE, cuckoos

Cuckoo   B237
Cuculus canorus Linnæus 1758
T2 p. 30 and pl. 25 **top left** (young and adult)
as cuckoo, *Cuculus canorus*, Linnæus

Possibly of palearctic origin, but breeds through virtually the whole of continental Africa south of the Sahara save the Congo forests; into the oriental region to Himalayan India, Assam, Burma and northern Indochina, and throughout the palearctic region north to the edge of the boreal zone, east to Anadyr, Kamchatka, Sakhalin and Japan, in the west from Morocco, Algeria, Tunisia, the Mediterranean islands and Asia Minor north to northern Norway, Lapland and Archangel. Migrates to Africa south to the Cape.

Breeding population of Britain-Ireland order 5; chief hosts meadow pipit and dunnock. Breeds in every county, though only in very small numbers in Shetland. Decreases have been reported in Ireland since early in the present century (this may lately have accelerated), and in England since the early 1950's.

Great Spotted Cuckoo   B238
Clamator glandarius (Linnaeus 1758)
T2 p. 32 and pl. 25 **top right**
as great spotted cuckoo, *Coccystes glandarius* (Linnæus)

An Old World species with a relict distribution; breeds in scattered areas in ethiopian Africa. Breeds in the palearctic in Nile Egypt, possibly still in north-west Africa, and has a headquarters in the Iberian Peninsula and Mediterranean France perhaps extending into northern Italy, and another in Asia Minor, perhaps extending into Macedonia. The palearctic birds winter in tropical and southern Africa, and wander to some extent.

Ten records 1842–1960; first 1 Omey Island, co. Galway 1842 about March; England 4; Wales 2; Scotland 1; Ireland 3; 3 April, 3 August, rest also spring or autumn.

Yellow-billed Cuckoo   B239
Coccyzus americanus (Linnaeus 1758)
T2 p. 33 and pl. 25 **mid left**
as American yellow-billed cuckoo, *Coccyzus americanus* (Linnæus)

A nearctic species breeding from southern Canada and the northern United States south to México and the West Indies; winters south to central Argentina.

A rare vagrant on transatlantic westerlies at full migration time (most, October) to south-west England and south Wales; has been recorded from other parts of England and Wales, and from Scotland and Ireland.

Black-billed Cuckoo   B240
Coccyzus erythropthalmus (Wilson 1811)
T2 p. 33, **not figured**
as American black-billed cuckoo, *Coccyzus erythrophthalmus* (Wilson)

A nearctic species breeding from southern Canada west to Saskatchewan, to the United States from Wyoming to South Carolina; winters in north-western South America.

Four records: 1 Killead, co. Antrim 1871 September 25; 1 Tresco, Scilly 1932 October 27; 'flock' near Southend in south Kintyre, Argyll 1950 November 6 and immature found dead November 8; exhausted bird caught Foula, Shetland 1953 October 11.

Order CORACIIFORMES

A modern systematic order of the families known in Britain-Ireland is Alcedinidae, Meropidae, Coraciidae, Upupidae.

Family MEROPIDAE, bee eaters

Bee Eater   B259
Merops apiaster Linnaeus 1758
T2 p. 28 and pl. 25 **bottom left**
as bee-eater, *Merops apiaster*, Linnæus

Possibly of steppe origin; a palearctic species breeding from Portugal, central Spain and the European Mediterranean shores (in North Africa only in Morocco and Algeria) through the Balkans and the Black Sea river systems to Asia Minor, Mesopotamia, the north and west Caspian rivers, Persia, Afghanistan to Pakistan, north-western India and from the Aral River systems to those of Lake Balkhash. A breeding outpost in Cape Province may be derived from palearctic migrants; the European elements winter to South Africa. Has bred sporadically north of its normal European range in about eight countries in hot summers.

A pair attempted to nest in a bank of the Esk at Musselburgh, Midlothian in 1920. In 1955 3 pairs bred in a sandpit in Sussex. Otherwise an annual vagrant, sometimes in small parties (not in winter) to south-east England, recorded also from the rest of England, Wales, Scotland and Ireland.

Blue-cheeked Bee Eater
Merops superciliosus Linnaeus 1766
Not illustrated

Breeds in the palearctic in Morocco, Algeria and possibly Tunisia, and from Egypt through Mesopotamia and Persia to north-west India, the Caucasus and Russian Turkestan to Lake Balkhash; and in eastern tropical Africa and Madagascar. Birds of the eastern palearctic race winter in Africa to the Cape, and those of the north-western African race normally south of the Sahara, where breeding has been recorded in Mauretania and French Sudan.

One English record: a bird (of unknown race) seen St Agnes, Scilly 1951 June 22.

Family UPUPIDAE, hoopoe

Hoopoe   B261
Upupa epops Linnaeus 1758
T2 p. 29 and pl. 25 **bottom right**
as hoopoe, *Upupa epops*, Linnæus

A palearctic, ethiopian and oriental species breeding in virtually all the continental Old World from Africa (and Canaries and Madagascar) and from India (and Ceylon) and Malaya (probably also Sumatra) north to southern boreal Russia from Estonia across the plains of the upper Volga and upper Ob systems to Lake Baikal and the Amur system; though absent from the Congo forests and the fully arid Sahara, parts of western India and Korea, north-westernmost Europe and Scandinavia (bred Denmark to 1876 or later; now only sporadic in south-easternmost Sweden). Most of the European population migrates to Africa. Has decreased in north-west Europe under some persecution in nineteenth century and very rare now as a breeder in northern France, though there are some signs of a north-westward trend at least by sporadic breeders to Britain, most marked in the last two decades.

Of about 32 probable breedings those unconfirmed include the only possible Irish breeding, ? co. Waterford 1934; and the 28 fully accepted records are all from England, the first in Sussex c 1835, and 15 (over half) of them in the present century. All confirmed breedings were of single pairs and can be regarded as sporadic, often associated with marked spring influxes, nearly always in warm seasons and were in Hampshire 7; Sussex 5; Wiltshire 4; Somerset, Kent, Surrey and Suffolk (2 each); Cornwall, Buckinghamshire, Herefordshire and Lincolnshire (1 each). About 2000 birds must have been recorded at one time or another in the four countries; years of marked spring immigration in the present century are 1906, 1948, 1950, 1954, 1955, 1959, 1960 and 1965. Spring influxes are usually most marked in south and eastern England but may reach east Ireland and co. Cork; hoopoes are more often encountered as autumn vagrants in the rest of England, Wales, Scotland (to Shetland) and rest of Ireland.

Pl. 25.

Cuckoo. (adult & young). Great Spotted Cuckoo
American Yellow-billed Cuckoo. Bee-eater. Hoopoe.

Plate 58 (Thorburn's plate 24)

Family ALCEDINIDAE, kingfishers

Kingfisher B258
Alcedo atthis (Linnaeus 1758)
T4 p. 26 and pl. 24 **bottom left**
as kingfisher, *Alcedo ispida* (Linnæus)

Old World; breeds in river systems of ethiopian Africa; the continental oriental region, Ceylon and Hainan; the australasian region from Celebes-Bali blend-zone through East Indies east to Papua and the Solomons; and the palearctic region from Morocco-Tunisia and western Europe east to Sakhalin, Japan, the Ryu Kyus and Taiwan, north to Denmark, south Sweden, Estonia, the upper Volga, and the moister Russian steppes and valleys through Lake Baikal and Amurland. The western European birds are mostly resident, some dispersing to coasts and estuaries in winter.

Breeding population of Britain-Ireland order 4; has recovered after persecution for feather trade but drops markedly after long hard winters. Has bred in every county of England, Wales, Ireland, Lowlands and south-east Highlands; its northward range may be limited by that of the minnow, and nesting records are only sporadic from Aberdeen co., Argyll, Arran, Islay and perhaps other northern counties.

Family CORACIIDAE, rollers

Roller B260
Coracias garrulus Linnaeus 1758
T2 p. 27 and pl. 24 **bottom right**
as roller, *Coracias garrulus*, Linnæus

Palearctic; breeds in Morocco-Tunisia, Portugal and Spain, principal Mediterranean islands, and from Italy north to Estonia and east to the upper Ob and Turkestanian steppes, and from Asia Minor to north-westernmost India. Outside this range it has very isolated breeding places in south France and Gotland in Sweden and is now sporadic elsewhere in western Europe; has probably withdrawn with more humid Atlantic summers and last bred Denmark *c* 1876. European birds migrate to Africa where some reach the south.

A vagrant, almost annual and with a mainly spring and autumn passage in eastern England; recorded from the rest of England, Wales, Scotland and (not since 1900) Ireland.

Order PICIFORMES

Family PICIDAE, woodpeckers

Wryneck B265
Jynx torquilla Linnaeus 1758
T2 p. 21 and pl. 24 **top left**
as wryneck, *Jynx torquilla*, Linnæus

A palearctic species breeding in Algeria and western Tunisia, and from Europe through the upper Siberian river systems east to the Sea of Okhotsk, Sakhalin and Hokkaido, north-eastern Korea and Manchuria, with an extension in the mountains of western China and outposts in Kashmir, the Crimea, and the Caucasus and north-west Russia. In Europe breeds from north Portugal and Spain, France (not Brittany), Sicily, Sardinia, perhaps Corsica, Italy, Jugoslavia, Macedonia and Bulgaria north to south Norway, south and east Sweden, south Finland and Archangel. The European elements migrate to tropical Africa. A closely related bird of ethiopian Africa is held by some to be the same species.

Breeding population of Britain (only) order **2**; *c* 100–200 pairs when surveyed by J. F. Monk in 1958, *c* 25–30 1965. In 1850 bred in virtually every county in England and Wales save Cornwall and Northumberland; by 1900 was rare and by 1925 extinct as a breeder in Wales and north England; in 1958 was proved to breed only in Bedfordshire, Buckinghamshire, Hampshire, Surrey and Kent; outside Kent nestings are now virtually sporadic. The decline could march with the phase of wetter, more Atlantic summers since the late nineteenth century. Has not bred Scotland, where vagrant, as in Ireland.

Green Woodpecker B262
Picus viridis Linnaeus 1758
T2 p. 23 and pl. 24 **top right** (♂)
as green woodpecker, *Gecinus viridis* (Linnæus)

Western palearctic; breeds from Morocco-Tunisia, Iberian Peninsula and Mediterranean north to Britain, south Scandinavia, Leningrad and the upper Volga; and from north-east Turkey to Caucasus and west Persia. Resident; disposed to wander.

Breeding population of Britain (only) order 5; breeds in virtually all England and Wales; colonised Isle of Wight after 1905 and Scotland in Berwick and Selkirk cos. 1951, Dumfries and Roxburgh cos. and East Lothian 1954, Midlothian 1955, Kirkcudbright st. 1959, Stirling co. 1960, Lanark co. 1961 and Clackmannan co. 1965. Population is reduced by very hard winters. Only thrice recorded Ireland, the last 1854!

Black Woodpecker
Dryocopus martius (Linnaeus 1758)
Not illustrated

Palearctic; breeds in pine forests in isolated groups in Spain, France and Italy, and from the Alps, Balkans, Greece, north Turkey and north-west Persia west to Rhineland, north to Fenno-Scandia and east through Siberia to Kamchatka, north Japan and highland China. Resident but wanders, and has spread west in Europe to breed Belgium *c* 1908, Holland 1915.

R. S. R. Fitter's analysis of 1959 could restore this species to the List; of 54 records, all England and Wales with no specific reason for rejection the 7 most reliable are: 1 shot Blandford, Dorset between 1764 and 1799; 1 seen Beningborough Wood near York *c* 1799; 1 shot Longleat, Wiltshire before 1887; 1 seen and heard Builth Wells, Brecon co. 1903 April 19; 1 seen around Park Hall near Mansfield, Nottinghamshire 1907 December; 1 seen Delamere Forest, Cheshire 1936 July; 1 seen Hitchin, Hertfordshire 1944 December.

Great Spotted Woodpecker B263
Dendrocopos major (Linnaeus 1758)
T2 p. 24 and pl. 24 **mid right** (♂ and young)
as great spotted woodpecker, *Dendrocopus major* (Linnæus)

Palearctic; breeds from Canaries, Morocco-Tunisia, Iberian Peninsula, Mediterranean, north Turkey and north-west Persia to Britain and south Fenno-Scandia and through Siberia to Kamchatka, Japan, Korea and China to reach oriental Burma and Assam. Resident with a tendency to irruptive wandering.

Breeding population of Britain (only) order 5; is now a vagrant to Ireland though may have bred there in late or post-Ice Age times (fossil co. Clare). Has slowly invaded northern Scotland through last 100 years; may have bred in virtually every English and Welsh county (though rare north England and extinct Scotland) before 1870's–1880's; by 1900 bred Cumberland and east and south Lowlands; by 1925 central and east Highlands; by 1950's virtually all Scottish mainland counties and Arran, Bute and possibly Mull. May previously have bred Inverness co. to 1840's and Easter Ross to 1865. The Scottish history may march with the destruction and rehabilitation of the forests.

Lesser Spotted Woodpecker B264
Dendrocopos minor (Linnaeus 1758)
T2 p. 25 and pl. 24 **mid left** (♂ ♀)
as lesser spotted woodpecker, *Dendrocopus minor* (Linnæus)

Palearctic; distribution closely resembles great spotted's though does not breed Canaries, Morocco, Scotland and Denmark or south of Manchuria and north Korea in the east. In Europe reaches further north: to Lapland and Kola; northern birds winter south within Europe.

Breeding population of Britain (only) order 4; breeds or has bred locally in every English and Welsh county save Northumberland. No breeding or other record for Scotland or Ireland is now accepted: the English-Welsh race is very sedentary and its smallish population seems stable.

Wryneck.   Green Woodpecker.
Lesser Spotted Woodpecker ♂ & ♀. Great Spotted Woodpecker. (adult ♂ & young)
           Kingfisher.   Roller.

Plate 59 (Thorburn's plate 22)

Order PASSERIFORMES

I have adopted a plate order corresponding as much as possible to the system of classification I prefer for the largest order of birds, which is set out on non-plate '83' in full.

Family ALAUDIDAE, larks

Short-toed Lark   B269
Calandrella cinerea (J. F. Gmelin 1789)
T2 p. 9 and pl. 22 **upper mid right**
as *Alauda brachydactyla* Leisler

Breeds from around the Mediterranean east through steppe-type country to Tibet and north China, also in Arabia and dry east and south ethiopian Africa. The western European population winters to North Africa and the Sudan.

An annual vagrant (most often in autumn) to England (particularly east and south), Scotland (particularly Fair Isle and other North Isles) and Ireland; recorded rarely from Wales.

Lesser Short-toed Lark
Calandrella rufescens (Vieillot 1820)
Not illustrated

A palearctic (and ethiopian) species possibly of Turkestanian steppe origin and with an Asian distribution similar to that of its close relation the short-toed lark, though breeds on no Mediterranean island and in Europe (west of Russia) only on the Mediterranean coast of Spain. Races in Somaliland, Ethiopia and Kenya have been included in this species. Most populations are sedentary with a tendency to wander.

Four Irish sight records: a flock of 30 Tralee Bay, co. Kerry 1956 January 4; 5 Great Saltee, co. Wexford 1956 March 30–31; 2 near Belmullet, co. Mayo 1956 May 21; 5 Great Saltee, co. Wexford 1958 March 22 (and up to 4 until March 25).

Calandra Lark   B267
Melanocorypha calandra (Linnaeus 1766)
Not illustrated

Breeds around most of the Mediterranean and in the Black Sea and Caspian systems, Asia Minor, Persia, north Afghanistan, and Turkestanian and Kirghiz steppes. Northern birds migrate, apparently not beyond the palearctic.

One record: 1 seen Portland Bill, Dorset 1961 April 2.

Bimaculated Lark
Melanocorypha bimaculata (Ménétries 1832)
Not illustrated

Breeds from Asia Minor to Afghanistan, and in the Kirghiz steppes. Migrates to west India, and north ethiopian Africa.

One record: 1 seen Lundy, Devon 1962 May 7–11.

White-winged Lark   B268
Melanocorypha leucoptera (Pallas 1811)
T2 p. 10 and pl. 22 **lower mid right**
as white-winged lark, *Alauda sibirica*, J. F. Gmelin

Breeds in Russia from the Crimea and Caucasus through the steppes east to beyond Lake Balkhash. Migrates and wanders within the palearctic.

Three records, all Sussex: female caught alive Brighton 1869 November 22; 3 seen west Hove 1917 November 15; 1 seen between Rye and Camber 1933 August 1919.

[Black Lark   B266
Melanocorypha yeltoniensis (J. R. Forster 1768)
T2 p. 11 and pl. 22 **bottom right** (♂ summer and winter)
as black lark, *Alauda yeltoniensis*, Forster

A Russian species rejected from the List, though figured by Thorburn in good faith. Six specimens, said to be obtained in 1907 and 1915 in Sussex and Kent, are 'Hastings Rarities'.]

Shore Lark   B273
Eremophila alpestris (Linnaeus 1758)
T2 p. 12 and pl. 22 **mid left** (♂)
as shore-lark, *Otocorys alpestris* (Linnæus)

The only lark that has naturally colonised the New World, where it breeds through most of the nearctic continent, including the Canadian arctic and south into the mountains of neotropical México and Colombia. In the palearctic 'tundra birds' breed from spinal Norway and Lapland to east Siberian Anadyrland and on some arctic islands, and 'steppe birds' breed from the Balkans through the steppes and mountains of Asia (its theatre of origin?) to Manchuria and Siberia east of Lake Baikal, with outpost in Moroccan Atlas.

A winter visitor from northern Europe and adjoining tundras, normally to east England, rarer in south England and east Scotland north to Fair Isle, in late years in decreasing numbers; vagrant elsewhere, including Wales and Ireland.

Crested Lark   B270
Galerida cristata (Linnaeus 1758)
T2 p. 8 and pl. 22 **bottom left**
as crested lark, *Alauda cristata*, Linnæus

Breeds from Arabia and Asia Minor through desert-edge, steppe and savannah to north China, Korea and north India; probably of palearctic steppe origin whence it has invaded oriental and ethiopian regions; in latter breeds south of the Sahara from Somaliland to west Africa. Now breeds from north Sahara through continental Europe to south Sweden, having colonised north-west slowly – by centuries 14 Czechoslovakia, 16 Switzerland and south-west Germany, 17 Austria and north France, late 19 Denmark; not yet Britain though nesting across the Channel.

At least fourteen British records before 1845 to 1965; first, 4 Littlehampton, Sussex before 1845; England (coastal south) 13; Scotland 1; most September–January, 4 spring, 1 June.

Wood Lark   B271
Lullula arborea (Linnaeus 1758)
T2 p. 7 and pl. 22 **top right**
as wood-lark, *Alauda arborea*, Linnæus

Doubtless of European origin; a palearctic species breeding into Asia from Asia Minor to north-west Persia, and in Africa in Morocco, Algeria and Tunisia. European range is from the Mediterranean and Caucasus north to Wales, England, Denmark, south Sweden, Baltic islands, south Finland, Lake Onega and upper Volga. Migrates within the palearctic.

Breeding population (England-Wales only) order 3; formerly bred Ireland where last cos. Wicklow 1894, Wexford c 1905, Cork 1954. Decreased Britain last century; last bred Cheshire c 1848, Westmorland c 1861, Lancashire 1870's, Yorkshire c 1880, Cumberland late 1880's; recovered 1920 to early 1950's when still bred north Wales and recolonised Yorkshire 1945; since 1954 markedly decreased to c 100 pairs 1965, virtually sporadic outside Cornwall, Devon, Dorset, Hampshire, Sussex, Suffolk and Norfolk. Probably reduced by bird catchers, later by habitat disturbance and 1962–63 winters. In Scotland it is a regular passenger.

Skylark   B272
Alauda arvensis Linnaeus 1758
T2 p. 5 and pl. 22 **top left** (2 birds)
as sky-lark, *Alauda arvensis*, Linnæus

A palearctic species breeding north into the boreal zone, in Asia in the upper systems of the Siberian rivers east to the Chukotski Peninsula, Kamchatka, the Komandorski and Kurile Islands, Japan and the Amur system, also from north Persia to the upper systems of the Aral and Balkhash basins. In the west breeds in Morocco, Algeria and Tunisia, and from the Mediterranean and the Caucasus north to Ireland, Britain, Faeroe, Fenno-Scandia and Archangel. North European birds winter to the Mediterranean. Introduced in New Zealand, the Hawaiian Islands and Vancouver Island.

Breeding population of Britain-Ireland order 6 or low order 7; nests with apparent stability in every county.

Pl. 22.

Sky-Lark.
Shore-Lark.
Crested Lark

Wood Lark.
Short-toed Lark.
White-winged Lark.
Black Lark (summer & winter)

A. Thorburn 1914

Plate 60 (Thorburn's plate 12)

Family MOTACILLIDAE, wagtails and pipits

Richard's Pipit   B374
Anthus novaeseelandiae (J. F. Gmelin 1789)
TI p. 81 and pl. 12 **mid**
as Richard's pipit, *Anthus richardi*, Vieillot

A cosmopolitan Old World species breeding in the eastern palearctic from the Irtysh east through the steppes and upper Siberian river systems to the Pacific, and in China; through the oriental and australasian regions and widely in ethiopian Africa. The western Siberian race normally winters into the oriental region, but wanders in some numbers into Europe (where it does not breed).

An irregular vagrant to south England, Norfolk and Fair Isle, very rare elsewhere in England, Scotland, Wales and Ireland; mostly in autumn, less often in winter and spring.

Tawny Pipit   B375
Anthus campestris (Linnaeus 1758)
TI p. 80 and pl. 12 **mid left**
as tawny pipit, *Anthus campestris* (Linnæus)

A palearctic species possibly of steppe origin, breeding from Morocco to Tunisia, on most Mediterranean islands, and north in continental Europe to the south Baltic shore and Leningrad, though not in the Channel and North Sea coastal regions; breeds also in two places in Denmark and in Sweden on the southernmost coast, Öland and Gotland. In Russia and Asia ranges through Asia Minor and the Black, Caspian, Aral Seas and Balkhash systems to Lake Baikal, the Gobi Desert, Tibet, Mongolia and the uppermost Amur system. The European birds winter to Africa north of the equator.

A breeding report in Sussex in 1905 has been rejected. Is an annual passage vagrant to south England, most frequent in Sussex, in autumn, and occasionally spring; has been recorded elsewhere in England, rarely in Wales and Scotland, and almost annually in Ireland where 9 records to 1966.

Tree Pipit   B376
Anthus trivialis (Linnaeus 1758)
TI p. 77 and pl. 12 **top right**
as tree-pipit, *Anthus trivialis* (Linnæus)

Possibly of steppe origin; a palearctic bird that breeds north into the boreal zone from the Cantabrian Mountains of Spain, the Pyrenees, the spinal mountains of Italy, the Balkans and northern Greece, northern Turkey and north-west Persia, north almost to the tree-line in Fenno-Scandia, and east through the systems of the north Caspian rivers and the upper and middle systems of the Siberian rivers to the Lena, with a salient into the central Asian wooded highlands through the Tian Shan, Pamirs and Karakorum to Garhwal in the Himalayas. Migrates to India, the Mediterranean and Africa south of the equator.

Breeding population of Britain-Ireland order 5; does not breed Isle of Man, or Ireland where only a passage migrant in small numbers (mainly east). Breeds in every county of England and Wales (though absent from west Cornwall) and the Lowlands, and rather locally to the central and north-west Highlands and Inner Hebrides. The population appears to be stable.

Olive-backed Pipit
Anthus hodgsoni Richmond 1907
Not illustrated

An eastern palearctic species, the 'Indian tree pipit' of most textbooks, breeding in the taiga and highland forests from the Pechora in Europe through the middle and upper systems of the Siberian rivers to Kamchatka, the Kuriles, Sakhalin, Hokkaido in Japan and through Amurland to Korea, highland China and the Himalayas west to Garhwal. Normally migrates into the oriental region, reaching the Philippines.

Two records of birds seen and trapped Fair Isle, Shetland 1964 October 17–19; 1965 September 29–30.

Pechora Pipit   B377
Anthus gustavi Swinhoe 1863
Not illustrated

Breeds on the tundras and in the taiga forest-edge of Russia from the middle Pechora through the middle or lower systems of the Siberian rivers to the Chukotski Peninsula, Komandorski Islands and Ussuriland. Normally migrates to East Indies.

Sixteen records, 1925–66, all September 18–November 19 save 1 'late August'; all but 1 Fair Isle, Shetland 1925–66, where first 1 seen 1925 September 23, shot the next day; 1 Spurn, Yorkshire 1966 September 26.

Meadow Pipit   B373
Anthus pratensis (Linnaeus 1758)
TI p. 78 and pl. 12 **bottom left**
as meadow-pipit, *Anthus pratensis* (Linnæus)

Virtually European; breeds from south-east Greenland, Iceland, Faeroe and the arctic coasts of Europe east to the Pechora and northern Urals, south to the upper Volga, northern Ukraine, Carpathians and Alps, and central France, with an outpost in the Abruzzi Mountains of Italy. Migrates, western European birds as far as Mediterranean Africa.

Breeding population of Britain-Ireland order 7; breeds stably in every county and may have fluctuated only with the ploughing of rough grassland and the disturbance of heaths.

Red-throated Pipit   B378
Anthus cervinus (Pallas 1811)
TI p. 79 and pl. 12 **mid right** (♂)
as red-throated pipit, *Anthus cervinus* (Pallas)

A palearctic species breeding on the tundra from Lapland east to the Chukotski Peninsula (bred 1931 at Wales, Alaska), and on Kolguev Island. Migrates into the oriental region and to ethiopian Africa around the equator.

A rare passage vagrant, nearly all records being from the North Isles (most Fair Isle), a few from south England and (1950's) Great Saltee, co. Wexford.

American, Water and Rock Pipits   B379
Anthus spinoletta (Linnaeus 1758)

Holarctic with a fragmented distribution, birds of the 3 racial groups being recognisable in the field by experts

American pipit, *Anthus spinoletta rubescens* (Tunstall 1771)

This race breeds in Siberia and North America from the Khatanga River to Canada, extending south to Maine and New Mexico, is a rare vagrant to Scotland and Ireland. A close race breeds in south-east Siberia to Amurland and Kuriles.

Water pipit, *Anthus spinoletta spinoletta*
TI p. 82 and pl. 12 **bottom right**
as alpine pipit, *Anthus spinoletta* (Linnaeus)

Breeds in the mountains of central Spain, the Pyrenees, the Massif Central of France, the Alps, spinal Italy, Corsica, perhaps Sardinia, the Balkans and Carpathians. A close race breeds in central Asia from the Pamirs to Lake Baikal.

A rare winter visitor recorded in all four countries.

Rock pipit, *Anthus spinoletta petrosus* (Montagu 1798)
TI p. 83 and pl. 12 **top left**
as rock pipit, *Anthus obscurus* (Latham)

The rock pipit group is purely coastal as breeders and confined to Europe. The British resident race (*petrosus*) breeds in Normandy, Brittany, Britain and Ireland; Faeroe and Shetland have another resident race, as does northern Europe where birds breed on all coasts of the Scandinavian Peninsula, on some Baltic islands, and through Murmansk and Kola to the White Sea. The northern race is migratory, some elements of it wintering in Britain and Ireland.

Breeding population of Britain-Ireland order 5; nests in virtually every coastal county save those of south-east England, where breeds only in the Isle of Wight and Sussex. There seems to be no recorded population change of any importance.

Pl. 12.

Rock Pipit
Tawny Pipit
Meadow-Pipit

Richard's Pipit

Tree Pipit
Red-throated Pipit
Alpine Pipit

Plate 61 (Thorburn's plate 11)

Family MOTACILLIDAE, wagtails and pipits (*continued*)

Yellow Wagtail   B382
Motacilla flava Linnaeus 1758

British yellow wagtail, *Motacilla flava flavissima* (Blyth 1834)
TI p. 76 and pl. 11 **bottom right**
as yellow wagtail, *Motacilla raii* (Bonaparte)

Central European yellow wagtail, *Motacilla flava flava*
TI p. 75 and pl. 11 **mid right** (upper bird)
as blue-headed wagtail, *Motacilla flava*, Linnæus

Fenno-Scandian yellow wagtail, *Motacilla flava thunbergi*
Billberg 1828
TI p. 75 and pl. 11 **bottom left** (left bird)
as grey-headed yellow wagtail (*Motacilla viridis*, Gmelin)

A palearctic bird with a broad breeding distribution reaching the northern tundra in places. Highly variable, with a complex of at least 18 races some of which can be distinguished in the field. Breeds from Morocco, Algeria, Tunisia, Mediterranean islands, Egypt, Asia Minor, Persia, Afghanistan, Russian Turkestan, Mongolia, Ussuriland, Sakhalin and Kamchatka, north to north Norway and Russia, in Siberia to the Arctic Ocean (in the east), and with a nearctic outpost in Alaska, probably extending to north Yukon. All winter to Africa or through the oriental region to the East Indies.

Breeding population of Britain-Ireland order 4; mostly of green-yellow-crowned *flavissima* race. Strongholds identified by Stuart Smith in 1948 were in Dorset, near the coast from Sussex to the Wash (of blue-headed *flava* type), and in the river systems of Welland, Trent, Mersey, Ribble, south Lake District, Yorkshire Dales and Tees. In present century has increased in north England, but decreased elsewhere; is very local in Devon and Cornwall, in Wales sporadic save in Towy system, Glamorgan and some Border areas, in Lowlands sporadic save in Ayr co. and Clyde system, in Highlands extinct (last successful breeding Aberdeen co. 1934), in Isle of Man sporadic (1914, 1916). In Ireland bred co. Dublin 1808 and had headquarters Connaught 1854–1928, Loughs Neagh and Beg 1850–*c* 1942, since when extinct save for colonists (of all 3 main racial types above) 1956–66 in scattered pairs in 6 counties. The general decline of the yellow wagtail is doubtless linked with the disturbance, 'reclamation' and 'improvement' of its preferred wetlands, marshes and sewage farms.

Citrine Wagtail
Motacilla citreola Pallas 1776
Not illustrated

A central palearctic species breeding from the tundras between the Kanin Peninsula and the Khatanga in Siberia south through the Yenisei and Ob systems to the middle Volga, and through the central Asian highlands to the Himalayas and eastern Persia. Normally winters into the continental oriental region.

Eight British records 1954–66; 6 from Fair Isle, Shetland where first, immature (trapped) 1954 September 20–24; 1 first winter (trapped) Minsmere, Suffolk 1964 October 17–November 14; 2 seen Stanpit Marshes, Hampshire 1966 October 15; all September–November.

Grey Wagtail   B381
Motacilla cinerea Tunstall 1771
TI p. 74 and pl. 11 **lower right mid**
as grey wagtail, *Motacilla melanope*, Pallas

Palearctic; breeds widely in eastern Siberia, and to Japan, north Korea and north China, and through the central Asian highlands to the Himalayas, Persia and Asia Minor; in the west from the Azores, Madeira, Canaries, Morocco, Algeria and the Mediterranean north to Ireland, Britain, southernmost Scandinavia, the Vistula and the Dnestr systems: has colonised north Germany, Holland and Scandinavia since 1856. Some birds migrate as far as tropical Africa and Papua.

Breeding population of Britain-Ireland order 5; nests in virtually every county save Shetland (bred Fair Isle 1950, sporadically) and Outer Hebrides, though decidedly local in south-east England, where has increased in Channel counties in present century. In Ireland since hard winter 1916–17 is scarce in the western coastal areas from co. Clare to co. Donegal. Our population is largely sedentary, or moves south in winter within Britain and Ireland.

Pied and **White Wagtails**   B380
Motacilla alba Linnaeus 1758

Pied wagtail, *Motacilla alba yarrellii* Gould 1837
TI p. 72 and pl. 11 **upper mid left**
as pied wagtail, *Motacilla lugubris*, Temminck

White wagtail, *Motacilla alba alba*
TI p. 73 and pl. 11 **lower mid left**
as white wagtail, *Motacilla alba*, Linnæus

Breeds in the whole (non-African) palearctic region, including the Angmagssalik area of east Greenland, save some arctic islands, the Yamal-Taimyr tundras and the Arabian-Persian deserts. Also breeds in Africa in Morocco, and through most of the ethiopian region from Aswan (Nile) to the Cape; and in oriental India and China. Western (white) race winters to tropical Africa.

Breeding population of pied wagtail (the British-Irish race with black-mantled breeding males) order 5; breeds in every county save Shetland where grey-mantled 'whites' are sporadic nesters. Numbers fluctuate and drop after hard winters: has decreased slightly in Scotland since 1939 but increased markedly in Ireland since early 1930's especially in coastal districts and isles of west and north. Most winter in our islands but some to Morocco.

Family CERTHIIDAE, creepers

Tree Creeper   B298
Certhia familiaris Linnaeus 1758
TI p. 70 and pl. 11 **top right**
as tree-creeper, *Certhia familiaris*, Linnæus

A palearctic bird of temperate and boreal woodlands breeding in a belt across Siberia to southern Kuriles, Japan, Korea and north China; also in the central Asian highlands, Persia, the Caucasus and Turkey. In Europe breeds from the south (where in major highlands only) to around the arctic circle in Fenno-Scandia and Russia. Some northern but not British-Irish birds range south in winter.

Breeding population of Britain-Ireland order 5; breeds in every county save Orkney and Shetland; in Outer Hebrides since 1962 and in wooded Inner Hebrides; seems generally stable in most mature woodlands; probably increasing in Scotland in new plantations and, relatively to nearly all other resident birds, unaffected by hard winters.

Family SITTIDAE

Subfamily TICHODROMADINAE, wallcreeper

For nuthatch subfamily, see pl. 63

Wallcreeper   B297
Tichodroma muraria (Linnaeus 1766)
TI p. 71 and pl. 11 **top left** (winter and summer)
as wall-creeper, *Tichodroma muraria* (Linnæus)

Palearctic and montane: breeds from the central Asian highlands through Persia to the Caucasus, south-east Turkey and north Syria. In Europe isolated populations are resident (though may wander) in Balkans, Carpathians, Alps, spinal Italy (rare), Pyrenees and north Spain.

Five records: 1 shot Stratton Strawless, Norfolk 1792 October 30; 1 Sabden near Pendle Hill, Lancashire 1872 May 8; 1 Winchelsea, Sussex *c* 1886 spring; 1 seen Mells, Somerset 1901 September; 1 seen near Dorchester, Dorset 1920 April 24.

Pl. II.

Wall-Creeper (summer & winter).   Tree-Creeper.
Pied Wagtail.   Blue-headed Wagtail.
White Wagtail.   Grey Wagtail.
Grey-headed Yellow Wagtail.   Yellow Wagtail.

Plate 62 (Thorburn's plate 10)

Family PARIDAE, titmice

Subfamily AEGITHALINAE, long-tailed tits

Long-tailed Tit   B294
Aegithalos caudatus (Linnaeus 1758)
T1 p. 64 and pl. 10 **top left**
as long-tailed titmouse, *Acredula caudata* (Linnæus)

Palearctic; breeds east to Kamchatka, Japan and north China, from Persia through the Caucasus and Asia Minor, in Europe from the Iberian Peninsula and the Mediterranean to Fenno-Scandia and the central Urals. Resident and wandering.

Breeding population of Britain-Ireland order 4 or low 5; breeds sparsely in every county save Isle of Man. Outer Hebrides (sporadic 1939), Orkney and Shetland. The population is markedly reduced by hardest winters and fluctuates.

Subfamily REMIZINAE, penduline tits and fire-capped tit

Penduline Tit
Remiz pendulinus (Linnaeus 1758)
Not illustrated

Palearctic wetlands; breeds locally in France, Spain, Italy and Sicily, sporadically in western Germany, Switzerland and Denmark (1964), and from the Oder and south-east Europe through Asian steppes to north China. Resident but not sedentary, may wander some distance and has reached western France and Finland.

One record: 1 seen Spurn, Yorkshire 1966 October 22–28.

Subfamily PARINAE, typical tits

Marsh Tit   B292
Parus palustris Linnaeus 1758
T1 p. 67 and pl. 10 **mid left**; also T4 pl. 80A (here pl. 82, compared with willow tit)
as marsh-titmouse, *Parus palustris*, Linnæus

Palearctic: breeds in Asia from south-east Siberia, south Kuriles and Hokkaido to north-east China and Korea; in Europe from north Spain, France, Italy and Balkans to Britain, south Sweden and Norway, Leningrad, the south Urals, and a Caucasian outpost. Resident and wandering.

Breeding population of Britain order 4 or low 5; breeds in every English and Welsh county, sparsely in north England, north-west Wales and west Cornwall and in Berwick co. since 1920's, Roxburgh co. and East Lothian since 1966. Does not breed Isle of Man; no wild record Ireland.

Willow Tit   B293
Parus montanus Conrad von Baldenstein 1827
See pl. 82 (pl. 80A of Thorburn)

Crested Tit   B291
Parus cristatus Linnaeus 1758
T1 p. 69 and pl. 10 **bottom right**
as crested titmouse, *Parus cristatus*, Linnæus

Purely European; breeding from Iberian Peninsula, southern France, Italian Alps and Balkans north (not in Black Sea lowlands) to about the arctic circle in Fenno-Scandia and Russia; east to southern Urals; with an outpost in Scotland. Resident with a tendency to dispersive wandering.

Breeding population of Scotland (only) order 3 or low 4; despite forest felling may have survived in Lowlands and west Highlands to early nineteenth century, but a hundred years later was virtually restricted to the Caledonian pine forests of eastern Inverness co. in the Spey system. With maturing of new conifer plantations, recolonised Easter Ross 1912, Nairn co. 1915, Moray 1918, Banff co. 1920's, Aberdeen co. 1939; and sightings in Wester Ross 1934, west Inverness co. 1943, 1945 and east Sutherland 1956, 1961 may presage a further spread. Vagrant England; no Welsh or Irish record.

Coal Tit   B290
Parus ater Linnaeus 1758

British coal tit, *Parus ater britannicus* Sharpe and Dresser 1871
T1 p. 66 and pl. 10 **bottom left**
as coal-titmouse, *Parus ater*, Linnæus

Irish coal tit, *Parus ater hibernicus* Ogilvie-Grant 1910
T4 p. 101 and pl. 80A **mid right**
as Irish coal-titmouse, *Parus hibernicus*, Ogilvie-Grant
See pl. 82

Palearctic; breeds in Asia from Kamchatka and Japan west through the taiga forests of Siberian rivers, south through Korea and northern China to the east Himalayas and north-east Burma, with an oriental outpost in Taiwan; also in the Tian Shan Mountains; and Persia, Caucasus, Asia Minor and Cyprus. In west breeds in Morocco-Tunisia, and from the Mediterranean to Ireland, Britain, central Fenno-Scandia, Archangel and central Urals. Resident, some birds wander.

Breeding population of Britain-Ireland order 5 or low 6; breeds in every county save Orkney and Shetland. Fluctuates with hard winters, but has increased in Scottish Highlands and west of Ireland with the maturing of new plantations.

Blue Tit   B289
Parus caeruleus Linnaeus 1758
T1 p. 68 and pl. 10 **mid right**
as blue titmouse, *Parus cæruleus*, Linnæus

Western palearctic; breeds from Canaries, the African Mediterranean, Asia Minor and west Persia to Ireland, Britain, southern Fenno-Scandia and the central Urals. Resident; some populations may move south or south-west irregularly.

Breeding population of Britain-Ireland order 6 or low 7; breeds in every county save Orkney and Shetland, having colonised Isle of Man 1896, Caithness 1907, Scilly late 1940's, Outer Hebrides *c* 1962; has spread with woodland recovery and free housing, food and, since *c* 1920, milk.

Great Tit   B288
Parus major Linnaeus 1758
T1 p. 65 and pl. 10 **mid**
as great titmouse, *Parus major*, Linnæus

Palearctic and oriental; breeds in virtually the whole of continental Eurasia north to Lapland and the upper systems of the Siberian rivers (save deserts from Arabia to central Asia, and parts of Burma, Siam and Indochina); and in Ireland, Britain, Morocco-Tunisia, Mediterranean islands, Ceylon and some of the East Indies, where enters australasian region. Resident, with a tendency to irregular wandering.

Breeding population of Britain-Ireland order 6 or low 7; range as blue tit after spread for the same reasons, having colonised Caithness, Sutherland, Skye and Scilly in present century, Outer Hebrides in 1966.

Family MUSCICAPIDAE

Subfamily PANURINAE, bearded tit and parrotbills

Bearded Tit   B295
Panurus biarmicus (Linnaeus 1758)
T1 p. 63 and pl. 10 **top right** (♀ ♂ ♂)
as bearded titmouse, *Panurus biarmicus* (Linnæus)

Palearctic reedbeds; breeds in the Amur-Ussuri system and from the Black Sea and Asia Minor in steppe wetlands to Balkhash and the Irtysh; but in Europe has a very fragmented distribution in 14 countries, with a now large population in Holland. Resident, but may make strong dispersive moves.

Breeding population England (only) order 3; *c* 269 breeding pairs 1965 by H. E. Axell's analysis, after Dutch invasions since 1959. By 1947, through drainage, human disturbance and hard winters, under 10 birds survived, in Norfolk-Suffolk; has now recolonised 3 of the 8 other counties in which bred in nineteenth century. Since invasions can be listed for Ireland (1 county), Wales (2), England (all but 5); not Scotland.

Pl. 10.

Marsh-Titmouse.   Long-tailed Titmouse.

Great Titmouse.   Bearded Titmouse.
♂ & ♀

Coal-Titmouse.   Crested Titmouse. Blue Titmouse.

Plate 63 (Thorburn's plate 9)

Family SITTIDAE
Subfamily SITTINAE, nuthatches
For wallcreeper subfamily, see pl. 61

Nuthatch B296
Sitta europaea Linnaeus 1758
TI p. 61 and pl. 9 **top right**
as nuthatch, *Sitta cæsia*, Wolf

Palearctic and oriental; breeds in virtually the whole Asian continent north to the upper Siberian river systems except the steppes, deserts and central highlands; also in Kuriles, Sakhalin, Japan and Taiwan. In west breeds from Morocco, Iberian Peninsula and Mediterranean north to Britain, south Scandinavia, Estonia, Lake Onega and central Urals. Resident, but northern birds explore south irregularly.

Breeding population of Britain (only) order 4; not listed wild for Ireland or Isle of Man; to Scotland vagrant save possible breeding Berwick co. 1850 and attempt breeding Wigtown co. 1927. Very sedentary England-Wales and scarce Cornwall and Wales, though increasing north-west Wales and Cheshire early 1940's. North limit is Lancashire, Westmorland (bred 1916 and since *c* 1955) and (lately) Northumberland.

Family CINCLIDAE, dippers

Dipper B300
Cinclus cinclus (Linnaeus 1758)
TI p. 60 and pl. 9 **bottom right**
as dipper, *Cinclus aquaticus*, Bechstein

Palearctic; breeds only in swift shallow rivers and thus has fragmented range, in Asia in Urals, Cyprus, Asia Minor, Caucasus, north-west Persia, the central highlands and south-east Siberia. In west breeds from Morocco, Algeria, the Iberian Peninsula and Mediterranean north to Ireland, Britain, Lapland and White Sea save in areas of plains and slow rivers. Resident, but northern birds disperse south.

Breeding population of Britain-Ireland order 4; does not normally breed in England south-east of Dorset, Wiltshire, Gloucestershire, Worcestershire, Staffordshire, Derbyshire and Yorkshire (rare East Riding), beyond which old or sporadic records Hampshire, Oxfordshire, Warwickshire and perhaps Leicestershire. Breeds rather stably in all counties of Ireland, Wales and Scotland save Orkney (colonised 1919 but lately extinct) and Shetland; not lately Isle of Man.

Family TROGLODYTIDAE, wrens

Wren B299
Troglodytes troglodytes (Linnaeus 1758)
TI p. 62 and pl. 9 **mid left**
as wren, *Troglodytes parvulus*, K. L. Koch

St Kilda wren, *Troglodytes troglodytes hirtensis* Seebohm 1884
T4 p. 101 and pl. 80A **bottom right**
as St Kilda wren, *Troglodytes hirtensis*, Seebohm
See pl. 82

Holarctic; the other member of its family in the palearctic which doubtless invaded in Ice Age times; from Newfoundland chains of races are resident and sedentary west through north and highland United States, provincial Canada, Alaska, Bering Sea islands, Kamchatka, Kuriles, Sakhalin, Japan, Taiwan (oriental), south-east Siberia and the great Asian highlands, north Persia, Caucasus, Asia Minor and the Levant, North Africa and the Mediterranean to central Fenno-Scandia and the White Sea, Ireland, Britain and Faeroe to a limit in Iceland. Northern birds may disperse and wander.

Breeding population of Britain-Ireland normally order 7; though it may possibly drop to order 6 after hard winters, which produce marked fluctuations, from which recovery is usually fairly swift; no trend of decrease, increase or shift seems detectable that hard winters cannot account for. Breeds in every county. The resident populations of Fair Isle, Shetland, the Outer Hebrides and St Kilda are racially distinct.

Family PRUNELLIDAE, accentors

Alpine Accentor B372
Prunella collaris (Scopoli 1769)
TI p. 59 and pl. 9 **bottom left**
as Alpine accentor, *Accentor collaris* (Scopoli)

Palearctic; breeds in boreal and alpine highlands in Hondo (Japan), Amur-Ussuriland, north Korea, the central Asian highlands, north-west Persia, Caucasus, Asia Minor, Morocco, and the principal mountain range of Europe north to northern Czechoslovakia. Resident, but may wander.

A rare vagrant to southern England, mainly in autumn; has been recorded from elsewhere in England and from Wales; in Scotland known only from Fair Isle where 2 confirmed records (1 June); not recorded Ireland.

Dunnock or **Hedge Sparrow** B371
Prunella modularis (Linnaeus 1758)
TI p. 58 and pl. 9 **mid right**
as hedge-sparrow, *Accentor modularis* (Linnæus)

'European', breeding in Asia Minor, Caucasus and north Persia, and from north Portugal and Spain, spinal Italy and Balkans north to Ireland, Britain, Lapland and Archangel, east to the Urals. Resident, but some northern birds winter to the Mediterranean.

Breeding population of Britain-Ireland order 7; resident in every county save Shetland; first bred Orkney 1862 where spreading. The Hebridean race has spread since 1880's; elsewhere stable save for hard winter fluctuations.

Family MUSCICAPIDAE

This huge family is divided here into subfamilies, for convenience; see pl. '83'.

Subfamily REGULINAE, goldcrests

Goldcrest B364
Regulus regulus (Linnaeus 1758)
TI p. 56 and pl. 9 **top left** (upper bird, ♂)
as goldcrest, *Regulus cristatus*, K. L. Koch

Palearctic; breeds in conifer and mixed forests, in Asia in Amur-Ussuriland, Sakhalin and Japan; the central highlands, the upper Ob system and the Sayan Mountains; and in north Persia, Caucasus and Asia Minor. In west breeds in Azores, and from central Spain, France, spinal Italy and Balkans north to Fenno-Scandia, Archangel and the central Urals. Mostly resident; some northern birds winter south and pass through Britain and Ireland.

Breeding population of Britain-Ireland order 5; rare in eighteenth and early nineteenth centuries, but spread since with maturing of new plantations; though rather vulnerable in hard winters, shows a general increase particularly in Scotland and Ireland. Breeds in every county save Shetland though but sporadically Orkney (1830, 1945); colonised north Inner Hebrides 1881, Outer Hebrides 1906, Scilly *c* 1920.

Firecrest B365
Regulus ignicapillus (Temminck 1820)
TI p. 57 and pl. 9 **top left** (lower bird, ♂)
as firecrest, *Regulus ignicapillus* (C. L. Brehm)

'European', breeding in Asia Minor; in Canaries, Madeira and Morocco-Tunisia; and from Spain and the Mediterranean north to south-west Ukraine, Pskov in west Russia, the south Baltic shore, Germany and east France. More migratory than the goldcrest; birds winter to south France and England.

Bred in the New Forest, Hampshire in 1962 and 1965, and may now thus be established as an English resident; a Lancashire breeding record of 1927 is unconfirmed. Otherwise a passage migrant along the coasts of south-east England and an occasional winterer; has otherwise been recorded vagrant inland in England, in Wales, in south Ireland and in eastern Scotland.

Pl. 9

Goldcrest
Firecrest
Wren
Alpine Accentor.

Nuthatch
Hedge-Sparrow
Dipper

Archibald Thorburn
1913.

Plate 64 (Thorburn's plate 1)

Subfamily TURDINAE, thrushes

A modern systematic order is B353 (pl. 70), 325 (pl. 67), 323 (pl. 68), 322, 324, 319, 321, 320, 318 (pl. 67), 317, 315, 311, 312, 313, 314, 316 (pl. 66), 310, blue rock thrush, Siberian thrush, 309, grey-cheeked thrush, olive-backed thrush, 307, 308, eyebrowed thrush (pl. 65), 306 (pl. 64), 305 (pl. 65), 302, 304, 303, 301, American robin (pl. 64).

American Robin
Turdus migratorius Linnaeus 1766
Not illustrated

A nearctic species that breeds to the tree limit in Alaska and Canada, reaching the shore of the Polar Basin in Mackenzie; and south through the North American continent, reaching into the neotropical region in the hills of southern México. Migrates to winter as far as Guatemala in Central America.

Fifteen records 1876–1966 seem acceptable, though some are unconfirmed by British-Irish List Committee at the time of writing; first 1 caught alive Dover, Kent 1876 April or May; England 7; Scotland 2; Ireland 6; 11 September–January especially 5 December, and 4 (April?–) May.

Mistle Thrush
B301
Turdus viscivorus Linnaeus 1758
T1 p. 1 and pl. 1 **top left**
as mistle-thrush, *Turdus viscivorus*, Linnæus

A bird (originally of mountain forests) of the palearctic, breeding into Siberian Asia through the upper Ob and Yenisei systems to near Lake Baikal, and in the mountain chain from the Sayan to the western Himalayas and west through northern Afghanistan and northern and western Persia to the Caucasus, Asia Minor and the Levant. In the west breeds in Africa in Morocco, Algeria and Tunisia, and in Europe in Sicily, Sardinia and Corsica, and from the Iberian and northern Mediterranean shores north to Ireland, Britain, eastern Norway, Swedish and Finnish Lapland, Archangel and the central Urals. Has spread into the plains of Europe and colonised parkland on a wide scale in the nineteenth century. Partially migratory within the palearctic.

Breeding population Britain-Ireland order 5; breeds in every county except Shetland. In Ireland appears to have been unknown before 1808, and in Scotland very rare at the same time; but in the early nineteenth century colonised every Irish county (by 1850), and since spread widely in Scotland, though early breeding records, some clearly sporadic, were very scattered in distribution from the Lowlands to the Highlands. Early in the present century (if not before) it was, however, firmly established on the whole Scottish mainland and most of the inner isles, and it has nested in the Outer Hebrides since 1906 and stably in Orkney (where sporadic records in the mid nineteenth century) since *c* 1910. Doubtless the spread in Ireland and Scotland was promoted primarily by replantation; but there is some evidence that a spread into cultivated and parkland areas like that on the Continent may have taken place in all four countries. Much earlier, in Upper Pleistocene times of more than ten thousand years ago, it was a native of Ireland (then connected with Britain), as witness fossil bones from the caves of cos. Cork, Clare and Sligo.

Song Thrush
B303
Turdus philomelos C. L. Brehm 1831
T1 p. 2 and pl. 1 **bottom**
as song-thrush, *Turdus musicus*, Linnæus

Hebridean song thrush, *Turdus philomelos hebridensis* Clarke 1913
T4 p. 98 and pl. 80A **bottom left**
as Hebridean song-thrush, *Turdus hebridensis*, Eagle Clarke (the type specimen from Barra), see pl. 82

Possibly of European origin; a western palearctic species breeding into Asia in the upper Ob and Yenisei systems to Lake Baikal, and in northern Asia Minor, the Caucasus and north-west Persia, and in Europe from north Spain, southern France, north Italy and northern Greece to northern Norway, Lapland, the White Sea and the northern Urals. Partially migratory, European elements wintering to North Africa.

Breeding population of Britain-Ireland order 7; breeds in every county, apparently stably, apart from fluctuations after hard winters; colonised Shetland where first bred possibly 1890's, certain 1906 (and has bred sporadically Fair Isle 1905, 1911, 1926). Birds of the Hebrides and Skye, some at least of which are migratory, are of a separate race. The north European race is a passenger and winter visitor.

Redwing
B304
Turdus iliacus Linnaeus 1766
T1 p. 3 and pl. 1 **mid right**
as redwing, *Turdus iliacus*, Linnæus

A palearctic bird mainly of the boreal zone, breeding from Iceland, Faeroe (a few pairs), north Scotland, the Scandinavian Peninsula and Finland, and from north-east Poland through Russia and Siberia in the upper Volga system and through the middle systems of the Siberian rivers east as far as the Kolyma, reaching the Arctic Ocean shore in Europe. Migratory, wintering in the palearctic, within Europe in the west. Has bred sporadically since the nineteenth century in western Europe, in Czechoslovakia, Austria, Germany, north-east France and Belgium.

Breeding population arrived in Scotland in the present century; small (order 1) but becoming less sporadic and probably now established in east Sutherland, where (sporadic) pair bred first 1925. Has bred somewhere in virtually every year since 1953, other first records being Moray 1932, Shetland (Fair Isle) 1935, (Unst) 1953, Inverness co. 1936, Ross 1959, west Sutherland 1964. Attempted to breed co. Kerry, Ireland, 1951. A large population from Iceland and Scandinavia winters with us in every county of all four countries, and some also pass.

Fieldfare
B302
Turdus pilaris Linnaeus 1758
T1 p. 4 and pl. 1 **top right**
as fieldfare, *Turdus pilaris*, Linnæus

A palearctic bird of taiga which has probably colonised west in Europe since the Ice Age, as doubtless has the redwing. Breeds from Germany, Austria and Hungary, north to the Arctic Ocean in Europe, though not in Denmark, and in Russia east in the upper systems of the Black Sea and Caspian rivers, and in the upper and middle systems of the Siberian rivers east to the Lena. Colonised most of central and western Germany since 1830, Switzerland in 1923, Greenland (after a long easterly storm) in 1937, Iceland after 1950 and the Jura in France in 1953; has bred sporadically east Holland. Migrates, most populations strongly, normally within the palearctic.

A large population winters in Britain and a substantial number in Ireland, mainly from Norway and Lapland, and many pass on coast routes; recorded from every county.

Black-throated Thrush
B306
Turdus ruficollis Pallas 1776
T1 p. 5 and pl. 1 **mid left** (♀ and ♂)
as black-throated thrush, *Turdus atrigularis*, Temminck

A boreal palearctic species with a central distribution; has 2 races so distinguishable that they have different vernacular names. The black-throated thrush *Turdus ruficollis atrogularis* Jarocki 1819 breeds just into Europe in the upper system of the Kama tributary of the Volga west of the Urals, and into Asia from the central Urals to the middle and upper systems of the Ob and the Yenisei and south into the Altai and Tarbagatai Mountains of western Mongolia and Russian and Chinese Turkestan. It hybridises in the south-east of this range with the red-throated thrush *Turdus ruficollis ruficollis*, whose distribution continues further east to Lake Baikal, and south to Mongolia. Black-throats migrate to India and Burma but some also as far west as Persia, occasionally Iraq, and (rare stragglers) further west into Europe.

Three records of black-throated race: male caught near Lewes, Sussex 1868 December 23, kept alive for some time; 1 (out of 2) shot near Perth 1879 February; male seen and trapped Fair Isle, Shetland 1957 December 8–1958 January *c* 22.

Pl. 1.

Mistle-Thrush

Black-Throated Thrush
♂ & ♀.

Song-Thrush

Fieldfare

Redwing

Plate 65 (Thorburn's plate 2)

Subfamily TURDINAE, thrushes (continued)

Dusky Thrush   B305
Turdus naumanni Temminck 1820
TI p. 6 and pl. 2 **top right**
as dusky thrush, *Turdus dubius*, Bechstein (1795)

A boreal Asian palearctic taiga bird with 2 races so distinguishable that they have different common names. Breeds from the east arm of Gulf of Ob through Siberia to Anadyr, Kamchatka and the Komandorski Islands, and the Stanovoi Mountains. The northern population is the (sooty-spotted) dusky thrush *Turdus naumanni eunomus* Temminck 1831, the central and southern the (chestnut-spotted) Naumann's thrush *Turdus naumanni naumanni*, which hybridises with the other in the Yenisei system. The species migrates through Mongolia and China, some reaching the oriental region, and both races have wandered into western Europe.

Three records of the dusky race: 1 shot near Gunthorpe, Nottinghamshire 1905 October 13; first winter male seen and trapped Hartlepool, co. Durham 1959 December 12–1960 February 24; first winter female seen and trapped Fair Isle, Shetland 1961 October 18–21.

Eyebrowed Thrush
Turdus obscurus J. F. Gmelin 1789
Not illustrated

A boreal Asian palearctic taiga bird breeding from the eastern Ob system to Kamchatka and the Amur system, with an outpost colony on Fujiyama, Japan. Migrates into the oriental region but has wandered into western Europe.

Three records, all seen in 1964: 1 Oundle, Northamptonshire October 5; 1 North Rona, Outer Hebrides October 16; 1 St Agnes, Scilly December 5.

Blackbird   B308
Turdus merula Linnaeus 1758
TI p. 9 and pl. 2 **bottom right** (♂ and ♀)
as blackbird, *Turdus merula*, Linnæus

Palearctic; breeds in Azores, Madeira and Canaries, and in Europe (where origin?) from the Iberian Peninsula and the Mediterranean to central Fenno-Scandia, Leningrad, south Urals and Crimea; and in a highland strip from Asia Minor and Caucasus through south-central Asia to oriental China. Resident and partial migrant within the palearctic.

Breeding population of Britain-Ireland order 7; must be close on ten million pairs; breeds in every county though in Shetland only since 1870's, at which time an increase and spread, which has continued, began to be noticeable in the northern Highlands and islands of Scotland. In the present century has spread and consolidated in peripheral Ireland.

Ring Ouzel   B307
Turdus torquatus Linnaeus 1758
TI p. 10 and pl. 2 **bottom left**
as ring-ouzel, *Turdus torquatus*, Linnæus

Palearctic; a race breeds in north-east Turkey, Caucasus and north Persia; main range (and origin?) is highland Europe in north Spain, France, Alps, Balkans, Carpathians, Scandinavia, Ireland and Britain; has bred, perhaps sporadically, also in north Russia, west Turkey, Cyprus and spinal Italy. Migrates to the Mediterranean, many to the Atlas Mountains.

Breeding population of Britain-Ireland order 4; present south-east limit is county chain Cornwall–Devon–Somerset–Monmouth–Herefordshire–Shropshire–Staffordshire–Derbyshire–Yorkshire (not East Riding) beyond which has bred sporadically or in the past in at least 7 other counties. Now scarce in West Country and Pembroke co.; decreasing in rest of Wales (absent 2 counties), as in England and Ireland, since *c* 1900; in Ireland bred only 11 counties 1965; in twice as many formerly. Breeds in every county of Scotland save Outer Hebrides and Shetland but decrease, noted 1920's, marked in 1940's. Continental birds join the east coast passage.

Swainson's or **Olive-backed Thrush**
Catharus ustulatus (Nuttall 1840)
Not illustrated

Nearctic; breeds in Alaska, Canada and the United States, in the mountains south to Colorado and West Virginia. Winters in Central and South America as far as northern Paraguay.

One record: 1 found dead Blackrock Lighthouse, co. Mayo 1956 May 26.

Grey-cheeked Thrush
Catharus minimus (Lafresnaye 1848)
Not illustrated

Nearctic; with a palearctic outpost in eastern Siberia; main breeding range is to the tree-line in Alaska and Canada. Winters from Central America and West Indies to western tropical South America south of the equator.

Five records: 1 trapped Fair Isle, Shetland 1953 October 5–6; 1 first winter Fair Isle 1958 October 29; 1 (died) Bardsey, Caernarvon co. 1961 October 10; 1 (died) St Kilda 1965 October 29; 1 found dying Lossiemouth, Moray 1965 November 26.

White's or **Golden Mountain Thrush**   B309
Zoothera dauma (Latham 1790)
T4 p. 7 and pl. 2 **top mid**
as White's thrush, *Turdus varius*, Pallas

An eastern palearctic, oriental and australasian species, breeding in Siberia from Yenisei to Amur-Ussuri and reportedly west through the Ob system to the European side of the Urals; and in many races from the central Asian highlands and Japan through south-east Asia to Papua, Australia and New Zealand. The Siberian race migrates into the oriental region and is vagrant west to Europe.

A rare vagrant to England, and recorded from Scotland and Ireland, most often in winter.

Siberian Thrush
Zoothera sibirica (Pallas 1776)
TI p. 8 and pl. 2 **top left**
as Siberian thrush, *Turdus sibiricus*, Pallas

A 'Siberian' palearctic species breeding from the Yenisei to the Sea of Okhotsk, Amurland, Manchuria, Sakhalin and Japan. Winters into the oriental region.

One acceptable record: adult male trapped Isle of May, Fife 1954 October 2.

Blue Rock Thrush
Monticola solitarius (Linnaeus 1758)
Not illustrated

Breeds in the southern palearctic in Morocco-Tunisia, the Iberian Peninsula, south Switzerland and the European Mediterranean countries and islands, and from Asia Minor through the central Asian highlands to Ussuriland, China, Korea and Japan; into the oriental region in Taiwan and a Malayan outpost. The European birds are partially migratory.

One record: 1 seen North Ronaldshay, Orkney 1966 August 29–September 6.

Rock Thrush   B310
Monticola saxatilis (Linnaeus 1766)
TI p. 11 and pl. 2 **mid right**
as rock-thrush, *Monticolo saxatilis* (Linnæus)

A Mediterranean and dry highland southern palearctic bird; breeds from Morocco-Algeria and the European Mediterranean to the Iberian Peninsula, Switzerland, south Poland, the Black Sea and through Asian highlands to Baikal, Amurland and north China. European birds migrate to tropical Africa.

Seven records 1843–1963: first 1 Therfield near Royston, Hertfordshire 1843 May 19; England 3; Scotland 4; 5 May-June, 2 October-November.

Pl. 2

Siberian Thrush   White's Thrush   Dusky Thrush

Ring-Ouzel   Blackbird   Rock Thrush

Plate 66 (Thorburn's plate 3)

Subfamily TURDINAE, thrushes (*continued*)

Black Wheatear B316
Oenanthe leucura (Gmelin 1789)
T1 p. 18 and pl. 3 **bottom mid**
as black wheatear, *Saxicola leucura* (Gmelin)

Probably of African-Mediterranean origin; a western pale-arctic dry hill species breeding in the Rio de Oro, Morocco, Algeria, western Libya, the Iberian Peninsula, southernmost France, the Ligurian Hills in Italy and, perhaps sporadically, in Sardinia and Sicily. Resident with a tendency to wander.

Five records of single birds: seen Fair Isle, Shetland 1912 September; Altrincham, Cheshire 1943 August 1; Fair Isle 1953 October 19; Dungeness, Kent 1954 October 17; Portnoo, co. Donegal 1964 June 10; the last could *possibly* have been of the black-crowned form of the white-rumped black wheatear *Oenanthe leucopyga* (C. L. Brehm 1855) of the Sahara and Arabian deserts, not on the List, but this is unlikely.

Pied Wheatear B314
Oenanthe pleschanka (Lepechin 1770)
T1 p. 17 and pl. 3 **top right** (upper bird, ♂)
as eastern pied wheatear, *Saxicola pleschanka* (Lepech)
T4 p. 99 and pl. 80B **mid** (♀)
as eastern pied wheatear, *Saxicola pleschanka* (Lepech)
the first British specimen, see pl. 81

Central palearctic; breeds from Rumania, south-east Ukraine and Crimea through the steppes and dry highlands of central Asia to Baikal, north China and the Himalayas, with outpost race in Cyprus. Western birds winter to tropical Africa.

Three records of females of the main race: Isle of May, Fife 1909 October 19; Swona, Orkney 1916 November 1; 1 trapped Portland, Dorset 1954 October 17–19.

Black-eared Wheatear B313
Oenanthe hispanica (Linnaeus 1758)

Western black-eared wheatear, *Oenanthe hispanica hispanica*
T1 p. 15 and pl. 3 **mid right** (right bird)
as black-eared wheatear, *Saxicola stapazina* (Linnæus)

Eastern black-eared wheatear, *Oenanthe hispanica melanoleuca* (Güldenstädt 1775)
T1 p. 14 and pl. 3 **mid right** (left bird)
as black-throated wheatear, *Saxicola occidentalis*, Salvadori

A south-western palearctic bird with 2 field-distinguishable races, breeding in Morocco-Tripoli, Iberian Peninsula, Mediterranean European coasts including Greek islands and Crete, and from Asia Minor to west Persia, and into Caucasus, Bulgaria and perhaps Rumania. Racial boundary is in Italy-Jugoslavia; winters to Africa south of Sahara and may wander.

Fifteen records of birds of both races 1878–1965: first, male shot near Bury, Lancashire 1878 May *c* 8; England 8; Scotland 6; Ireland 1; 8 March–June (half May), 7 August–November (most September).

Desert Wheatear B312
Oenanthe deserti (Temminck 1825)
T1 p. 16 and pl. 3 **mid left**
as desert wheatear, *Saxicola deserti*, Rüppell

A southern palearctic desert and semi-desert species breeding in Africa in hill oases of the northern Sahara and along virtually the whole coastal strip from the Rio de Oro to the Nile, whence into the Sudan, Palestine, north-west Arabia and through Iraq into the southern Caucasus, Persia, Afghanistan, and north through the steppes east of the Caspian, in Russia through the Aral and Lake Balkhash systems to those of the uppermost Ob and Yenisei, and into Mongolia, the Gobi and virtually the whole of highland west China south to Tibet and the Himalayas. Such British records as have been determined belong to the 2 south Mediterranean races which may normally winter to north-east Africa and Arabia.

Fifteen records 1880–1962: the first a male near Alloa, Clackmannan co. 1880 November 26; England 9; Scotland 6; 12 October–February (half October), 1 each April, June, August.

Wheatear B311
Oenanthe oenanthe (Linnaeus 1758)
T1 p. 12 and pl. 3 **top left** (♂ and ♀)
as wheatear, *Saxicola Œnanthe* (Linnæus)

An holarctic species of palearctic origin, which may have colonised North America rather lately. In the Old World breeds from Morocco-Algeria, the European Mediterranean, Asia Minor, Persia, the central Asian highlands and Mongolia north (not around the Sea of Okhotsk or in Kamchatka) to Ireland, Britain, Faeroe, Iceland, Jan Mayen and the European and Siberian arctic shore. Extends from eastern Siberia through central Alaska into Yukon and (just) Mackenzie, and from Europe to Greenland, Canadian Franklin and Labrador. All birds, including west and east nearctic groups, winter to tropical Africa, the 'Greenland' race *normally* making a full Atlantic crossing in autumn to Ireland, Britain and western Europe.

Breeding population of Britain-Ireland order 5; breeds, or fairly recently recorded as breeding in virtually every county, though has been decreasing (partly with the agricultural development of poor land) probably since the nineteenth, certainly in the present century in many parts of England, south Scotland and central Ireland, and perhaps in Orkney. It is still common on undeveloped moorland and downland, especially near the coast where such land remains undisturbed.

Isabelline Wheatear B315
Oenanthe isabellina (Temminck 1829)
T1 p. 13 and pl. 3 **top right** (lower bird)
as isabelline wheatear, *Saxicola isabellina* (Rüppell)

A south-central palearctic dryland species breeding in Europe only from the lower systems of the Volga, Ural River and the eastern Don into the Caucasus; and in Asia from Asia Minor through the steppes and central Asian highlands to Amurland and north China. Migrates to India and tropical Africa; a vagrant in western Europe.

One record: a female Allonby, Cumberland 1887 November 11

Stonechat B317
Saxicola torquata (Linnaeus 1766)
T1 p. 19 as stonechat, *Pratincola rubicola* (Linnæus), and
T2 pl. 38 **bottom left** (as prey of merlin), see pl. 28

Western European stonechat, *Saxicola torquata hibernans* (Hartert 1910)
T1 pl. 3 **bottom right**, the resident race in Britain and Ireland
as stonechat

Eastern European stonechat, *Saxicola torquata rubicola* (Linnaeus 1766)
T1 pl. 3 **bottom left**
as eastern stonechat

Origin possibly Asian; palearctic and ethiopian. Breeds from Morocco-Tunisia, the Iberian Peninsula and European Mediterranean, Asia Minor, Caucasus and central Asian highlands north to the White Sea, Urals and the boreal Siberian river systems, east to the Sea of Okhotsk; Sakhalin, south Kuriles, Japan and Korea; in western Europe north to Ireland, Britain, Holland, Denmark, Germany, Poland and Ukraine. Several races breed in ethiopian Africa and Madagascar and one in south-west Arabia. Western birds, partial migrants, may winter to Saharan borders; eastern European birds are autumn vagrants to Britain.

Breeding population of Britain-Ireland order 4; has bred in every county in the present century, though in Shetland not provedly until 1961. J. D. Magee shows a decrease since 1900 which he ascribes primarily to the exploitation of marginal land and general human (including recreational) disturbance. The stonechat's population is also very sensitive to hard winters. This applies less to coastal areas; but the bird is now very local, sporadic or no longer a breeder in many inland counties of England; indeed the only major areas that may have a stable population resembling that of former days appear to be the West Country in England, western Wales, the western isles and parts of highland Scotland, and Ireland.

Pl. 3.

Wheatear ♂ & ♀
Desert Wheatear
Eastern Stonechat

Pied Wheatear
Isabelline Wheatear
Black-throated & Black-eared Wheatears.
Black Wheatear   Stonechat.

A. Thorburn. 1913

Plate 67 (Thorburn's plate 4)

Subfamily TURDINAE, thrushes (*continued*)

Whinchat   B318
Saxicola rubetra (Linnaeus 1758)
TI p. 20 and pl. 4 **mid** (♂)
as whinchat, *Pratincola rubetra* (Linnæus)

A western palearctic species doubtless of European origin,
breeding from north Spain and the Pyrenees, France, Corsica
north Italy, Macedonia, Balkans and European Black Sea
coast north to Ireland, Britain, north-central Fenno-Scandia,
the White Sea and central Urals, with extensions into Asia
to the Altai foothills, and into the Caucasus and north Persia.
Winters to tropical Africa south of the Sahara.

Breeding population of Britain-Ireland order 5; has a history
of general decrease similar to the stonechat's, though now
breeds more densely inland than stonechat, and being a
summer visitor, is not affected by our hard winters. Breeds in
every British county save Orkney (where now sporadic or
extinct) and Shetland; may have colonised Outer Hebrides
in 1841. In Ireland decreased in first half of present century
but since then has increased and bred for the first (known)
time in 5 counties; has bred in 25 of the 32 since 1900.

Redstart   B320
Phoenicurus phoenicurus (Linnaeus 1758)
TI p. 21 and pl. 4 **top left** (♂)
as redstart, *Ruticilla phoenicurus* (Linnæus)

A western palearctic species breeding into Asia as far as Lake
Baikal, and from Cyprus, Asia Minor and Caucasus to Persia.
In the west breeds in Morocco-Algeria and from the Iberian
Peninsula, European Mediterranean, the Black Sea rivers
(not their lower systems) and the Crimea north to Ireland (now
sporadic), Britain, northern Scandinavia, the White Sea and
the northern Urals. Winters to tropical Africa.

British breeding population order 4; breeds or has bred in
every British county save Isle of Man, Outer Hebrides
(sporadic 1914), Orkney, and Shetland (sporadic attempt
1901); sporadic also Cornwall (1957, 1959, 1960). In Ireland
bred cos. Wicklow and Tyrone 1880's and 1890's; but present
century nestings – cos. Kerry 1946, Antrim 1955, Tyrone
1955, Wicklow 1959–60 – are doubtless sporadic. In second
half nineteenth century may have slightly increased and
spread north in Scotland, but in present century has decreased
in Scotland and rather markedly in Midland and south-east
England, perhaps as a consequence of the destruction and
recreational disturbance of open marginal woodland and
scrub.

Black Redstart   B321
Phoenicurus ochruros (S. G. Gmelin 1774)
TI p. 22 and pl. 4 **mid left**
as black redstart, *Ruticilla titys* (Scopoli)

A palearctic species, breeding in the east in dry uplands from
the Crimea, Asia Minor-Palestine and Caucasus through the
central Asian highlands to Mongolia. In the west breeds in
Morocco, and in Europe from the Iberian Peninsula and the
Mediterranean north to England, southern Scandinavia,
Poland and the Ukraine. In Europe has colonised north-west
in last hundred years, reaching Norway in 1944. Western
birds appear to winter in Africa north of the Sahara.

Bred sporadically in England (co. Durham 1845, Sussex
1909) before invasion of 1920's, since when some first records
are 1923 Sussex, 1926 Middlesex, 1929 Cornwall, 1937 Cambridgeshire, 1938 Suffolk, 1940 Kent, 1942 Devon, 1943
Hampshire and Warwickshire, 1944 Surrey, 1945 Yorkshire,
1949 Essex, c 1962 Staffordshire, 1964 Berkshire, 1965 Buckinghamshire, 1967 Northamptonshire. The breeding pairs were
order 1 (under 10) to 1942 but rose to over 30 in late 1940's
and are now doubtless high in order 2 (under 100). The
natural spread north-west in Europe brought the birds to
England in the 1920's but the ease of colonisation was helped
by the partial ruination of English cities, particularly London,
in the early 1940's which provided preferred habitat. Some
winter in south England, south Wales and eastern Ireland;
and the species is a regular passenger through all four

countries, more common on the east side of Scotland than on
the west.

Red-flanked Bluetail   B319
Erithacus cyanurus (Pallas 1773)
Not illustrated

'Siberian' palearctic; breeds through the upper taiga systems
of the Siberian rivers from the Pechora to the Sea of Okhotsk,
in Kamchatka and Komandorski Islands, and from Japan and
Amur-Ussuriland through the western Chinese highlands to
the Himalayas. May be spreading west; bred Kola 1937 and
has summered in Finland since 1949; normally winters in
oriental region.

Four records: 1 seen North Cotes, Lincolnshire 1903
September; 1 shot Whalsay, Shetland 1947 October 7; immature male found dead Sandwich, Kent 1956 October 28;
female or first winter male seen Hartley, Northumberland
1960 October 16.

Bluethroat   B324
Erithacus svecicus (Linnaeus 1758)

Red-spotted bluethroat, *Erithacus svecicus svecicus*
TI p. 23 and pl. 4 **bottom right**
as arctic bluethroat, *Cyanecula suecica* (Linnæus)

White-spotted bluethroat, *Erithacus svecicus cyaneculus* (Meisner
1804)
TI p. 24 and pl. 4 **bottom left**
as white-spotted bluethroat, *Cyanecula leucocyana*, Brehm

Northern palearctic with a nearctic outpost in northern
Alaska, where has bred in 3 places. Breeds through most
Siberian river systems to coastal tundras and in central Asian
highlands and Caucasus-Persia. In Europe red-spotted race
breeds from the arctic coast through Lapland and down spinal
Norway, and to Lake Ladoga; white-spots from Leningrad to
the Caspian Sea and west to east France, the Low Countries
and south Denmark, with outposts in south-west France and
central Spain; birds winter to Africa north of the Sahara.

Scarce passenger (small white-spot minority) from north
Scotland to east England, regular in autumn, rare in spring;
vagrant in rest of Britain, including Wales, and in Ireland.

Robin   B325
Erithacus rubecula (Linnaeus 1758)
TI p. 25 and pl. 4 **top right**
as redbreast, *Erythacus rubecula* (Linnæus)

Western palearctic; breeds from Azores, Madeira, Canaries,
Morocco-Tunisia and the European Mediterranean, into
Asia only to Caucasus-Persia and from southern Urals to the
upper Ob, north to Ireland, Britain, central Fenno-Scandia,
White Sea and upper Pechora. Resident, and partial migrant
within the palearctic.

Breeding population of Britain-Ireland order 7; breeds in
every county save Shetland, its stability and tameness fostered
in many areas by human customs and the food table.

Nightingale   B322
Erithacus megarhynchos (C. L. Brehm 1831)
TI p. 26 and pl. 4 **mid right**
as nightingale, *Daulias luscinia* (Linnæus)

Western palearctic; breeds in Asia from Crimea, Asia Minor
and Syria east to the Pamir-Tarbagatai highlands; in the
west from Morocco-Cyrenaica and the European Mediterranean to Britain, Holland, Denmark, central Germany and
Poland and the Ukraine. Winters to tropical Africa.

Breeding population of Britain order 5; in present century
despite slight decrease with woodland changes has not altered
much in range, normal limits of which to west and north are
Devon – Somerset – Glamorgan – Monmouth – Herefordshire – Shropshire – Staffordshire – Derbyshire – Notting-
shire – West Riding – Lincolnshire; has bred sporadically 4
other Welsh counties, Cheshire and other Yorkshire Ridings.
Is a vagrant beyond breeding range, rare in Scotland where
has sung in May, and in Ireland where all 11 records, last
1963, were from cos. Wexford and Kildare in May (some also
sang).

Pl. 4

Redstart   Redbreast

Black Redstart   Whinchat   Nightingale

White-spotted Bluethroat   Arctic Bluethroat

Archibald Thorburn
1915

Plate 68 (Thorburn's plate 5)

Subfamily TURDINAE, thrushes (*continued*)

Thrush Nightingale   B323
Erithacus luscinia (Linnaeus 1758)
TI p. 26 and pl. 5 **bottom left**
as thrush-nightingale or 'sprösser', *Daulias philomela*

Central palearctic; breeds from Denmark, south Sweden and
Finland to north Germany, Poland, east Czechoslovakia and
Baltic Russia east to the lower Danube, and through the south
Urals into Asia as far as the upper Ob and Turkestan. In
present century has withdrawn from middle Elbe and upper
Danube, but colonised Fenno-Scandia mostly since 1940.
Winters to tropical Africa south of the equator.

Seven records 1911–65: the first 1 Fair Isle, Shetland
1911 May 15; England (Northumberland) 2 in September,
October; Scotland (Fair Isle) 5 in May.

Subfamily SYLVIINAE, Old World warblers

A modern systematic order is B326, 329, river warbler, 330,
327, 328, 331, 338, 337 (pl. 71), 336, 335, 334, 333 (pl. 70),
332, thick-billed reed warbler (pl. 71), 340, 339, 341, 342
(pl. 70), 344, 345, 346, 343, 347, 348, 349, 350 (pl. 68), 351,
352, 354, 356, 358, 357, 362 (pl. 69), 363 (pl. 70), 360, 361,
359, 355 (pl. 69).

Barred Warbler   B344
Sylvia nisoria (Bechstein 1795)
TI p. 33 and pl. 5 **lower mid left**
as barred warbler, *Sylvia nisoria* (Bechstein)

Palearctic; the steppe race breeds from the upper Ob to
Mongolia in Turkestan and the western central Asian highlands; the European race from north Italy, eastern Alps,
upper Danube, eastern France, Elbe and south Denmark east
through Baltic and Danubian countries to south Urals and
Caucasus. Migrates to tropical east Africa.

An annual autumn passage vagrant (mostly immature
birds) to the North Isles and eastern Scotland and England;
has been recorded in other parts of England and in Wales, and
20 times by 1966 in Ireland, almost annual co. Wexford lately.

Orphean Warbler   B345
Sylvia hortensis (J. F. Gmelin 1789)
TI p. 29 and pl. 5 **upper mid right**
as *Sylvia orphea*, Temminck

Western palearctic; breeds from Morocco to Cyrenaica, in the
Iberian Peninsula, and in virtually all European and Asian
Mediterranean borderlands, extending to western Switzer-
land, formerly (not for 100 years) Luxemburg and south
Germany, and through Caucasus-Persia to Turkestan and
West Pakistan. Western birds migrate to south of Sahara in
Africa.

Two records: female shot near Wetherby, Yorkshire 1848
July 6; 1 trapped Portland, Dorset 1955 September 20.

Garden Warbler   B346
Sylvia borin (Boddaert 1783)
TI p. 32 and pl. 5 **bottom right**
as garden-warbler, *Sylvia hortensis*, Bechstein

Western palearctic; breeds from central Portugal and Spain,
France, north Italy, Albania, Bulgaria, Crimea and Caucasus
north to Ireland, Britain, around the arctic circle in Fenno-
Scandia and White Sea, and east in Siberia to the western
upper Yenisei. Migrates to tropical Africa.

Breeding population of Britain-Ireland order 5; seems
stable. Breeds in virtually every English and Welsh county,
though scarce Cornwall and Anglesey and sporadic Isle of Man.
In Scotland scarce in Lowlands outside Clyde-Forth system;
in Highlands stable in Perth co., Fife, Bute and south Argyll;
has bred Easter Ross 1919, Orkney 1964. In Ireland has
nested in 11 counties but seems stable only around Loughs
Ree and Erne in Shannon valley and co. Fermanagh.

Blackcap   B343
Sylvia atricapilla (Linnaeus 1758)
TI p. 31 and pl. 5 **upper mid left** (♂ and ♀)
as blackcap, *Sylvia atricapilla* (Linnæus)

Western palearctic; breeds from Cape Verdes, Azores,
Madeira, Canaries, Morocco-Tunisia, Iberian Peninsula,
European and Asian Mediterranean and Caucasus-Persia to
Ireland, Britain, around arctic circle in Fenno-Scandia, Lake
Onega and central Urals, whence extends into upper Ob
Siberia. Some winter to Africa beyond equator but others
winter in the palearctic.

Breeding population of Britain-Ireland order 5; breeds in
virtually every county of England and Wales, sporadically in
Isle of Man, and through Scottish Lowlands to headquarters
in Clyde and south Argyll, and Perth co.; in rest of Highlands
occasional breedings in 5 other counties north to Ross, and in
Orkney 1910, 1949 and Shetland 1945–46, 1948, may indicate
a spread. In Ireland headquarters are in cos. Wicklow and
Cavan, and it has bred in 5 other counties.

Whitethroat   B347
Sylvia communis Latham 1787
TI p. 27 and pl. 5 **top left**
as whitethroat, *Sylvia cinerea*, Bechstein

Western palearctic; breeds from Morocco-Tunisia, the
Iberian Peninsula, the European and Asian Mediterranean
and north Persia and Afghanistan north to Ireland, Britain,
south Fenno-Scandia, Archangel, the central Urals, Turkestan
and the central steppelands east to Mongolia. Migrates to the
ethiopian region, some reaching southern Africa.

Breeding population of Britain-Ireland order 7; apparently
stable. Nests in every county except Shetland, though rare in
Caithness and sporadic in Orkney (?1910, unsuccessfully
1941).

Lesser Whitethroat   B348
Sylvia curruca (Linnaeus 1758)
TI p. 28 and pl. 5 **top right**
as lesser whitethroat, *Sylvia curruca* (Linnæus)

Western palearctic; breeds from north and east France, north
Italy, Macedonia, Asia Minor, the Levant and north Persia
and Afghanistan north to south Fenno-Scandia, Archangel,
the north Urals and middle and upper Siberian river systems,
east to the upper Lena and the west central Asian highlands.
Western birds winter to north-eastern Africa.

Breeding population of Britain (only) order 4; has bred in
virtually all English and Welsh counties, and Isle of Man,
though in many sporadic or local. Sporadic also in Scotland,
where has bred 7 counties north to Inverness 1929, Wester
Ross 1896, latest Argyll 1948, Midlothian 1949. Normally
a passage visitor to Scotland, and a scarce but regular one to
Ireland where (though but 39 records to 1966) has been
recorded almost annually on the south coast since 1951.

[Rüppell's Warbler   B349
Sylvia ruppelli Temminck 1823
See pl. 81 (not on the British-Irish List).]

Sardinian Warbler   B350
Sylvia melanocephala (J. F. Gmelin 1789)
TI p. 30 and pl. 5 **lower mid right**
as Sardinian warbler, *Sylvia melanocephala* (Gmelin)

A palearctic species restricted to the Canaries and Mediterranean (unless Ménétries's warbler *Sylvia mystacea* Ménétries
1832 of Iraq and the steppelands be included in the species).
Breeds in the Canaries, Morocco, Algeria, Tunisia, Cyrenaica
and in the Nile delta, on all the principal Mediterranean
islands including Aegean islands, Rhodes and Cyprus, in
Portugal, southern Spain, southern France, Italy, the Jugo-
slav and Albanian coastal areas, Greece, south Bulgaria, Asia
Minor, Syria and Palestine. At least a partial migrant, some
birds moving to Africa north of the Sahara and Arabia.

One record: an adult male trapped Lundy, Devon 1955
May 10.

Pl. 5.

Whitethroat
Blackcap
588   Barred Warbler
Thrush-Nightingale

Lesser Whitethroat
Orphean Warbler
Sardinian Warbler
Garden-Warbler

Plate 69 (Thorburn's plate 6)

Subfamily SYLVIINAE, Old World warblers (continued)

Subalpine Warbler   B351
Sylvia cantillans (Pallas 1764)
TI p. 34 and pl. 6 **top left**
as subalpine warbler, *Sylvia subalpina*, Bonelli

Palearctic; breeds only in Morocco, Portugal and the European and some Asian and African Mediterranean countries; winters normally to Africa south of the Sahara.

A very rare vagrant, though almost annually recorded by coastal observatories since 1950's, to England, Wales, Scotland and Ireland in May–July, a few September–October.

Dartford Warbler   B352
Sylvia undata (Boddaert 1783)
TI p. 35 and pl. 6 **mid left**
as Dartford warbler, *Sylvia undata* (Boddaert)

West European; the typical race breeds in Morocco-Tunisia, Iberian Peninsula, Balearics, south France, Corsica, Sardinia and south Italy; *Sylvia undata dartfordiensis* Latham 1787 in north-west France to Seine, Channel Islands and south England. Resident but not strictly sedentary.

English stock has long history of decrease with destruction of furze habitat, disturbance and collection. Has bred in 15 counties or more but in present century only 9 and in 1961 (C. R. Tubbs) but 5, 1966 3. Population, *c* 400–450 pairs 1961 (*c* 300 New Forest, Hampshire), was reduced to *c* 10 1963–64 after hard winters, since when 15–20 1965, 20–30 1966 when 1 or 2 New Forest, *c* 4 Sussex and rest Dorset. A male of our race co. Wexford 1912 October 27 is the only Irish record; there is none for Wales or Scotland.

Willow Warbler   B354
Phylloscopus trochilus (Linnaeus 1758)
TI p. 40 and pl. 6 **mid**
as willow-wren, *Phylloscopus trochilus* (Linnæus)

Palearctic; breeds in boreal Siberia to the upper Anadyr and in Europe from central France, north Italy and Jugoslavia, Carpathians and Ukraine north to Ireland, Britain, north Norway, Kola, the middle Pechora and north Urals. Migrates to ethiopian Africa, some reaching the south.

Breeding population of Britain-Ireland order 6; breeds in every county, apparently stably, though only locally in Outer Hebrides and Orkney and sporadically in Shetland.

Chiffchaff   B356
Phylloscopus collybita (Vieillot 1817)
TI p. 39 and pl. 6 **bottom right**
as chiffchaff, *Phylloscopus rufus* (Bechstein)

Palearctic; breeds into Asia to the Kolyma in Siberia and Caucasus-Persia, in west in Canaries and Algeria and in Europe from Mediterranean to Ireland, Britain, central Fenno-Scandia, White Sea and Urals. Western birds migrate to reach ethiopian Africa north of the equator.

Breeding population of Britain-Ireland order 6; breeds in every county of England, Wales and Lowlands though sparsely in north, and in at least 6, probably more mainland Highland counties and several western isles, where present signs of spread. In *c* 1850 bred in but 7 counties of Ireland but by *c* 1900 in all 32, and increase here probably continues.

Bonelli's Warbler   B358
Phylloscopus bonelli (Vieillot 1819)
Not illustrated

Palearctic; breeds in Morocco-Tunisia and from European and Asian Mediterranean to central France, Switzerland, Austria, Czechoslovakia, and south Germany where spreading north.

Eighteen records 1948–66; the first a female trapped Skokholm, Pembroke co. 1948 August 31; England 9; Wales 6; Scotland 1; Ireland 2; 2 April–June, 16 August–October.

Wood Warbler   B357
Phylloscopus sibilatrix (Bechstein 1793)
TI p. 41 and pl. 6 **bottom left**
as wood-wren, *Phylloscopus sibilatrix* (Bechstein)

Western palearctic; breeds from Pyrenees, Italy, Balkans, Crimea and Caucasus, in south in isolated highland groups, to Ireland, Britain, south Fenno-Scandia and the middle North Dvina in north Russia; may nest on the Asian side of the south Urals. Winters to equatorial Africa.

Breeding population of Britain-Ireland order 5; breeds in virtually every county of Britain save Isle of Man and North Isles, though local in East Anglia, and in north Highlands which were colonised 1847–1914, and in western isles. In Ireland bred for a few years in co. Galway at end of nineteenth century, since then sporadically in 4 other counties, last co. Cork 1938; males have sung in 7 others.

Dusky Warbler   B362
Phylloscopus fuscatus (Blyth 1842)
TI p. 38 and T2 pl. 27 (prey of Tengmalm's owl)
as dusky warbler, *Phylloscopus fuscatus* (Blyth), see pl. 55

Palearctic; breeds in Siberia and the central Asian highlands, normally wintering to the oriental region.

Four records: female Auskerry, Orkney 1913 October 3; 1 trapped Fair Isle, Shetland 1961 October 14; 1 trapped St Agnes, Scilly 1964 October 19; 1 trapped Spurn, Yorkshire 1965 October 26–31.

Yellow-browed Warbler   B360
Phylloscopus inornatus (Blyth 1842)
TI p. 36 and pl. 6 **top right**
as yellow-browed warbler, *Phylloscopus superciliosus* (J. F. Gmelin)

Palearctic; breeds from the Pechora in Europe through Siberia to north China and the central Asian highlands, normally wintering into the oriental region.

An annual vagrant (autumn, few spring), from Shetland to east England, recorded elsewhere in Britain, in Ireland rather often since 1950's at coastal observatories.

Pallas's Willow Warbler   B361
Phylloscopus proregulus (Pallas 1811)
TI p. 37 and pl. 6 **upper mid right**
as Pallas's willow warbler, *Phylloscopus proregulus* (Pallas)

Palearctic; breeds in Siberia and the central Asian highlands, normally wintering into the oriental region.

Since 1960's known as a rare annual autumn vagrant, all 21 records 1896–1966 being October 11–November 23, all but 1 (Fair Isle, Shetland 1966) being from east and south England, most Spurn, Yorkshire 4, St Agnes, Scilly 4.

Arctic Warbler   B359
Phylloscopus borealis (Blasius 1858)
Not illustrated

Holarctic; breeds to the tree-line from Lapland through Russia to western Alaska and south to highland Japan and Korea; all birds normally migrate into the oriental region.

Over 30 times vagrant in autumn mainly at Fair Isle, otherwise on the east coast south to Norfolk and in Ireland (2).

Greenish Warbler   B355
Phylloscopus trochiloides (Sundevall 1837)
TI p. 38 and pl. 6 **lower mid right**
as greenish willow-warbler, *Phylloscopus viridanus*, Blyth

Palearctic; breeds in Siberia and the central Asian highlands, and has spread into Baltic Europe steadily through present century; normally winters into the oriental region.

Autumn vagrant (few summer), most Fair Isle to east England, 9 Ireland, also Wales; all but 1 of *c* 40 since 1945.

Pl. 6.

Subalpine Warbler
Dartford Warbler   Willow Wren
Wood-Wren

Yellow-browed Warbler
Pallas's Willow-Warbler
Greenish Willow-Warbler
Chiffchaff

Plate 70 (Thorburn's plate 7)

Subfamily SYLVIINAE, Old World warblers (*continued*)

Radde's Willow Warbler   B363
Phylloscopus schwarzi (Radde 1863)
TI p. 43 and pl. **7 mid right**
as Radde's bush-warbler, *Lusciniola schwarzi* (Radde)

Palearctic; breeds in Siberia and from Manchuria to northern Korea; normally migrates into the oriental region.
Seven records 1898–1966: the first 1 shot North Cotes, Lincolnshire 1898 October 1; the rest since 1961; England 6; Scotland 1; all October 1–20, east coast and Kent.

Subfamily TURDINAE

The rufous bush robin was believed by most ornithologists to be a warbler until some time after Thorburn did this painting; it has now been shown to be a member of the thrush subfamily.

Rufous Bush Robin   B353
Cercotrichas galactotes (Temminck 1820)
TI p. 42 and pl. **7 mid left**
as rufous warbler, *Aëdon galactodes* (Temminck)

Palearctic and ethiopian; breeds on both sides of the Sahara, in south Portugal and Spain, and from the Balkans and Greece, Asia Minor and Persia to Russian Turkestan and the Indus; European races normally migrate across the Sahara.
Eight records 1854–1963: the first 1 Plumpton Bosthill near Brighton, Sussex 1854 September 16; England 6; Ireland 2; all September–October.

Subfamily SYLVIINAE, Old World warblers (*continued*)

Booted Warbler   B342
Hippolais caligata (Lichtenstein 1823)
Not illustrated

Palearctic; in Asia breeds in central Siberia, the western central highlands and through the steppes to central Persia; in Europe from the Ural River system through the Volga to Lakes Onega and Ladoga, Leningrad and Pskov; migrates normally to India and southern Arabia.
Four records: female Fair Isle, Shetland 1936 September 3; 1 trapped Fair Isle 1959 August 29–31; 1 Fair Isle 1966 August 28–31; 1 St Agnes, Scilly 1966 October 23.

Olivaceous Warbler   B341
Hippolais pallida (Hemprich and Ehrenberg 1833)
See pl. 81

Melodious Warbler   B339
Hippolais polyglotta (Vieillot 1817)
TI p. 45 and pl. **7 top left**
as melodious warbler, *Hypolais polyglotta* (Vieillot)

Palearctic; breeds provedly in Morocco-Tunisia, Portugal, Spain and south-central France; migrates to west Africa.
An annual autumn vagrant, mostly on south coasts from Dorset west to co. Cork and in Wales. Has been recorded in May–July and from eastern England and Scotland.

Icterine Warbler   B340
Hippolais icterina (Vieillot 1817)
TI p. 44 and pl. **7 top right**
as icterine warbler, *Hypolais icterina* (Vieillot)

Palearctic; breeds from central Europe to western Asia between Mediterranean and south Fenno-Scandia to the North Dvina system; winters to ethiopian Africa, some to south.
Bred Wiltshire 1907; normally annual passenger in autumn, but also spring when males have stayed and sung; most east and south coasts west to co. Cork; no record for Wales.

Paddy-field Warbler   B336
Acrocephalus agricola (Jerdon 1845)
Not illustrated

Palearctic; breeds in Europe in the river deltas of the north Black Sea, in Asia mainly in the Kirghiz and Turkestanian steppes, also in Manchuria and probably India and Burma; western birds migrate normally to Persia and India.
Two records, Fair Isle, Shetland: male shot 1925 October 1; 1 trapped 1953 September 16.

Blyth's Reed Warbler   B335
Acrocephalus dumetorum Blyth 1849
Not illustrated

Palearctic; breeds from Estonia and southernmost Finland to the Urals, and in Asia to Lake Baikal and in the steppes to Persia and Afghanistan. Winters normally in India.
Six records 1910–28: the first Fair Isle, Shetland 1910 September 19–20; east England 3; Fair Isle 3; September 20–October 21.

Marsh Warbler   B334
Acrocephalus palustris (Bechstein 1798)
TI p. 47 and pl. **7 bottom left**
as marsh-warbler, *Acrocephalus palustris* (Bechstein)

Palearctic; breeds from north and east France, north Italy, the Danube system, Black Sea and Caucasus north to England, Denmark, south Sweden (since 1930), south Finland, Leningrad and the Volga system, east to the Urals and the Caspian Sea; winters to eastern tropical Africa.
Breeding population England (only) order 3; now breeds stably only in Somerset, Dorset, Kent, Gloucestershire and Worcestershire. Has nested in present century in 15 other counties, last Oxfordshire 1960, and though some records were doubtless sporadic shows a clear decline and present relict distribution, assisted by the conversion of wetlands, human inteference and the destruction of osier beds with the decline of basketmaking. Known in Scotland as passenger, mostly in spring, only at Fair Isle c 25 and St Kilda 1; no proved record for Wales or Ireland.

Reed Warbler   B333
Acrocephalus scirpaceus (Hermann 1804)
TI p. 46 and pl. **7 bottom right**
as reed-warbler, *Acrocephalus streperus* (Vieillot)

A western palearctic species breeding in Asia in Palestine, Syria, Cyprus, probably Asia Minor and from the Caucasus through north and central Persia and Russian Turkestan north to the Tarbagatai in the east and the lower Volga in the west. In the west breeds in Morocco and Algeria, and in Europe from the Iberian Peninsula and the Mediterranean north to Britain, southern Fenno-Scandia, Norway since 1947, western Estonia and east to the Don. Migrates to tropical Africa.
Breeding population Britain (only) order 4; declining slowly with the drainage and reclamation of reedy wetlands, though some populations are increasing in protected reserves. Breeds, or has bred, in virtually every county of England save Northumberland, though has few colonies and sometimes a tenuous hold in Cornwall, Devon, Monmouth co., Herefordshire, and North Country. Strong colonies where suitable habitat remains are in the Midlands, south and east and are roughly bounded by, and breed in the chain Dorset – cast Somerset – Gloucestershire – Worcestershire – Shropshire – south Cheshire – Staffordshire – south Derbyshire – Nottinghamshire – Lincolnshire – East Riding. Into Wales penetrates as a breeder into Glamorgan, Brecon, Flint and Denbigh cos. and probably the other border counties of Radnor and Montgomery. Has never bred in the Isle of Man and Scotland, and but once (obviously sporadically) in Ireland in co. Down 1935; otherwise in Ireland is a rare autumn and rarer spring passage vagrant, as it also is in western Wales and in Scotland (North Isles and east coast) – though it is annual in autumn on Fair Isle in very small numbers.

Pl. 7

Melodious Warbler.   Icterine Warbler.
Rufous Warbler.   Radde's Bush-Warbler.
Marsh-Warbler.   Reed Warbler.

Plate 71 (Thorburn's plate 8)

Subfamily SYLVIINAE, Old World warblers (continued)

Thick-billed Reed Warbler
Acrocephalus aedon (Pallas 1776)
Not illustrated

Palearctic; breeds in north China and Outer Mongolia, and in east Siberia where spread west from Yenisei to Novosibirsk on Ob in present century; migrates to oriental region.

One record: 1 trapped Fair Isle, Shetland 1955 October 6.

Great Reed Warbler   B332
Acrocephalus arundinaceus (Linnaeus 1758)
TI p. 48 and pl. 8 **mid**
as great reed-warbler, *Acrocephalus turdoides* (Meyer)

Palearctic; in west breeds from Morocco-Tunisia, Iberian Peninsula, European Mediterranean, north Palestine, Iraq and Caspian-Persia north to France (not Brittany and Channel coast), Denmark (since mid nineteenth century), southernmost Sweden and Finland (since *c* 1917 and *c* 1930), Estonia, Ukraine, Don and lower Volga systems and the Russian steppes; migrates to Africa where some reach south; a form in eastern Asia and Japan may be a full species; migrates to the oriental region.

An annual vagrant, most frequently spring but also summer and autumn, to south-east England; has been recorded from Scotland, twice from Ireland, never from Wales.

Sedge Warbler   B337
Acrocephalus schoenobaenus (Linnaeus 1758)
TI p. 49 and pl. 8 **top left**
as sedge-warbler, *Acrocephalus phragmitis* (Bechstein)

Western palearctic; breeds from Algeria, Morocco and northern Spain (possibly), central France and Italy, the Balkans, Caucasus and Russian steppes, north to Ireland, Britain, Fenno-Scandia, Murmansk and the edge of the Siberian tundra east to the Yenisei; absent from central Norway and Sweden; migrates to Africa where some reach south.

Breeding population of Britain-Ireland order 5; breeds in every county save Shetland where has sung in May; may not have bred in Outer Hebrides until 1937; population seems to have been generally stable.

Aquatic Warbler   B338
Acrocephalus paludicola (Vieillot 1817)
TI p. 50 and pl. 8 **bottom right**
as aquatic warbler, *Acrocephalus aquaticus* (J. F. Gmelin)

Wholly European; breeds in a very fragmented range, to limits some of which it may no longer reach, from Majorca, France, Italy's Po valley, Sicily, Balkans and Crimea north to east Holland, the Baltic from Germany to Latvia, east to the middle Volga and Ufa, Urals. Migrates to tropical Africa.

An annual passage vagrant, mostly August to early October (extremely few spring) between Norfolk and Hampshire; has been recorded elsewhere, in all four countries.

Moustached Warbler   B331
Lusciniola melanopogon (Temminck 1823)
See pl. 81.

Lanceolated Warbler   B328
Locustella lanceolata (Temminck 1840)
TI p. 53, **not figured**
as lanceolated warbler, *Locustella lanceolata* (Temminck)

Asian palearctic; breeds in Siberia from the upper Ob to the Sea of Okhotsk and west Kamchatka, from Amur-Ussuriland to north Korea, and in the south Kuriles and Japan; has bred in Europe by upper Kama tributary of Volga and possibly further west; normally migrates into the oriental region.

Twelve records 1909–1961: first, male shot North Cotes, Lincolnshire 1909 November 18; England 1; Scotland 11 (Fair Isle 10); all September 9–November 18 save 1 May 4.

Grasshopper Warbler   B327
Locustella naevia (Boddaert 1783)
TI p. 51 and pl. 8 **bottom left**
as grasshopper-warbler, *Locustella nævia* (Boddaert)

Western palearctic; breeds from north-east Spain, most of France, north Italy and Jugoslavia, the Danube, Caucasus and Aral-Balkhash steppes north to Ireland, Britain, the south Baltic, south Sweden, south-east Finland and Russia from Lake Onega through upper Volga, Ob and Yenisei systems. European birds winter to south Europe, occasionally North Africa.

Breeding population of Britain-Ireland order 4; breeds in every county of England, Wales, Lowlands (probably), Ireland and Isle of Man. On Highlands mainland local in Dumbarton co., Argyll, Perth co., Inverness co. and Fife, and may breed Moray and Wester Ross. The British population may be stable but that of Ireland has changed; was known to nest in but 5 counties *c* 1900, 15 by 1953, all 32 by 1965; old nestings may have been overlooked but increase seems certain.

Pallas's Grasshopper Warbler   B330
Locustella certhiola (Pallas 1811)
TI p. 52, **not figured**
as Pallas's grasshopper-warbler, *Locustella certhiola* (Pallas)

Asian palearctic; breeds in Siberia east from the eastern Ob, in Russian Turkestan and north and highland China; a form in Japan, Sakhalin, Kuriles and Kamchatka may be of the same species; migrates into the oriental region.

Three records: male Rockabill Lighthouse, co. Dublin 1908 September 28; immature seen Fair Isle, Shetland 1949 October 8–9; immature trapped Fair Isle 1956 October 2.

River Warbler
Locustella fluviatilis (Wolf 1810)
Not illustrated

Western palearctic; breeds from south Urals to middle Irtysh in Asia and east Europe from Danube-Sava system and north Black Sea to Oder and east Baltic, Helsinki in Finland since 1950's and upper North Dvina and Volga systems; migrates to eastern tropical Africa.

One record: a first winter bird trapped Fair Isle, Shetland 1961 September 24–25.

Savi's Warbler   B329
Locustella luscinioides (Savi 1824)
TI p. 54 and pl. 8 **top right**
as Savi's warbler, *Locustella luscinioides* (Savi)

Western palearctic; breeds in Kirghiz and Turkestanian steppes, in Algeria and isolated European and Asian Mediterranean places, and north to England, Holland, Elbe, Oder, Vistula, Dnepr, Don and lower Volga. Winters to tropical Africa.

Formerly bred Cambridgeshire and Huntingdonshire to 1840's, Norfolk to 1856, since when one record (2 birds Fair Isle 1908 May 14, 1 shot) until 1954; spring or summer birds recorded Cambridgeshire 1954, Somerset 1960, Suffolk 1964, Kent and Wiltshire 1965; has now recolonised England (Kent) after an absence of over a century.

Cetti's Warbler   B326
Cettia cetti (Temminck 1820)
TI p. 55 and pl. 8 **mid left**
as Cetti's warbler, *Cettia cetti* (Marmora)

South-west palearctic; breeds in Morocco-Tunisia, Iberian Peninsula and from European and Asian Mediterranean countries east through Iraq and Persia into Turkestanian and Kirghiz steppes, north in Europe to Crimea, lower Danube, Po valley and France, where spread of this resident bird began 1957, reaching Brittany and by 1961 north-east; coincides with records of birds in Germany, Jersey and England.

Two records: 1 netted Titchfield Haven, Hampshire, present 1961 March 4–April 8; juvenile netted the Crumbles, near Eastbourne, Sussex 1962 October 9.

Pl. 8.

Sedge-Warbler   Savi's Warbler
Cetti's Warbler   Great Reed-Warbler   Aquatic Warbler
        Grasshopper-Warbler

Plate 72 (Thorburn's plate 14)

Subfamily MUSCICAPINAE, Old World flycatchers

Pied Flycatcher   B368
Ficedula hypoleuca (Pallas 1764)
TI p. 94 and pl. 14 **bottom left** (♂ and ♀)
as pied flycatcher, *Muscicapa atricapilla*, Linnæus

A western palearctic bird of deciduous woodland, breeding in
Asia only from the central and south Urals east around
Krasnoyarsk. In the west breeds in Morocco-Tunisia and
very locally in north Portugal, Spain and southern France;
apart from Britain its main range in Europe is not west of
the Rhineland (where it reaches eastern France) or south of
northernmost Italy, northern Jugoslavia, Hungary and the
Ukraine and the uppermost Don and upper Volga, whence
north to inland Belgium and Holland, Denmark, northern
Lapland and Finland, the White Sea, the lower North Dvina
system and the uppermost Pechora. It reached Holland in
present century probably through readaptation to parkland.

Breeding population Britain order 5; by Bruce Campbell's
analysis bred in 36 counties of England, Wales and Scotland
1901–39, in 41 1940–52, in 39 1953–62. Has bred (or at least
attempted to) at one time or another in all English counties
save 9; not in the Isle of Man; in all Welsh counties save 2; in
all Scottish Lowland counties save 2, and in the Highland
counties of Perth, Clackmannan, Inverness, Argyll, Easter
Ross and in 1864 Orkney. Presently has a strong headquarters in the Forest of Dean, and good populations in the
hill woods from west Herefordshire and Shropshire through
central Wales to eastern Carmarthen and Cardigan,
Merioneth and eastern Caernarvon; and in the Lake District,
the Pennines south to central West Riding, the North York
Moors and the Dumfries-Kirkcudbright border in the Lowlands. Elsewhere is local and sporadic, though apparently
less sporadic lately in the Highlands; appears in the past to
have colonised, sometimes temporarily, after 'influx' years
such as 1864–66, 1885, 1898–99, 1901. There is some evidence
that a very gradual spread (allowing for fluctuations)
gathered some further way in 1940–52 but has slowed or
stabilised since. It is a regular passage migrant through most
non-breeding areas including Ireland and the Isle of Man.

Collared Flycatcher   B369
Ficedula albicollis (Temminck 1815)
TI p. 95 and pl. 14 **mid** (♂)
as collared flycatcher, *Muscicapa collaris*, Bechstein

Origin probably European; has a race from Greece and the
Caucasus into Asia Minor and north Persia; main range of
western European race is from Czechoslovakia and Austria
through Hungary, Jugoslavia, and north-west Rumania and
the northern Ukraine as far as the central Volga. Beyond this
is rather sporadic with stable breeding grounds in the French
Alps, the Black Forest and (very isolated) Öland and Gotland
islands in Sweden. Migrates to tropical Africa.

Five records: adult male shot Whalsay, Shetland 1947
May 11; male seen Bardsey, Caernarvon co. 1957 May 10;
1 North Fambridge, Essex 1962 September 21–23; male
Newhill on Harray, Orkney 1963 May 30; adult male found
dead Eskmeals, near Ravenglass, Cumberland 1964 June 2.

Red-breasted Flycatcher   B370
Ficedula parva (Bechstein 1794)
TI p. 96 and pl. 14 **mid left** (♂)
as red-breasted flycatcher, *Muscicapa parva*, Bechstein

A palearctic species of temperate hills and the boreal zone
breeding normally from Bulgaria, Jugoslavia, Austria, Germany, the south-east Baltic and south Finland east through
most of Siberia as far as Kamchatka; with an outpost from the
Caucasus to north Persia. Has lately colonised southernmost
Sweden and Denmark. Winters into the oriental region.

A rather scarce but regular autumn passage migrant on the
east coast of Scotland and England north to Shetland; has
been recorded in spring and elsewhere in England, Wales and
Scotland; virtually annual in autumn on the Irish coast.

Spotted Flycatcher   B366
Muscicapa striata (Pallas 1764)
TI p. 92 and pl. 14 **mid right**
as spotted flycatcher, *Muscicapa grisola*, Linnæus

Western palearctic; breeds in Morocco-Tunisia and from the
European and Asian Mediterranean north to Ireland, Britain,
northern Fenno-Scandia and Russia, east to beyond Lake
Baikal and the western highlands of central Asia. Western
birds migrate to ethiopian Africa, some reaching the south.

Breeding population of Britain-Ireland order 5; breeds in
every county save Shetland, though but sporadically in
Orkney and perhaps also Outer Hebrides. May have spread
into Highlands in first half of nineteenth century, though the
population seems to have been more stable in the present.

Brown Flycatcher   B367
Muscicapa latirostris Raffles 1822
TI p. 93 and pl. 14 **top right**
as brown flycatcher, *Muscicapa latirostris*, Raffles

Eastern palearctic; breeds in Siberia from the upper Yenisei
to Sakhalin and in Kuriles, Japan, Manchuria and north
Korea; with an outpost on the Indian side of the Himalayas
in the oriental blend-zone. Migrates into the oriental region.

Two records: 1 seen Holy Island, Northumberland 1956
September 9; 1 first winter Great Saltee, co. Wexford 1957
September 6.

Family ORIOLIDAE, Old World orioles

Golden Oriole   B278
Oriolus oriolus (Linnaeus 1758)
TI p. 90 and pl. 14 **bottom right** (♂)
as golden oriole, *Oriolus galbula*, Linnæus

Western palearctic and oriental, possibly of European origin;
breeds from the Indian subcontinent (not Ceylon) north to
the upper Yenisei through the steppes, and west to Morocco
(probably) and most of continental Europe between the
Iberian Peninsula and the Mediterranean, and the Baltic;
reached southernmost Sweden 1944; sporadic in Denmark
and Britain. Winters to tropical Africa.

A spring passenger and occasional summerer to east and
south England and south Wales, irregular rest of Wales,
England and Ireland, rare Scotland. Bred Kent 1836, since
when about two dozen successful nestings in 8 English
counties (most Kent, northernmost north Lancashire 1958),
and unproved or failed breedings in 7 others.

Family BOMBYCILLIDAE, waxwings

Waxwing   B383
Bombycilla garrulus (Linnaeus 1758)
TI p. 91 and pl. 14 **top left**
as waxwing, *Ampelis garrulus*, Linnæus

Holarctic; normally breeds through the boreal conifer and
birch zone from Lapland to Kamchatka, and from Alaska
through western Canada to central Washington, northern
Idaho and north-west Montana. Fluctuates markedly in
numbers and sometimes in breeding distribution, in northern
Europe largely with the winter rowan berry crop (bred far
into the southern Scandinavian Peninsula in 1956 and 1957).

In years when the berry crop in southern Scandinavia and
north-west Europe is used up by late autumn or early winter
marked invasions occur, at irregular intervals, of Britain and
Ireland. In the present century such invasions have been
logged in 1903–04*, 1913–14, 1921–22, 1931–32, 1932–33*,
19(36–)37, 1941–42, 1943–44, 1946–47*, 1948–49, 1949–50,
19(56–)57, 1957–58*, 1958–59*, 1959–60 and 1965–66*.
Those marked * reached Ireland in some strength, some of
those not marked were mainly in eastern British counties. The
invasion of 1946–47 seems to have been the largest analysed,
with an estimated 12,500 visiting birds. Has been recorded
from every county of England and Scotland, nearly all of
Wales and most of Ireland.

Waxwing.   Spotted Flycatcher.   Brown Flycatcher.

Red-breasted Flycatcher.

Pied Flycatcher.   Collared Flycatcher. Golden Oriole
♂ & ♀

3

Plate 73 (Thorburn's plate 13)

Family LANIIDAE, shrikes

Red-backed Shrike   B388
Lanius collurio Linnaeus 1758
TI p. 87 and pl. 13 **top left** (♂ ♀)
as red-backed shrike, *Lanius collurio*, Linnæus

A broadly distributed palearctic species breeding in Asia from
Asia Minor, Cyprus, the Caucasus, Iraq, central Persia and
Afghanistan, the Himalayas, highland west China and east
China south of the Yangtze north to the middle and upper
Siberian river systems, east to the upper Anadyr, the Sea of
Okhotsk, south Kamchatka and Sakhalin and Japan. The
eastern Asian birds are separated by some authorities as the
brown shrike, *Lanius cristatus* Linnaeus 1758. In Europe breeds
from the hills of north Portugal and Spain, the Pyrenees, south
France, Corsica, Sardinia, central Italy and Greece north to
England, south-eastern Norway, south Sweden and Finland,
Lake Onega, the upper North Dvina and the central Urals.
Has decreased since *c* 1950 in Sweden, Denmark, Holland,
Belgium and Germany; but may have spread in Norway.
Western elements migrate to ethiopian Africa, some reaching
the south.

Breeding population of Britain in 1960 under 200 pairs by
D. B. Peakall's analysis, after over a century of decrease and
withdrawal. Has probably bred in every county of Wales and
England in the past, but not in the Isle of Man or Ireland
(where rare vagrant) or provedly in Scotland (record 1933
Midlothian unconfirmed) where a scarce east coast passenger.
The specially British race is one of the few European birds on
the danger list of the International Union for Conservation of
Nature. Last bred in the Tyne counties and Cornwall nineteenth century, in the Mersey counties 1926, in Yorkshire
1934, in the Lake counties 1938, in the Trent counties 1947,
north Wales and south Wales early 1950's, in the Severn
counties 1950's (may possibly hang on in Gloucestershire).
1960 proved range entirely in south and south-east and limited
by chain Devon–Somerset–Wiltshire–Hampshire–Surrey–
Middlesex – Buckinghamshire – Hertfordshire – Cambridgeshire–Norfolk, with headquarters in Hampshire and Suffolk
and over 10 pairs also in Surrey, Essex and Norfolk. Peakall
and others assign the decline to the warmer, wetter summers
of the present century with a consequent reduction in the
population of large flying insects; though the heath and scrub
habitat has been reduced in some traditional breeding areas.

[Masked Shrike   B387
Lanius nubicus Lichtenstein 1823
TI p. 89 and pl. 13 **mid** (♂)
as masked shrike, *Lanius nubicus*, Lichtenstein

A palearctic species with a very limited distribution, breeding
through Asia Minor (mainly coastal) to Cyprus and in the
Levant south to Palestine; also in eastern Iraq and western
Asia. Migrates to tropical Africa. Now rejected from the
British-Irish List, though figured by Thorburn in all good
faith. An adult male, said to have been obtained at Wood-
church, Kent 1905 July 11 is a 'Hastings Rarity'.]

Woodchat Shrike   B386
Lanius senator Linnaeus 1758
TI p. 88 and pl. 13 **bottom left** (♂)
as woodchat, *Lanius pomeranus*, Sparrman

A basically Mediterranean palearctic species breeding in Asia
from Asia Minor, Cyprus, Syria-Palestine east through Iraq
into western Persia, and along the south Persian Baluchistan
coast; in Africa in Morocco, Algeria, Tunisia and Cyrenaican
Libya; and in Europe from the Iberian Peninsula, the Mediterranean north coast and its principal islands north to Spain
(not extreme north-west), France, Belgium and Holland (not
Brittany or the Channel-North Sea coastal areas), central

Germany, Czechoslovakia, Poland (outpost near Warsaw),
Hungary, western and southern Jugoslavia, and southern
Bulgaria. Winters in ethiopian Africa to about the equator.

An annual passage and summer vagrant to east and south
England, south Wales and co. Wexford, Ireland, recorded
rarely elsewhere in these countries and Scotland.

Lesser Grey Shrike   B385
Lanius minor J. F. Gmelin 1788
TI p. 86 and pl. 13 **bottom right** (♂)
as lesser grey shrike, *Lanius minor*, J. F. Gmelin

A western palearctic species breeding in Asia from Asia
Minor and the Caucasus to eastern Iraq, northern Persia and
Afghanistan north through the Caspian, Aral and Balkhash
steppe systems to the upper Ural River and the upper Ob
system; in Europe from Mediterranean France, central Italy
and central Greece north to central and north-east France,
south Belgium, central Germany, north Czechoslovakia,
south and east Poland, Lithuania and in Russia the Dnepr,
Don and lower Volga systems. Winters to ethiopian Africa
south of the equator.

A rare spring passage vagrant to south and east England
which has been recorded elsewhere in England, in Wales and
Scotland, once in Ireland, and in autumn.

Great Grey Shrike   B384
Lanius excubitor Linnaeus 1758
TI p. 84 and pl. 13 **top right** (♂)
as great grey shrike, *Lanius excubitor*, Linnæus

An holarctic species that breeds also into the oriental and
ethiopian regions, with a curiously discontinuous western
palearctic distribution which suggests to K. H. Voous that
Europe was populated after the last glacial period from south-
west via France and from east via Russia, which may explain
the big Baltic-Atlantic and Mediterranean-Caspian gaps in
the breeding range. Breeds in the Canaries and in the whole
of northern Africa to the Mediterranean, from south of the
Sahara, Lake Chad, the Sudan, Ethiopia, north Somalia and
Socotra; and through Arabia and Iraq, Persia and Afghanistan
into the northern Indian subcontinent south of the Himalayas;
and through the Turkestanian steppes to Mongolia and the
middle systems of the Siberian rivers east to Anadyr, the Sea
of Okhotsk and Sakhalin but not the Amur-Ussuri system
where replaced by the closely allied Chinese great grey shrike,
Lanius sphenocercus Cabanis 1873. In North America extends
through the Yukon-Kuskokwim systems of Alaska and Yukon
to the Mackenzie system, the Seward Peninsula of Alaska, and
and the northernmost parts of the provinces of British
Columbia, Alberta, Saskatchewan and Manitoba, and in a
band from Québec north-east of James Bay to central Newfoundland Labrador; further south in Canada and through
the United States and México is replaced by the closely allied
loggerhead shrike, *Lanius ludovicianus* Linnaeus 1766.

In Europe breeds in the Iberian Peninsula and from
southern and eastern France, Switzerland, north-east Italy,
northern Jugoslavia, Hungary, northern and eastern Rumania,
north-east Bulgaria, the Crimea and the northern border of
the Caucasus, north to Germany, Danish Jutland and the
south Baltic, and the White Sea, North Dvina and middle
Pechora systems in Russia, and through central Finland and
Lapland to the spinal mountains of central Sweden and
Norway. The western European birds migrate to winter
within the palearctic region.

An Early Upper Pleistocene fossil from Chudleigh, Devon
indicates that England was in visiting or breeding range in
Ice Age times (though a fossil does not mean a breeding bird).
Is presently a winter visitor and passage migrant to Britain-
Ireland (rare in Ireland), mostly in eastern Scotland and
England, less commonly in other parts of England, Wales and
western Scotland.

Pl. 13.

Red-backed Shrike. ♂ & ♀.   Great Grey Shrike
Woodchat Shrike.   Masked Shrike   Lesser Grey Shrike

Plate 74 (Thorburn's plate 15)

Family HIRUNDINIDAE, swallows

Sand Martin   B277
Riparia riparia (Linnaeus 1758)
TI p. 100 and pl. 15 **top mid**
as sand-martin, *Cotile riparia* (Linnæus)

Holarctic; breeds in virtually the whole region north to near the tree-line, not on islands north of Britain or regularly in North Africa; and enters the oriental region some distance in east China, probably Burma, and India. European birds winter to Africa, some south of the equator.

Breeding population of Britain-Ireland order 5; breeds in every county save Outer Hebrides where now extinct or sporadic, Orkney where sporadic, and Shetland (one record, 1887). Colonies change and fluctuate with the availability of sandbanks, but there seems little evidence for the decrease in the present century that was suggested in the 1940's.

Swallow   B274
Hirundo rustica Linnaeus 1758
TI p. 97 and pl. 15 **mid left**
as swallow, *Hirundo rustica*, Linnæus

Holarctic; breeds in virtually the whole region, though less close to the north tree-line than sand martin, but in North Africa, Faeroe irregularly and Iceland lately; enters the oriental region in China and Taiwan and the neotropical to central México. European birds migrate to ethiopian Africa, some reaching the Cape.

Breeding population of Britain-Ireland order 6; nests in every county though locally in Orkney and irregularly in several places in the Outer Hebrides; in Shetland over fifteen sporadic records, including Fair Isle and Foula. There is evidence of fluctuation in population but no good evidence of a general trend of decrease or increase.

Red-rumped Swallow   B275
Hirundo daurica Linnaeus 1771
TI p. 98 and pl. 15 **top left**
as red-rumped swallow, *Hirundo rufula*, Temminck

Old World; breeds in a rather fragmented range in the savannah of ethiopian Africa and south-west Arabia; in oriental India and south-east Asia, Taiwan, the Philippines, and from Java to australasian Timor; in the eastern palearctic from Lake Baikal and Amur-Ussuriland to China and south Japan, and from the Turkestanian steppes through Persia to Asia Minor; Palestine and Cyprus; in the western palearctic only in Morocco-Algeria, central and southern Portugal and Spain, and from southern Jugoslavia and Bulgaria to Greece, until 1965 when discovered nesting in southern France, Corsica and Sardinia. Western birds migrate to east Africa.

Thirteen records 1906–66: the first, 1 shot and 2 others seen Fair Isle, Shetland 1906 June 2; England 10; Scotland (Fair Isle) 2; Ireland (co. Wexford) 1; 10 May–June, August, October, November.

House Martin   B276
Delichon urbica (Linnaeus 1758)
TI p. 99 and pl. 15 **top right**
as martin, *Chelidon urbica* (Linnæus)

Palearctic; breeds in virtually the whole region north to near the tree-line; not in Kamchatka, in the Russian steppes or in China save Manchuria, the boreal western highlands, the south-east and Taiwan. Has bred once Spitsbergen 1924; otherwise on no island north of Britain. Western birds migrate to Africa, some to South Africa where groups of migrant origin have bred sporadically in at least 3 areas.

Breeding population of Britain-Ireland order 6; breeds (or has bred) in every county save Outer Hebrides; but probably extinct as breeder Orkney since 1940's, and in Shetland sporadic. General decrease in urban England and north Highlands during the middle of the present century, and recent increase in Ireland, have been recorded.

Family FRINGILLIDAE, finches

A modern systematic order is B407, 408, 399, 400 (pl. 75), 392, 394, 393 (pl. 74), 396 (pl. 76), 395, 397 (pl. 75), 398 (pl. 82), 402, 403, 405, 404, 406, 401 (pl. 76), 391 (pl. 74).

Hawfinch   B391
Coccothraustes coccothraustes (Linnaeus 1758)
TI p. 102 and pl. 15 **bottom mid** (♂)
as hawfinch, *Coccothraustes vulgaris*, Pallas

Palearctic oakland; breeds in east in Turkestanian steppes, and from upper Ob to Amur-Ussuriland, Manchuria, Korea and Japan; in west from Morocco-Tunisia, Mediterranean Europe, north Asia Minor and Persia, north to Britain, Denmark, south Sweden, Leningrad and central Russia; sporadic in Norway and Finland. Partial migrant within the palearctic.

Breeding population of Britain (only) order 4; breeds (Guy Mountfort) in virtually every county of England save Cornwall, and of Wales save 4; decreasing border counties. Probably colonised north England at end nineteenth century, Lowlands in first decade of twentieth though scarce in west; in Highlands nesting Perth co. since c 1944 and has bred 2 others. Does not breed Isle of Man; in Ireland known as postglacial fossil co. Clare, once nested, co. Kildare 1902, now vagrant.

Greenfinch   B392
Carduelis chloris (Linnaeus 1758)
TI p. 101 and pl. 15 **bottom right** (♂)
as greenfinch, *Ligurinus chloris* (Linnæus)

Western palearctic; breeds in Turkestanian steppes and from Azores (introduced), Morocco-Tunisia, Mediterranean, Palestine, Asia Minor and north Persia to Ireland, Britain, central Fenno-Scandia and north-central European Russia. Resident.

Breeding population of Britain-Ireland order 6; breeds in every county save Shetland; colonised other North Isles since 1880's and has spread in Highlands and inner isles since 1920's; in Ireland decreasing some areas but spreading in coastal ones.

Siskin   B394
Carduelis spinus (Linnaeus 1758)
TI p. 104 and pl. 15 **mid** (♂)
as siskin, *Carduelis spinus* (Linnæus)

Palearctic; breeds in Amur-Ussuriland, Manchuria and Japan; in some highlands of southern Europe, Asia Minor, Caucasus and north Persia, and more continuously from Alps and Carpathians through central Europe, and in Asia into the upper Ob system, north to central Fenno-Scandia and north-central Russia; also in Ireland and Britain. Migrates within the palearctic.

Breeding population of Britain-Ireland perhaps in order 5; unstable, with a headquarters in east Highlands (Perth co. to Sutherland-Caithness), groups in west Highlands; and shifting populations in Lowlands, (mostly north) England, north Wales and all four provinces (not all counties) of Ireland where spreading, though perhaps not increasing, lately.

Goldfinch   B393
Carduelis carduelis (Linnaeus 1758)
TI p. 103 and pl. 15 **bottom left** (♀)
as goldfinch, *Carduelis elegans*, Stephens

Western palearctic; breeds from Azores, Madeira, Canaries, North Africa, Palestine, Iraq, Persia, north Afghanistan and the west Himalayas north to Ireland, Britain, southernmost Fenno-Scandia and central Russia east to the upper Yenisei; absent from the arid Russian steppes. Partial migrant within the palearctic; introduced in Americas and Australasia.

Breeding population of Britain-Ireland order 5; probably bred 150 years ago in every mainland county; by 1900, widely decimated by bird trade and marginal land cultivation, was virtually extinct in Highlands and much of Lowlands, where recovery is incomplete; has returned Ross (1938) but not yet Sutherland-Caithness; breeds some western isles, not North Isles. In Ireland lately increasing in west, decreasing in east.

Pl. 15.

Red.rumped Swallow.   Sand.Martin.

Swallow.   Siskin.   Martin.

Goldfinch.   Hawfinch.   Greenfinch.

Plate 75 (Thorburn's plate 16)

Family FRINGILLIDAE, finches (*continued*)

Chaffinch   B407
Fringilla coelebs Linnaeus 1758
TI p. 109 and pl. 16 **bottom left** (♂)
as chaffinch, *Fringilla cœlebs*, Linnæus

Western palearctic; breeds from Azores, Madeira, Canaries, Mediterranean countries and Caspian-Persia north in Europe to near the tree-line, slowly spreading north in Fenno-Scandia; extending into Siberia in the upper Ob system. Resident save northern birds which migrate within palearctic.

   Breeding population of Britain-Ireland order 7; breeds in every county (Orkney first 1839, Outer Hebrides 1841, Shetland sporadically); has increased in Scotland with woodland recovery, and decreased in parts of England in last decades.

Brambling   B408
Fringilla montifringilla Linnaeus 1758
TI p. 110 and pl. 16 **mid left** (winter and summer)
as brambling, *Fringilla montifringilla*, Linnæus

Palearctic; breeds through the birch zone and taiga-edge of the boreal north from Norway to eastern Siberia. Western birds winter south within the palearctic.
   Bred Sutherland 1920 and may have bred Perth and Inverness cos. and Ross. A regular winter visitor, but irregularly reaching Wales, west England and Ireland in strength.

Citril Finch   B399
Serinus citrinella (Pallas 1764)
TI p. 105 and pl. 16 **top right lower** (♂)
as citril finch, *Chrysomitris citrinella* (Linnæus)

Palearctic; confined to Alps and other mountains of south-west Europe where resident but not sedentary.
   One record: female caught Great Yarmouth Denes, Norfolk 1904 January 29.

Serin   B400
Serinus serinus (Linnaeus 1766)
TI p. 106 and pl. 16 **top right upper** (♂)
as serin, *Serinus hortulanus*, K. L. Koch

Western palearctic; breeds in Morocco-Tripolitania and the European and Asian Mediterranean, whence has colonised most of continental western Europe since 1800 to south Baltic, reaching southernmost Sweden 1942, Channel coast 1956. Northern birds winter to the Mediterranean.
   An annual vagrant (rare in summer), in increasing numbers lately, to Channel England; rare Wales, Scotland and Ireland.

Linnet   B395
Acanthis cannabina (Linnaeus 1758)
TI p. 112 and pl. 16 **upper mid right** (♂)
as linnet, *Linota cannabina* (Linnæus)

Western palearctic; breeds from Madeira, Canaries, Morocco-Cyrenaica and the Mediterranean north to Ireland, Britain, south Fenno-Scandia and north-central Russia; and into Asia from Asia Minor through Persia to Turkestan, and to the western Ob. Northern birds winter to south palearctic.
   Breeding population of Britain-Ireland order 6; nests in every county save Shetland, rather sparsely in north Highlands and Hebrides. Decreased in England and Scotland with bird trade and wasteland 'reclamation' of nineteenth century; has now recovered, and is increasing south England, elsewhere rather stable.

Redpoll   B397
Acanthis flammea (Linnaeus 1758)

Mealy redpoll, *Acanthis flammea flammea*
TI p. 113 and pl. 16 **top left upper** (♂)
as mealy redpoll, *Linota linaria* (Linnæus)

Greenland redpoll, *Acanthis flammea rostrata* (Coues 1862)
T4 p. 103 and pl. 80A **mid left**
as greater redpoll, *Linota rostrata* (Coues), see pl. 82

Lesser redpoll, *Acanthis flammea cabaret* (P. L. S. Müller 1776)
TI p. 114 and pl. 16 **top left lower** (♂)
as lesser redpoll, *Linota rufescens* (Vieillot)

Holarctic; with races recognisable in field. Lesser redpoll breeds in Ireland, Britain, Alps and Czechoslovakian border mountains; mealy redpoll in birch forests and tundra scrub from Norway through Siberia and Alaska to Canada; Greenland redpoll in Baffin Island and Greenland. Iceland has a race. All but resident lesser redpoll migrate within holarctic.
   Breeding population of Britain-Ireland order 5; may have bred in every county save Cornwall, Isle of Wight, Orkney and Shetland (only once Outer Hebrides). Increased since decline of bird trade and recovery of plantations but local outside strongholds in north Wales, north England, and large Scottish forests; has spread in north Highlands and Inner Hebrides in last fifty years. Fairly stable in Ireland. Other races are irregular visitors from Shetland south, mealies usually on east coasts, Greenland (and Iceland?) birds on west.

Arctic Redpoll   B398
Acanthis hornemanni (Holbøll 1843)
See pl. 82

Family PLOCEIDAE, weavers and true sparrows

In Thorburn's time the sparrows were generally thought to be finches; hence this interruption. They are weaver birds.

House Sparrow   B424
Passer domesticus (Linnaeus 1758)
TI p. 107 and pl. 16 **bottom right** (♂ ♀)
as house-sparrow, *Passer domesticus* (Linnæus)

Natural breeding range is virtually the whole palearctic region, where has been successfully colonising Siberia for over one hundred years, with extensions into oriental India, Ceylon and Burma and into ethiopian Africa in the Sudan; north island limit is Faeroe since *c* 1935. Has been introduced into all other major faunal regions. Generally resident.
   Breeding population of Britain-Ireland order 7; *c* 9½ million breeding *birds* in *Britain c* 1958 (D. Summers-Smith). Has been increasing with spread of man and farms for ages and since colonisation Outer Hebrides *c* 1833 breeds in every county. Increase paused in urban areas with motorisation but has now resumed with public feeding; is decreasing in areas of lapsed peripheral farms in Scotland and Ireland.

Spanish Sparrow
Passer hispaniolensis (Temminck 1820)
Not illustrated

Palearctic; breeds in Cape Verdes, Canaries, Mediterranean countries and from Asia Minor to Turkestan. Mostly resident.
   One record: 1 Lundy, Devon 1966 June 9.

Tree Sparrow   B425
Passer montanus (Linnaeus 1758)
TI p. 108 and pl. 16 **lower mid right**
as tree-sparrow, *Passer montanus* (Linnæus)

Breeds through virtually the whole palearctic region and through south-east Asia to Java; introduced in nearctic and australasian regions; a partial migrant.
   Breeding population of Britain-Ireland order 5; virtually sporadic outside local strongholds in Midlands, east and north England, in rest of Britain has bred in most counties but very irregularly; in Ireland was extinct by 1959–60 but bred in 15 (mostly coastal) of the 32 counties 1966.

Pl. 16.

Mealy Redpoll.   Serin.

Lesser Redpoll.   Citril Finch.   Linnet.

Brambling (Summer & Winter).   Tree Sparrow.

Chaffinch.   House Sparrow (♂ & ♀)

Plate 76 (Thorburn's plate 17)

Family PLOCEIDAE, weavers and true sparrows (*continued*)

[Snow Finch   B426
Montifringilla nivalis (Linnaeus 1766)
TI p. 111 and pl. 17 **top right** (♂)
as snow-finch, *Montifringilla nivalis*, Linnæus

Palearctic; a resident in mountains of south Europe, Caucasus-Persia and central Asia.

Rejected from the List, though figured by Thorburn in all good faith; based on 'Hastings Rarities', Sussex-Kent 1905–16.**]**

Family FRINGILLIDAE, finches (*continued*)

Twite   B396
Acanthis flavirostris (Linnaeus 1758)
TI p. 115 and pl. 17 **top mid** (♂)
as twite, *Linota flavirostris* (Linnæus)

Palearctic; breeds in Ireland, Britain, Faeroe, Norway and Murmansk; in Caucasus, east Turkey and west Persia; and in the Kirghiz steppes and central Asian highlands. European birds migrate within the palearctic.

Breeding population of Britain-Ireland order 4; has bred once Isle of Man and perhaps once Wales; formerly bred in the 9 hill counties of England south to Pennine Staffordshire and in all but 4 counties of Scotland; since last century has withdrawn from much of the Pennines and Lowlands, remains strong in Highlands and North Isles. Breeds stably in coastal Ireland and on some dry inland hills.

Scarlet Grosbeak   B402
Carpodacus erythrinus (Pallas 1770)
TI p. 117 and pl. 17 **mid right** (♂)
as scarlet grosbeak, *Pyrrhula erythrina* (Pallas)

Palearctic; breeds from the Baltic through Russia and Siberia to Kamchatka and from the Black Sea to the central Asian highlands; normally winters into the oriental region.

An annual autumn vagrant to Fair Isle, Shetland (2 April records) has been recorded elsewhere on coasts of Scotland, England, Wales and (3 times) Ireland.

Pine Grosbeak   B403
Pinicola enucleator (Linnaeus 1758)
TI p. 118 and pl. 17 **bottom right** (♂)
as pine-grosbeak, *Pyrrhula enucleator* (Linnæus)

Holarctic; breeds in the taiga from northern Fenno-Scandia through Siberia and in Alaska, Canada, Maine and the highland United States west; migrates within the holarctic.

At least ten valid records 1769–1890; the first, several seen Invercauld Forest, Aberdeen co. 1769 August 5; England 8; Scotland 2; August–February.

Parrot Crossbill   B405
Loxia pytyopsittacus Borkhausen 1793
TI p. 119, **not figured**
as parrot-crossbill (*Loxia pityopsittacus*, Bechstein)

Northern European; breeds in pine forest from central and south Fenno-Scandia and the Baltic to the upper Pechora in Russia. Resident but prone to invasions beyond regular range.

Crossbill irruption of 1962–63 brought parties (September–May) to 4 places in England, 5 Scotland (North Isles) and 2 Ireland; previous records, perhaps only 6, first 1818, were all English (September–January).

Crossbill   B404
Loxia curvirostra Linnaeus 1758
Continental crossbill, *Loxia curvirostra curvirostra*
TI p. 119 and pl. 17 **bottom mid** (♂)
as crossbill, *Loxia curvirostra*, Linnæus

Scottish crossbill, *Loxia curvirostra scotica* Hartert 1904
T4 p. 104 and pl. 80B **top right** (♀ and subadult ♂)
as Scottish crossbill, *Loxia scotica* Hartert, see pl. 81

Holarctic; breeds widely through conifer forests in northern Eurasia and North America and in their highland south with neotropical outposts to Nicaragua and oriental outposts in South Viet Nam and the Philippines. Resident, but in years of food shortage may 'irrupt' beyond regular range.

Breeding population of Britain-Ireland order 4; native Scottish race is perhaps increasing and resident in 8 counties centred on Inverness co. Continental race, after irregular irruptions (about 28 1800–1966), has bred in all but 6 counties of England, half those of Wales and of Scotland not occupied by native race, and about two-thirds of those of Ireland. Many colonies die out unless refreshed; those of Wales are sporadic, but Ireland has had a fluctuating population since 1839 and the English Breckland and New Forest headquarters have been occupied since 1910.

White-winged Crossbill   B406
Loxia leucoptera (J. F. Gmelin 1789)
TI p. 120 and pl. 17 **lower mid** (♂)
as two-barred crossbill, *Loxia bifasciata* (C. L. Brehm)

Holarctic; breeds in larch-fir forests, in Russia from Lake Onega to Lena and upper Amur, in North America and an outpost on Hispaniola, West Indies. Resident but irruptive.

Rare vagrant England; recorded Wales, Scotland, Ireland.

Bullfinch   B401
Pyrrhula pyrrhula (Linnaeus 1758)
TI p. 116 and pl. 17 **bottom left** (♀ ♂)
as bullfinch, *Pyrrhula europæa*, Vieillot

Palearctic; breeds in Azores (extinct?), from Norway through north Russia and Siberia to Kamchatka, Manchuria and Japan, in west Europe south to hills of Mediterranean countries, and in Black Sea-Caspian uplands. Resident but irruptive.

Breeding population of Britain-Ireland order 5; breeds in every county save North Isles; an invasion of Scotland may have started before 1800; has lately spread in Ireland and increased in England despite lifting of protection.

Family EMBERIZIDAE

This large family is divided into subfamilies and tribes, for convenience, see pl. '83'.

Subfamily EMBERIZINAE
Tribe EMBERIZINI, buntings

A modern systematic order is B422, 423 (pl. 77), 410 (pl. 76), 409 (pl. 77), 411 (pl. 76), 417, 418, 416, 415, 420, 419, 414 (pl. 77), 412, 413 (pl. 76), 421 (pl. 77).

Corn Bunting   B410
Emberiza calandra Linnaeus 1758
TI p. 124 and pl. 17 **top left**
as corn-bunting, *Emberiza miliaria*, Linnæus

Western palearctic; breeds from Canaries and Mediterranean to Britain, Ireland, southernmost Scandinavia, the south Baltic and south Russia, and through north Persia to the Turkestanian steppes. Resident and partial migrant.

Breeding population of Britain-Ireland order 4; formerly bred in nearly every county but in present century became extinct in many inland, and local in favoured habitat of open farming on limy soil and near coasts; decrease fits the decline of marginal agriculture and hedge destruction on best arable land. The North Isles remain a stronghold.

For reasons of space (Thorburn *did* crowd this plate), texts for B412 black-headed bunting (**mid left**), B413 red-headed bunting (**not illustrated**) and B411 pine bunting (**upper mid mid**) are transferred to a column **opposite plate 80.**

Pl. 17.

Corn Bunting.
Black-headed Bunting.
Bullfinch (♂♀).

Twite.
Pine Bunting.
Two-barred Crossbill.
Crossbill.

Snow Finch.
Scarlet Grosbeak.
Pine Grosbeak.

Plate 77 (Thorburn's plate 18)

Tribe EMBERIZINI, buntings (*continued*)

Yellowhammer   B409
Emberiza citrinella Linnaeus 1758
TI p. 125 and pl. 18 **top right** (♂)
as yellow bunting or yellow hammer, *Emberiza citrinella*,
Linnæus

Western palearctic; breeds from north Spain, the hills of other
north Mediterranean countries and Caucasus to Fenno-
Scandia and north Russia, and in Siberia east to the upper
Viluyi tributary of the Lena. Resident and partial migrant.
 Breeding population of Britain-Ireland order 7; breeds in
every county save Outer Hebrides and Shetland, rather
stably save in England where declining with hedge destruction.

Rock Bunting   B417
Emberiza cia Linnaeus 1766
TI p. 128 and pl. 18 **lower mid mid** (♂)
as meadow-bunting, *Emberiza cia*, Linnæus

Southern palearctic; breeds round Mediterranean and in
highlands from central Europe to China. Resident, but may
wander.
 Four records: 2 netted by bird catchers near Shoreham,
Sussex 1902 October late; 1 seen Faversham, Kent 1905
February *c* 14; 1 seen Dale Fort, Pembroke co. 1958 August
15; 1 seen Spurn, Yorkshire 1965 February 19–March 10.

[Meadow Bunting   B418
Emberiza cioides Brandt 1843
TI p. 129 and pl. 18 **lower mid left** (♂)
as Siberian meadow-bunting, *Emberiza cioides*, Brandt

Eastern palearctic; breeds from Turkestan to China; the 1886
Yorkshire record is now rejected from the British-Irish List
though figured by Thorburn in all good faith.]

Ortolan   B416
Emberiza hortulana Linnaeus 1758
TI p. 127 and pl. 18 **bottom left** (♂)
as ortolan, *Emberiza hortulana*, Linnæus

Western palearctic; breeds from the Mediterranean and
north Persia to central Fenno-Scandia, White Sea and in
Siberia east to the upper Yenisei; not to the Channel and
North Sea coasts. Migrates to the Mediterranean and
Somaliland.
 A scarce annual passenger most frequent Fair Isle, south
Ireland and Wales, Devon-Cornwall; very rare elsewhere.

Cirl Bunting   B415
Emberiza cirlus Linnaeus 1766
TI p. 126 and pl. 18 **upper mid left** (♂)
as cirl bunting, *Emberiza cirlus*, Linnæus

Western palearctic; breeds in Morocco-Tunisia, Asia Minor
and in south-west Europe from Mediterranean to Britain,
Belgium, Rhineland Germany, Alps and Balkans. Resident.
 Breeding population of Britain (only) order 3; nests only
sporadically north of chain Hereford–Worcester–Gloucester–
Oxford–Buckingham–Hertford shires and Middlesex–Surrey–
Kent though has bred in 7 Welsh counties north to Denbigh
co. and 26 English counties in all north to Cumberland. Is very
local and fluctuating save on some limy downlands. It is only
a vagrant to Scotland and Ireland.

Little Bunting   B420
Emberiza pusilla Pallas 1776
TI p. 131 and pl. 18 **top mid**
as little bunting, *Emberiza pusilla*, Pallas

Northern palearctic; breeds in taiga-edge and tundra scrub
from Lapland (lately colonised) and White Sea through
Siberia to the Anadyr; normally winters to the oriental region.
 An annual passage vagrant; in autumn regular Fair Isle
and fairly so east Scotland and England. Recorded Wales and
10 times from Ireland, and occasionally in spring.

Rustic Bunting   B419
Emberiza rustica Pallas 1776
TI p. 130 and pl. 18 **top left** (♂)
as rustic bunting, *Emberiza rustica*, Pallas

Palearctic; breeds from north Sweden and Finland and east
Estonia through middle and upper Siberian river systems to
Anadyr and Kamchatka; migrates mainly to Japan and China.
 An annual vagrant, twice as often in autumn as in spring,
principally to Fair Isle and other North Isles, also down east
coast to Sussex; 1 record south Ireland; none Wales.

Yellow-breasted Bunting   B414
Emberiza aureola Pallas 1773
TI p. 122 and pl. 18 **upper mid mid** (♂)
as yellow-breasted bunting, *Emberiza aureola*, Pallas

Palearctic; breeds from north Finland (lately colonised)
through Russia-Siberia to Kamchatka, Kuriles, Hokkaido
(Japan), Manchuria and north Korea; migrates to oriental
region.
 Twenty-one records 1905–66; the first Cley, Norfolk 1905
September 21; England (Norfolk) 3; Scotland 16 (Fair Isle 9,
Isle of May 5); Ireland 2 (cos. Donegal, Cork); all July–
October, most September (18).

Reed Bunting   B421
Emberiza schoeniclus (Linnaeus 1758)
TI p. 132 and pl. 18 **upper mid right** (♂)
as reed-bunting, *Emberiza schœniclus*, Linnæus

Palearctic; breeds from Iberian Peninsula, Mediterranean,
Asia Minor, north Persia, Turkestan, highland China and
Hokkaido north to Ireland, Britain, European arctic coast, the
middle systems of Siberian rivers east to the Lena, Amurland
and Kamchatka. Western birds winter south in the palearctic.
 Breeding population of Britain-Ireland order 5; breeds in
every county – in Shetland since 1949; increasing in Scotland
in late decades, and on marine islands; common in most of
Ireland and fairly stable in most of England and Wales.

Lapland Bunting   B422
Calcarius lapponicus (Linnaeus 1758)
TI p. 134 and pl. 18 **lower mid right** (♂)
as lapland bunting, *Calcarius lapponicus* (Linnæus)

Holarctic; breeds beyond tree-line in virtually all the apron
tundras of the mainland north and some north boreal zones
(not Iceland) and in Greenland and polar islands save those
of highest arctic. Winters south to central holarctic.
 A regular autumn passenger (numbers vary; many from
Canada and Greenland) to the east and north-west coasts
including Ireland; a few winter, and pass in spring when
nearly annual Fair Isle. Vagrant inland, in south England
and in Wales.

Snow Bunting   B423
Plectrophenax nivalis (Linnaeus 1758)
TI p. 135 and pl. 18 **bottom right** (summer ♂ and autumn)
as snow-bunting, *Plectrophenax nivalis*, Linnæus

The passerine king of the arctic: a circumpolar holarctic bird
breeding to the northern land limits on all mainland apron
tundras, and on *every* arctic archipelago, and on boreal islands
and highlands of Kodiak, Bering Sea, Aleutians, Komandor-
skis, Kamchatka, Shelekhova Gulf (Sea of Okhotsk), Iceland,
Faeroe (regular breeding no longer certain), Scotland,
Norway and Lapland. Winters south to central holarctic,
largely on plateaus, coastal plains and estuaries.
 Breeding population of Britain order 1; from D. Nethersole-
Thompson's deep analysis to 1965 must breed annually in
Scotland, with a headquarters in the Cairngorms (Inverness,
Banff and Aberdeen cos.); has bred irregularly or sporadically
in Perth co., Ross, Sutherland and St Kilda (Outer Hebrides),
probably (unconfirmed) in Shetland, and has been seen in
summer on the mountains of Argyll. Otherwise a winter
visitor to coastal and hilly areas in England, Wales, Scotland
and Ireland, some elements being of the Iceland race.

Rustic Bunting.   Little Bunting.   Yellow Bunting or Yellow Hammer.
      Cirl Bunting. Yellow-breasted Bunting. Reed Bunting.   Lapland Bunting.
   Siberian Meadow-Bunting. Meadow-Bunting.   Snow-Bunting.
         O-tolan.   (Summer & Autumn)

Plate 78 (Thorburn's plate 19)

Family STURNIDAE, starlings

Rosy Starling B390
Sturnus roseus (Linnaeus 1758)
TI p. 137 and pl. 19 **top right** (adult and young)
as rose-coloured starling, *Pastor roseus* (Linnæus)

A Turkestanian steppe bird with a very fluctuating southern palearctic range (follows locust swarms), breeding in Asia from Asia Minor, Lebanon, Syria and the Caucasus east to Persia and Afghanistan and north through the Turkestanian and Kirghiz steppes of Russia to a varying distance in the upper Ob system, sometimes reaching the upper Yenisei; in Europe breeds in the plains of the middle and lower Ural River and lower Volga into the middle and lower Don, the Crimea and the southern Ukraine, extending west to Rumania and Bulgaria, often to Hungary, sometimes to Dalmatian Jugoslavia. Has irruption years with marked westerly movement in some of which huge populations have nested in Hungary, and in one of which (1875) a sporadic breeding of 6000–7000 pairs was recorded in holes in the ramparts of a castle in north Italy.

Marked invasions in the present century bringing unusual numbers to Britain-Ireland were in 1908, 1924–26, 1932–34, 1937 and 1945, since when vagrants have been few though annual. Birds have reached North Isles (including St Kilda) and western Ireland but main concentration of records is in eastern Scotland and eastern and southern England; few are reported in Wales. Most records are June–August.

Starling B389
Sturnus vulgaris Linnaeus 1758
TI p. 136 and pl. 19 **top left** (winter and summer)
as starling, *Sturnus vulgaris*, Linnæus

Presently almost cosmopolitan, and one of the world's most abundant land birds, by virtue of successful introduction into the nearctic, ethiopian and australasian regions, the starling was until the nineteenth century a western palearctic breeding bird of European or steppe origin; and in its natural range breeds from the Azores, south-central France, Italy (not extreme south-east), Jugoslavia, northern Greece, Asia Minor, northern Iraq, western and northern Persia, northern Afghanistan, Kashmir and the western Himalayas, east to western Chinese Turkestan, western Mongolia, Lake Baikal and the upper Yenisei, north to Iceland (since 1935), Faeroe, northern Fenno-Scandia, and in Russia the White Sea, the North Dvina and Volga systems, the central Urals and the upper Ob system. Has an outpost race in Sind at the mouth of the Indus in West Pakistan. Is absent from northern Russian Turkestan and the southern Kirghiz steppes; and has bred sporadically in Corsica, Bear Island and Spitsbergen. Some European birds migrate to reach North Africa.

Breeding population of Britain-Ireland order 7; breeds in every county. From fossil evidence was a member of the British-Irish fauna in Upper Pleistocene Ice Age times; but in historical times has had interesting vicissitudes. In the eighteenth century may have been as widely distributed as at present, but decreased markedly in the early nineteenth century to the extent that it became almost extinct in north England, Scotland and Ireland, though populations survived in Caithness and in the North Isles (those of the Outer Hebrides and Shetland belong to a recognisable race). Between 1830 and 1860 the British population recovered, recolonising north England and Scotland and increasing in the rest of England and Wales; and since 1850 Ireland was also progressively recolonised. The reasons for the crash and recovery are unknown. Increases and spreads have continued in Ireland in the last two decades, and were still noticeable in parts of Scotland in the early present century. In England the breeding population is now high and probably rather stable, but the density of breeding birds remains relatively very low in western Wales. The British winter population is possibly nearly doubled (very few of our birds emigrate to the Continent) by immigrant birds mainly from the Baltic countries, and the Irish winter population much increased by birds mainly from Scandinavia and northern Britain.

Family CORVIDAE, crows

A modern systematic order is B286 (pl. 78), 284 (pl. 79), 285, 287 (pl. 78), 283 (pl. 79), 282, 280, 281 (pl. 80), 279 (pl. 79).

Jay B286
Garrulus glandarius (Linnaeus 1758)
TI p. 140 and pl. 19 **bottom left**
as jay, *Garrulus glandarius* (Linnæus)

Palearctic and oriental; breeds in west from Morocco-Tunisia, Mediterranean, Palestine, Iraq and west Persia to Ireland, Britain, south Norway and north-central Sweden, Finland and Russia, whence through upper systems of Siberian rivers to Amurland and Sakhalin and through Japan, Manchuria and Korea to China, Taiwan, Himalayas, Assam, north Burma and Indochina. Resident; but northern birds may invade west Europe.

Breeding population of Britain-Ireland order 5; by 1900 regarded as vermin and source of plumage, and was local in Wales and most of England, scarce in Scotland and north England, and confined to a limited area of south-east Ireland. Recovered in Ireland since 1900 and by 1966, still increasing, bred in all but 4 counties. British recovery began *c* 1920; now breeds in every county of England and Wales though not in Isle of Man, and in Scotland not on principal islands but north to Argyll, Perth co., Angus and perhaps Kincardine, though still absent from some Lowland counties.

Nutcracker B285
Nucifraga caryocatactes (Linnaeus 1758)
TI p. 139 and pl. 19 **mid left**
as nutcracker, *Nucifraga caryocatactes* (Linnæus)

Palearctic; breeds fairly continuously in boreal conifer forests from south Fenno-Scandia and the Baltic States of Russia through Siberia to Kamchatka, the Kuriles, Japan, north Korea; also in Taiwan, central Asian highlands, and highland central Europe from Balkans. Carpathians and Alps to Czechoslovakia and south Germany. Northern birds migrate irregularly, sometimes irrupting into west Europe.

A rare vagrant to Britain, not recorded in Ireland; most frequent in south-east England in autumn and December; has been recorded a very few times in Scotland and Wales.

Chough B287
Pyrrhocorax pyrrhocorax (Linnaeus 1758)
TI p. 138 and pl. 19 **bottom right**
as chough, *Pyrrhocorax graculus* (Linnæus)

Palearctic; breeds on inland and coastal cliffs; most continuous range is from Lebanon, east Asia Minor and Caucasus through the central Asian highlands to Mongolia and north China; western range is highly fragmented, with a distant ethiopian outpost in the Simen Mountains of Ethiopia, headquarters in highland Portugal and Spain and coastal Ireland, and isolated groups in Crete, Greece, Jugoslavia, Italy, Sardinia, Switzerland, France and Ouessant in Brittany; last bred Channel Islands *c* 1929. Resident.

Breeding population of Britain-Ireland (a good race) order 3; in 1963 (Richard Rolfe) about 98 breeding pairs Wales, 11 Scotland, 20 Isle of Man, 600 Ireland. In England approximate last breeding dates were Sussex 1830, Kent 1849, Somerset and Cumberland 1860, Yorkshire 1861, Isle of Wight 1882, Dorset 1887, Devon 1910 – and Cornwall 1952 where 2 birds occupied a cave to 1967 when 1 killed. In Wales formerly bred 9 counties; now 7, but recolonising inland sites. Last bred Lowlands in Berwick co. *c* 1866, Ayr co. 1929. In Highlands last bred Sutherland 1848, Arran before 1863, Iona 1890, Skye 1904, previously bred 3 or more eastern counties also, survives only in Argyll where headquarters 1963 Islay. In Ireland stable; bred 1963 in all 12 counties with full Atlantic coasts from Waterford to Antrim, except Derry; has formerly bred in cos. Dublin, Wicklow and Wexford. In Britain the collapse may be partly due to human persecution and collecting, but Rolfe shows it also fits the hard winter period 1820–80, which was worse there than in Atlantic Ireland.

Pl. 19.

Starling. (Summer & winter)   Rose-coloured Starling.
Nutcracker.   (adult & young)
    Jay.   Chough.

A. Thorburn
1913

Plate 79 (Thorburn's plate 20)

Family CORVIDAE, crows (*continued*)

Magpie   B284
Pica pica (Linnaeus 1758)
TI p. 141 and pl. 20 (frontispiece) **top left**
as *Pica rustica* (Scopoli)

An holarctic and oriental bird breeding in the Old World
from Morocco, Algeria, Tunisia, the European Mediterranean
shore, Sicily, Asia Minor, Cyprus, Iraq, Persia, Afghanistan,
West Pakistan, Chinese Turkestan, Mongolia, highland west
China (not the Gobi Desert, the main Tibetan plateau, or
the western and central Himalayas), Assam, north Burma and
Laos, central Viet Nam, Hainan, Taiwan and south China,
north to Ireland, Britain, northern Fenno-Scandia, and in
Russia Kola and the systems of the North Dvina, upper
Pechora, middle and upper Ob, upper Yenisei, Lake Baikal
and the Amur, with outposts in the Asir Mountains of south-
west Arabia (virtually in the ethiopian region), Kyushu in
Japan (introduced 1598), and in Kamchatka-Anadyr and the
neighbouring Gizhiga coast of the Sea of Okhotsk. In the
nearctic breeds from the Alaska Peninsula and coastal central
Alaska through south-west Yukon, British Columbia, Alberta,
southern Saskatchewan and south-western Manitoba south to
central California, Nevada, Kansas, Nebraska and South
Dakota. Resident though not entirely sedentary.

Breeding population of Britain-Ireland order 5 or low order
6; may breed in every county save Bute, Inner Hebrides,
Ross and Sutherland where bred in nineteenth century
(Sutherland to 1923, Ross possibly still but unproved) and
Outer Hebrides, Orkney, and Shetland (where fossil found of
Viking times *c* A.D. 800–900). Through human persecution
with the advent of the shotgun suffered a marked decrease in
south and east England and in Scotland (where nearly exterminated) in the nineteenth century. Began to recover in many
parts of England and Scotland after the relaxation of keeping
in First World War, though not in eastern England until after
Second World War, where has decreased again in last decade.
Is now common throughout England and Wales but still local
and scarce in most parts of Scotland, e.g. Argyll where returned in very small numbers in 1960's. In Ireland, where
known as a fossil from several horizons of the Upper Pleistocene Ice Age period, was (for reasons unknown) extinct in
early historical times; birds colonised co. Wexford *c* 1676 and
had spread into every county a long time ago.

Jackdaw   B283
Corvus monedula Linnaeus 1758
TI p. 142 and pl. 20 (frontispiece) **top right** (2 birds)
as jackdaw, *Corvus monedula*, Linnæus

A western palearctic species breeding in Morocco, Algeria,
Sardinia, Sicily, Malta, Crete and Cyprus, and from the
Iberian Peninsula, the European Mediterranean shore, Asia
Minor, Syria, northern Iraq, Persia and Afghanistan, Kash-
mir and the Karakorum north to Ireland, Britain, south

Norway, Sweden and Finland, and in Russia Lake Onega, the
North Dvina and Volga systems, the central Urals, the upper
Ob; east just beyond the upper Yenisei near Abakan and just
into western Mongolia and Chinese Turkestan. Northern
populations are migratory within the palearctic.

Breeding population of Britain-Ireland order 6 or low 7;
breeds in every county, having been increasing in Scotland
for some time, where colonised the Outer Hebrides in 1895,
Shetland in 1943. Is increasing also in Ireland. The causes of
increase are unknown, though doubtless human persecution
has been relaxed in many areas in last decades.

Raven   B279
Corvus corax Linnaeus 1758
TI p. 143 and pl. 20 (frontispiece) **bottom** (ptarmigan prey)
as *Corvus corax*, Linnæus

A very widely distributed bird of the holarctic region extending into the ethiopian and neotropical regions, thus from the
tropics to the high arctic. In the Old World breeds from the
Cape Verdes, Canaries, the south border of the Sahara east to
the Sudan, eastern Ethiopia, Somaliland and Kenya, Socotra,
Arabia, Persia, West Pakistan, north-west India, the Himalayas, highland west China, the Amur-Ussuri system, north
Sakhalin, the northern Kuriles, Kamchatka and the Komandorski Islands, north to Iceland, Faeroe, and the Eurasian
arctic shore (except the Yamal and Taimyr Peninsulas)
and Wrangel Island; within this range is absent only from
much of the central Asian plateau and from most of Europe
east of Brittany, north of the Alps, west of the Vistula and
south of Sweden. In the New World breeds in Alaska and all
its islands, through virtually the whole of Canada except for
the true prairie, in central and southern Greenland on both
coasts, and south through the western United States and
México to Nicaragua, and into the eastern United States to
Minnesota, northern Michigan and Maine, also breeding in
the southern Appalachians as far as Georgia. Generally
resident throughout its range.

Breeding population of Britain-Ireland order 4; doubtless
bred in every county in early historical times but by the nineteenth century had been cleared, probably by human
persecution and interference and the absence of carrion, from
most of England save the West Country and the north; last
south and east survivors seem to have bred in Essex to 1890,
Sussex to 1895 (1 pair bred in 1938–45), Isle of Wight to 1956
(possibly 1960). Apart from sporadic breedings, especially in
Welsh border counties, is now confined to English counties
from Somerset-Dorset west, and from Lancashire-Yorkshire
north: occupation is tenuous in Lancashire and Durham and
in Yorkshire where extinct since 1860, a few pairs recolonised
since 1945. In Wales breeds in every county and in Ireland in
virtually every coastal county and a few inland, and in both
countries has been increasing in present century. In Scotland
breeds in every county except those of the Forth and the
coastal east Highlands save Banff, and appears to be stable in
the west and north Highlands and the major islands.

Pl. 20.

Magpie. Raven. Jackdaw.

Plate 80 (Thorburn's plate 21)

Family CORVIDAE, crows (*continued*)

Rook   B282
Corvus frugilegus Linnaeus 1758
T2 p. 3 and pl. 21 **top**
as rook, *Corvus frugilegus*, Linnæus

A palearctic bird breeding in Asia from north-eastern Asia Minor, the Caucasus, northern Iraq, western and northern Persia, the Russian steppes in the east Caspian, Aral and Balkhash systems, and the upper Ob east through the upper Yenisei and Lena systems and Lake Baikal to the Amur-Ussuri and south through Manchuria to north-east China and the Yangtze. In Europe has outpost populations in north-western Spain and north Italy but otherwise breeds from the Loire, Rhine and Danube systems north to Ireland, Britain, the Baltic and the North Dvina and upper Volga in Russia, with outposts in south-east Norway, south Sweden and western Finland. The northerly European birds migrate south within the palearctic.

Breeding population of Britain-Ireland order 7; about one and a half million occupied nests in Britain (not Ireland) estimated in the middle 1940's, when population high with abnormally intensive cereal cultivation; has decreased since with the partial reversion to prewar farming systems. Breeds in every county after the recolonisation of the North Isles since the recovery of their plantations – in Orkney since 1846, the Outer Hebrides since 1895 and Shetland since 1952.

Crow   B280 and B281
Corvus corone Linnaeus 1758

Carrion crow, *Corvus corone corone*
T2 p. 1 and pl. 21 **bottom left**
as carrion crow, *Corvus corone*, Linnæus

Hooded crow, *Corvus corone cornix*, Linnaeus 1758
T2 p. 2 and pl. 21 **bottom right**
as hooded crow, *Corvus cornix*, Linnæus

Though quite different-looking in the field, carrion crows and hoodies are only racially distinct and hybridise over a wide zone where their ranges meet in Europe and Britain. The species is widely distributed in the palearctic, breeding from the Iberian Peninsula, the Mediterranean and its principal islands, the Nile valley in Egypt south to about Aswan, Cyprus, Palestine, Asia Minor, Iraq, western and northern Persia, northern Afghanistan and West Pakistan, Kashmir, western Tibet, Chinese Turkestan, highland west China, Inner Mongolia, Manchuria, Korea and Japan; east to the Kuriles, Kamchatka and Anadyrland; north to Ireland, Britain, Faeroe, northernmost Fenno-Scandia, south Kola and the White Sea, and all but the lowest parts of the systems of the northward-flowing Siberian rivers.

Breeding population of Britain-Ireland order 6; one race or the other breeds in every county, hoodies normally in Ireland and most of Scotland, carrion crows in England, Wales and the east Lowlands; normal zone of overlap and hybridisation is between Ayr co. and east Sutherland, and is moving north. During the present century the hoodie has markedly decreased in the Lowlands and the southern Highlands with human persecution, and markedly decreased in Ireland until fairly lately when it has noticeably increased and spread west in co. Donegal. It is stable, or probably so, in the western and northern Highlands and the isles. In England and to a lesser extent Wales, the carrion crow has decreased for the same reasons except perhaps in the neighbourhood of towns, suburbs and urban parks where it has increased, and has stabilised or even begun to increase again lately in most country districts except East Anglia. In the Lowlands and south-east Highlands has been increasing and penetrating slowly north at the expense of the hoodie; the zone of hybridisation has remained fairly narrow.

Tribe EMBERIZINI, buntings (*continued text to pl. 76*)

Black-headed Bunting   B412
Emberiza melanocephala Scopoli 1769
T1 p. 121 and pl. 17 **mid left** (♂)
as black-headed bunting, *Emberiza melanocephala*, Scopoli

A palearctic species breeding in Europe on the Italian and Jugoslavian coasts of the Adriatic to Greece, Bulgaria and eastern Rumania in the Dobruja; in Crete, Rhodes and Cyprus, and from Asia Minor and Palestine east to north Iraq and central Caspian-Persia and north through the Caucasus to the lower Don system and lowest reaches of the Volga. Normally migrates into the oriental region in India, but some elements wander west in Europe.

Fifteen records (though a couple might possibly be escapes from captivity) 1868–1965; the first a female near Brighton, Sussex 1868 November *c* 3; England 4; Wales 3; Scotland 7; Ireland 1; 6 in May, rest June–November.

Red-headed Bunting   B413
Emberiza bruniceps Brandt 1841
Not illustrated

Despite the marked difference in the coloration of the male, this should probably be treated as a race of the black-headed bunting, with which its distribution marches, overlapping only in eastern Caspian-Persia where the two hybridise and intermediate types are found in the population. A palearctic Turkestanian bird breeding from east of the Volga (where also close to the black-headed bunting's range) through the lower Ural river system east in the Kirghiz steppes to the Altai foot-hills, and south through the Balkhash and Aral systems, some

distance into Chinese Turkestan between the Tian Shan and the Pamirs, and to eastern Afghanistan and neighbouring parts of West Pakistan (perhaps also Kashmir) and to north-east Persia. Normally migrates into the oriental region in India; some straggle west to Europe.

Perhaps only one acceptable record: an adult male North Ronaldshay, Orkney 1931 June 19. Since then much more than a score of encounters in the 1950's and 1960's, particularly 1966 July–August when recorded in over 12 counties from Anglesey to Shetland; all these coincide with a period of quite heavy importation of the species (or race) as a cage bird, especially males – and males make up the bulk of the records.

Pine Bunting   B411
Emberiza leucocephala S. G. Gmelin 1771
T1 p. 123 and pl. 17 **upper mid mid** (♂ summer)
T4 p. 104 and pl. 80B **bottom left** (♂ winter, from first British specimen), see pl. 81
as pine-bunting, *Emberiza leucocephala*, S. G. Gmelin

Despite a marked difference in coloration, this should probably be treated as a race of the yellowhammer (pl. 77) which it replaces to the east; the two meet in the Ob and Yenisei systems of western Siberia where they freely hybridise and produce intermediate types. A palearctic species breeding from Perm in eastern Russian Europe east across the Urals through the middle and upper systems of the Ob, Yenisei and Lena to the upper Kolyma, Sea of Okhotsk, lower Amur and Sakhalin, and south perhaps to the Tian Shan; has an outpost race in the Koko-Nor area of highland west China (Tsinghai-Kansu). Normally winters into the northern oriental region; some straggle west to Europe.

Two records: male Fair Isle, Shetland 1911 October 30; male seen Papa Westray, Orkney 1943 October 15.

Pl. 21.

Carrion Crow.   Rook.   Hooded Crow.

Plate 81 (Thorburn's plate 80B)

Lesser Yellowlegs B164
Tringa flavipes (J. F. Gmelin 1789)
T4 p. 46 and fig. 80B **bottom right**
as yellowshank, *Totanus flavipes* (J. F. Gmelin)

A nearctic species with a mainly boreal distribution; breeds in the open forest and muskeg of North America from central Alaska through Yukon, western Mackenzie and south-westernmost Keewatin to the northern half of provincial Canada from British Columbia to Ontario, just entering Québec at Moar Bay in James Bay. Winters normally from the south-eastern United States and México south to Argentina and Chile, and in the West Indies.

An annual vagrant to England, Wales, Scotland and Ireland, mainly in the autumn.

Pied Wheatear B314
Oenanthe pleschanka (Lepeckin 1770)
See pl. 66. A female (**mid**); the first British specimen

Moustached Warbler B331
Lusciniola melanopogon (Temminck 1823)
T4 p. 100 and pl. 80B **mid left**
as moustached warbler, *Lusciniola melanogopogon* (Temminck)

A south-western palearctic bird possibly of Turkestanian steppe origin; the Asian race breeds in the Caucasus and the lower Volga and Ural river systems and the other systems of the Caspian Sea, the Aral Sea systems and to Lake Balkhash, and through Russian Turkestan to central Persia, perhaps Afghanistan and to Iraq, with an outpost at Lake Huleh in Palestine; has been seen in the breeding season at Hofuf in eastern Saudi Arabia. The western race breeds in Africa near Cape Bon in Tunisia, in Spain in the Coto Donaña, near Valencia, in the Ebro delta and on Majorca, in the Camargue of southern France, in Sicily and Italy, and in the Danube-Sava systems of eastern Austria, Hungary, Jugoslavia, Rumania and perhaps Bulgaria; and normally winters in the eastern Mediterranean.

Five records: pair reared 3 young Cambridge sewage farm, Cambridgeshire, seen 1946 August 3–20 (a sensational sporadic record); 2 seen Eling Great Marsh near Totton, Hampshire 1951 August 13; 1 seen Cliffe, Kent 1952 April 14; 1 seen Lundy, Devon 1959 May 2; 1 trapped Wendover, Buckinghamshire 1965 July 31.

Olivaceous Warbler B341
Hippolais pallida (Hemprich and Ehrenberg 1833)
T4 p. 100 and pl. 80B **top left**
as olivaceous warbler, *Hypolais pallida* (Hempr. and Ehr.)

A western palearctic and northern ethiopian species possibly of Mediterranean origin; breeds in Asia from Asia Minor, Caucasus, Iraq, Persia and northern Afghanistan and east of the Caspian and the Aral Seas in Russian Turkestan to the western Tian Shan; in Africa in Morocco, Algeria, Tunisia, lower Egypt and in several Saharan oases south to Lake Chad in the ethiopian region; in Europe in eastern and southern Spain, and from south Hungary to Jugoslavia, southern and eastern Bulgaria, south-easternmost Rumania, Turkey-in-Europe and Greece, including some Aegean Islands and Crete. Northern limit fluctuates in Balkan Peninsula. Winters to eastern tropical Africa, the race of eastern Europe vagrant to western Europe.

Seven records 1951–66: first 1 trapped Skokholm, Pembroke co. 1951 September 23–October 3; England 5; Wales 1; Ireland 1; all August 16–October 4.

[Rüppell's Warbler B349
Sylvia ruppelli Temminck 1823
T4 p. 99 and pl. 80B **mid top** (♀ ♂)
as Rüppell's warbler, *Sylvia rüppelli*, Temminck

A rare palearctic bird with a purely eastern Mediterranean breeding distribution in Greece (mainly the Aegean Islands and Crete), southern Asia Minor and the Levant; has been reported breeding sporadically outside this range; may be more or less resident but not sedentary. Now rejected from the British-Irish List, though figured by Thorburn in all good faith. Two males, said to have been obtained at Baldslow, Sussex 1914 May 5 are 'Hastings Rarities'.]

Pine Bunting B411
Emberiza leucocephala S. G. Gmelin 1771
See pl. 76. A winter male, from the first British specimen (**bottom left**)

Crossbill B404
Loxia curvirostra Linnaeus 1758
See pl. 75. The form here (**top right,** ♀ and subadult ♂) is the Scottish crossbill, *Loxia curvirostra scotica* Hartert 1904

PL. 80.

Olivaceous Warbler.   Rüppell's Warbler.
Moustached Warbler.   Pied Wheatear.
Pine Bunting   Yellowshank.   Scottish Crossbill.

Plate 82 (Thorburn's plate 80A)

Wren   B299
Troglodytes troglodytes (Linnaeus 1758)
See pl. 63. The form here (**bottom right**) is the St Kilda wren, *Troglodytes troglodytes hirtensis* Seebohm 1884

Song Thrush   B303
Turdus philomelos C. L. Brehm 1831
See pl. 64. The form here (**bottom left**) is the Hebridean song thrush, *Turdus philomelos hebridensis* Clarke 1913

Marsh Tit   B292
Parus palustris Linnaeus 1758
See pl. 62 (here **top left**)

Willow Tit   B293
Parus montanus Conrad von Baldenstein 1827
British willow tit, *Parus montanus kleinschmidti* Hellmayr 1900
T4 p. 102 and pl. 80A **top right**
as willow-titmouse, *Parus kleinschmidti*, Hellmyr

A palearctic bird of the temperate and boreal zones formerly thought to be of the same species as the North American black-capped chickadee but now regarded as fully separate. Has a fairly wide temperate and boreal range from Anadyr and Kamchatka, the Sea of Okhotsk, Sakhalin and Japan, west into Europe in the river systems of the Amur-Ussuri and the upper systems of the Siberian rivers from the Lena westwards. A group of races from Manchuria through highland west China to Russian Turkestan in the Tian Shan Mountains is regarded by some authorities as of the same species. In Europe breeds from the Rhône valley and north-eastern France, the Alps and the Danubian system (not in the Black Sea lowlands) north to Britain, northern Norway, Lapland, the White Sea and the north-central Urals (in Denmark only in south Jutland). Resident but not sedentary; northern elements wander or partially migrate.

Breeding population of Britain order 4; not recorded from Ireland and does not breed in the Isle of Man. Status is still uncertain owing to the difficulty of distinguishing from marsh tit. Doubtless breeds in virtually every county of England and Wales, though has not yet been formally proved to do so in some (e.g. Isle of Wight where present in breeding season 1961–62, Rutland); first proved breeding Cornwall 1948. Staffordshire and Cheshire may still be the only counties where it is widespread, and it is decidedly local in many peripheral counties such as those of the West Country, Wales (except perhaps Pembroke co.) and eastern England. In Scotland may no longer breed all Lowland counties, but has a headquarters in the Clyde valley, and may still extend very locally but regularly into Stirling, Perth and Fife cos.; nine-

teenth-century breeding records are of the period when marsh and willow tits were not separated, but assuming they were of the latter extended (a very few) to Aberdeen co.; in the present century breeding has been proved (some cases obviously sporadic) in Angus, Inverness and Moray cos. and in Easter Ross (1919) and Wester Ross (1919, 1942). The few birds that have been recorded in Argyll were probably vagrants, and there is no suspicion of breeding in any of the Scottish isles.

Coal Tit
Parus ater Linnaeus 1758
See pl. 62. The form here (**mid right**) is the Irish coal tit, *Parus ater hibernicus* Ogilvie-Grant 1910

Redpoll   B397
Acanthis flammea Linnaeus 1758
See pl. 75. The form here (**mid left**) called greater redpoll is, in fact, the Greenland redpoll, *Acanthis flammea rostrata* (Coues 1862)

Arctic Redpoll   B398
Acanthis hornemanni (Holbøll 1843)
T4 p. 103 and pl. 80A **mid**
as Greenland redpoll, *Linota hornemanni*, Holböll; not, in fact, the Greenland redpoll (above)

An holarctic bird of the tundra zone breeding round the Polar Basin from Lapland and the north Scandinavian mountains along the whole Russian tundra apron to Anadyrland and on south Novaya Zemlya (and reportedly to northern Kamchatka); in Alaska on the coastal apron and in neighbouring mountains south to Hooper Bay; in Canada from the coastal tundras of Yukon and Mackenzie east through north-east Mackenzie and Keewatin to the Nelson River in Manitoba, with an outpost in Ungava Bay in northern Québec, and on Southampton, north-east Baffin, Devon, Ellesmere and perhaps Prince Patrick, and Victoria Islands (on the last at Cambridge Bay); also in northern west and northern east Greenland. Some authorities hold this bird to be conspecific with the (common) redpoll, with which it may hybridise in Lapland, and the Iceland race, classed as a common redpoll, may be of hybrid origin. But in most of the overlapping range round the Polar Basin and particularly in North America and Greenland the two behave as different species.

A very rare autumn and winter vagrant (not many more than twenty records), the Greenland race and the race found in Lapland about equally divided; about half Fair Isle, rest Unst in Shetland, Mull (1; only certain record in west Britain), co. Durham, Yorkshire and Norfolk; 1 in April, all rest September–January, about half October.

Pl. 80.^A

Marsh. Titmouse.

Greenland Redpoll.   Willow. Titmouse.

Greater Redpoll.   Irish Coal-Titmouse.

Hebridean Song-Thrush.   St. Kilda Wren.

Order PASSERIFORMES

A systematic order of the present families of the British-Irish List, with some junior taxa. Those marked with an asterisk* are American taxa whose British-Irish records are described in the list that follows.

A *taxon* is simply a group of related organisms, e.g. a family or tribe. The members of the American taxa marked * were not accepted to the British-Irish List in Thorburn's time, but have been since, now that the possibilities of the wind-borne crossing by small passerines of the Atlantic Ocean are proved.

C. J. O. Harrison (1967 March) has just demonstrated that the habit of 'double-scratching' is confined to the group of American Emberizinae known as the American sparrows, and not found in the Old World buntings, or in the snow buntings and longspurs that also extend to the New World. On this characteristic there is some practical justification for making the groups different tribes of the Emberizinae – Emberizini for the Old World buntings based on the oldest genus, *Emberiza* Linnaeus 1758, *Systema Naturae*, ed. 10, p. 176; and Pipilonini for the American sparrows, based on the towhee genus, *Pipilo* Vieillot 1816 April, *Analyse*, p. 32. This, and *Arremon* of the same publication, p. 32 5 lines above, are the oldest names available, and I have chosen *Pipilo*.

Fairly recent authorities have included the bearded tit, which is certainly not a typical tit, in a 'rag-bag' Paridae group of similar but unrelated sets of species. The bearded tit is placed here with the parrotbills, a subfamily Panurinae of the Muscicapidae. Charles Vaurie, writer of the standard work on palearctic birds, would separate the long-tailed tits as a full family Aegithalidae, close to the bearded tit's group the Panurinae (or Panuridae if it is made a full family); the typical tits as a differently constituted family Paridae with the nuthatches and wallcreeper; and the penduline tits and their allies, close to the tropical flowerpecker family Dicaeidae, as a full family Remizidae. Here I hold the last three groups, for convenience, as subfamilies of the Paridae, in the sequence Aegithalinae, Remizinae and Parinae, and keep the nuthatches and wallcreeper as the full family Sittidae.

Passerines of peculiarly American groups
Family MIMIDAE, thrashers and mockers

Brown Thrasher
Toxostoma rufum (Linnaeus 1758)

Nearctic; breeds from southern provincial Canada (from Alberta to Québec) and from Maine south to eastern Colorado, Texas, the Gulf of México and Florida. Northern elements winter south within the nearctic.

One record: 1 Durlston Head near Swanage, Dorset 1966 November 18 onwards.

Family EMBERIZIDAE
Subfamily EMBERIZINAE
Tribe PIPILONINI, American sparrows

Rufous-sided Towhee
Pipilo erythrophthalmus (Linnaeus 1758)

Nearctic and neotropical; breeds from southernmost Canada and north-central New England south to Guatemala. Northern elements are normally migratory within the nearctic.

One record: 1 Lundy, Devon 1966 June 7.

Slate-coloured Junco
Junco hyemalis (Linnaeus 1758)

Nearctic; breeds from the tree-line in Alaska and Canada south to north-east British Columbia, central Alberta and Saskatchewan, Manitoba, Minnesota, Wisconsin, Michigan, Ohio, Pennsylvania, New York and Connecticut, and south in the Appalachians to Georgia. Migrates to winter virtually within the nearctic as far as north México.

One record: 1 shot Loop Head Lighthouse, co. Clare 1905 May 30.

White-throated Sparrow
Zonotrichia albicollis (J. F. Gmelin 1789)

Nearctic; breeds from the middle Mackenzie system and south-eastern Yukon, Manitoba, Ontario, north-central Québec and southern Newfoundland Labrador south to central British Columbia, Alberta, Saskatchewan, Minnesota, Michigan, Ohio, West Virginia, New York and Massachusetts. Migrates to winter virtually within the nearctic as far as north México.

Three records: male shot Eilean Mòr of Flannan Isles, Outer Hebrides 1909 May 18; 1 Needs Oar Point, near Beaulieu, Hampshire 1961 May 19; 1 trapped Walney, Lancashire 1965 June 17.

Fox Sparrow
Passerella iliaca (Merrem 1786)

Nearctic; breeds from northern Alaska, Yukon and the Mackenzie system, Manitoba, Ontario, northern Québec and northern Newfoundland Labrador south to Washington, southern California in the western United States mountains, Nevada, Utah, Colorado, the central parts of Saskatchewan, Manitoba, Ontario and Québec, Québec Labrador, Newfoundland, islands in the Gulf of St Lawrence and Nova Scotia. Migrates to winter as far as the México border.

One record: 1 trapped Copeland Islands, co. Down 1961.

Song Sparrow
Passerella melodia (Wilson 1810)

Nearctic; breeds from the Aleutian Islands, southern Alaska, south-central Yukon and Mackenzie, western provincial Canada, southern Québec and western Newfoundland south to western México, New Mexico, Arkansas, Tennessee, Georgia and South Carolina. Migrates to winter virtually in the nearctic as far as north México.

Two records: male trapped Fair Isle, Shetland 1959 April 27–May 10; 1 trapped, Spurn, Yorkshire 1964 May 18.

Subfamily CARDINALINAE, cardinals, etc.

Rose-breasted Grosbeak
Pheucticus ludovicianus (Linnaeus 1766)

Nearctic; breeds from south-west Mackenzie, north-east British Columbia, northern Alberta, central Saskatchewan, southern Manitoba, Ontario and Québec, and the maritime provinces of Canada south to North Dakota, Kansas, Missouri, Tennessee, Georgia, North Carolina and New Jersey. Winters south to northern South America.
Three records: adult male seen Shane's Castle, co. Antrim 1957 November 24; first winter male, Cape Clear Island, co. Cork 1962 October 7; 1 St Agnes, Scilly 1966 October 6–11.

Subfamily TANAGRINAE, tanagers

Summer Tanager
Piranga rubra (Linnaeus 1758)

Nearctic; breeds from California, New Mexico, Nebraska, Iowa, Ohio, Maryland and Delaware south to northern México and Florida. Winters to western South America as far south as Bolivia.
One record: immature male trapped Bardsey, Caernarvon co. 1957 September 11–25.

Family PARULIDAE, wood warblers

Black-and-White Warbler
Mniotilta varia (Linnaeus 1766)

Nearctic; breeds from the middle Mackenzie system, east-central British Columbia, northern Alberta, central Saskatchewan and southern Manitoba, Ontario and Québec – and Newfoundland – south to Montana, Texas, Louisiana, Alabama, Georgia and North Carolina. Winters south to northern South America.
One record: 1 found dead near Scalloway, Shetland 1936 October mid.

Parula Warbler
Parula americana (Linnaeus 1758)

Nearctic; breeds from south-easternmost Manitoba, southern Ontario and Québec, and the maritime provinces of Canada south to the Gulf Coast of the United States from Texas to Florida. Winters to south to Nicaragua and the West Indies.
One record: 1 Tresco, Scilly 1966 October 16–17.

Yellow Warbler
Dendroica petechia (Linnaeus 1766)

Nearctic and neotropical; breeds from about the tree-line (though not far into the spruce barrens of Ungava and Newfoundland Labrador) in north-central Alaska and Canada south to central Peru. Northern elements winter south to Peru and Brazil.
One record: 1 trapped Bardsey, Caernarvon co. 1964 August 29–30.

Myrtle Warbler
Dendroica coronata (Linnaeus 1766)

Nearctic; breeds from north-central Alaska, northern Yukon, the Mackenzie system, Manitoba, Ontario, central Québec, northern Newfoundland Labrador and Newfoundland south to central British Columbia and Alberta, southern Saskatchewan and Manitoba, Minnesota, Michigan, New York, Pennsylvania and Massachusetts. Winters south to Panama.
Two records: 1 Newton St Cyres near Exeter, Devon 1955 January–February 10; 1 trapped Lundy, Devon 1960 November 5–14.

Northern Waterthrush
Seiurus noveboracensis (J. F. Gmelin 1789)

Nearctic; breeds from north-central Alaska, northern Yukon, the Mackenzie system, northern Saskatchewan, Manitoba, Ontario and Québec, and Newfoundland, south to Idaho, central Saskatchewan, southern Manitoba, Montana, North Dakota, Wisconsin, Michigan, Ohio, Pennsylvania and Massachusetts. Winters to north-west South America round the equator.
One record: 1 trapped St Agnes, Scilly 1958 September 30–October 12.

Yellowthroat
Geothlypis trichas (Linnaeus 1766)

Nearctic and neotropical; breeds from southern Yukon, British Columbia and Alberta, and from central Saskatchewan, Manitoba, Québec and Newfoundland south to southern México. Winters south to Panama and the West Indies.
One record: immature male trapped Lundy, Devon 1954 November 4–5.

Family VIREONIDAE, vireos

Red-eyed Vireo
Vireo olivaceus (Linnaeus 1766)

Nearctic; breeds from the middle Mackenzie system, central British Columbia, Saskatchewan, southern Manitoba and Ontario, south-west Québec, Anticosti Island and the maritime provinces of Canada south to Oregon, Idaho, Wyoming, Colorado, Oklahoma, Texas and Florida. Winters to north-west South America as far as eastern Peru.
Three records: 1 found dead Tuskar Rock Lighthouse, co. Wexford 1951 October 4; adult and immature St Agnes, Scilly 1962 October 4–17; immature St Agnes 1966 October 6.

Family ICTERIDAE, icterids

Baltimore Oriole
Icterus galbula (Linnaeus 1758)

Nearctic; breeds from south-east Alberta, central Saskatchewan, southern Manitoba, Ontario and Québec, New Brunswick and Nova Scotia south to Oklahoma, Texas, Louisiana, Georgia, South Carolina, Virginia and Delaware. Winters to north-western South America.
Four records: immature trapped Lundy, Devon 1958 October 2–9; adult male Beachy Head, Sussex 1962 October 5–6; immature male trapped Calf of Man 1963 October 10–16; 1 Gwennap Head, Cornwall 1966 October 15.

Bobolink
Dolichonyx oryzivorus (Linnaeus 1758)

Nearctic; breeds from the southern large provinces (not Newfoundland) and the maritime provinces of Canada south to California, Utah, Colorado, Kansas, Illinois, Ohio, West Virginia, Pennsylvania and New Jersey. Winters to northern Argentina.
One record: 1 trapped St Agnes, Scilly 1962 September 19–20.

Index

176

Index

Index

Index

Index

Index

Reference to Vice-Counties

England and Wales

Peninsula
1 West Cornwall with Scilly
2 East Cornwall
3 South Devon
4 North Devon
5 South Somerset
6 North Somerset

Channel
7 North Wilts.
8 South Wilts.
9 Dorset
10 Isle of Wight
11 Hants. South
12 Hants. North
13 West Sussex
14 East Sussex

Thames
15 East Kent
16 West Kent
17 Surrey
18 South Essex
19 North Essex
20 Herts.
21 Middlesex
22 Berks.
23 Oxford
24 Bucks.

Anglia
25 East Suffolk
26 West Suffolk
27 East Norfolk
28 West Norfolk
29 Cambridge
30 Bedford and detached part of Hunts.
31 Hunts.
32 Northampton

Severn
33 East Gloucester
34 West Gloucester
35 Monmouth
36 Hereford
37 Worcester
38 Warwick
39 Stafford and Dudley
40 Shropshire

South Wales
41 Glamorgan
42 Brecon
43 Radnor
44 Carmarthen
45 Pembroke
46 Cardigan

North Wales
47 Montgomery
48 Merioneth
49 Caernarvon
50 Denbigh and parts of Flint
51 Flint
52 Anglesey

Trent
53 South Lincoln
54 North Lincoln
55 Leicester with Rutland
56 Nottingham
57 Derby

Mersey
58 Cheshire
59 South Lancashire
60 Mid Lancashire

Humber
61 South-east York
62 North-east York
63 South-west York
64 Mid-west York
65 North-west York

Tyne
66 Durham
67 Northumberland, South
68 Cheviotland or, Northumberland, North

Lakes
69 Westmorland with North Lancashire
70 Cumberland
71 Isle of Man

Scotland

W. Lowlands
72 Dumfries
73 Kirkcudbright
74 Wigtown
75 Ayr
76 Renfrew
77 Lanark and E. Dumbarton

E. Lowlands
78 Peebles
79 Selkirk
80 Roxburgh
81 Berwick
82 East Lothian
83 Midlothian
84 West Lothian

E. Highlands
85 Fife with Kinross
86 Stirling
87 South Perth with Clackmannan, and parts of Stirling
88 Mid Perth
89 North Perth
90 Angus or Forfar
91 Kincardine
92 South Aberdeen
93 North Aberdeen
94 Banff
95 Moray or Elgin
96 Easterness (East Inverness with Nairn)

W. Highlands
97 Westerness (West Inverness with North Argyll)
98 Argyll (Main)
99 Dumbarton (West)
100 Clyde Isles
101 Cantire
102 South Ebudes (Islay, etc.) and Scarba
103 Mid Ebudes (Mull, etc.)
104 North Ebudes (Skye, etc.)

N. Highlands
105 West Ross
106 East Ross
107 East Sutherland
108 West Sutherland
109 Caithness

North Isles
110 Outer Hebrides
111 Orkney
112 Shetland

Ireland
1 South Kerry
2 North Kerry
3 West Cork
4 Mid Cork
5 East Cork
6 Waterford
7 South Tipperary
8 Limerick
9 Clare with Aran Isles
10 North Tipperary
11 Kilkenny
12 Wexford
13 Carlow
14 Leix
15 South-east Galway
16 West Galway
17 North-east Galway
18 Offaly
19 Kildare
20 Wicklow
21 Dublin
22 Meath
23 Westmeath
24 Longford
25 Roscommon
26 East Mayo
27 West Mayo
28 Sligo
29 Leitrim
30 Cavan
31 Louth
32 Monaghan
33 Fermanagh
34 East Donegal
35 West Donegal
36 Tyrone
37 Armagh
38 Down
39 Antrim
40 Derry

Reference to National and Irish Grid

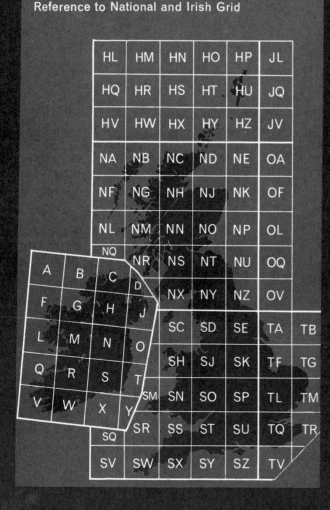

HL	HM	HN	HO	HP	JL
HQ	HR	HS	HT	HU	JQ
HV	HW	HX	HY	HZ	JV
NA	NB	NC	ND	NE	OA
NF	NG	NH	NJ	NK	OF
NL	NM	NN	NO	NP	OL
NQ	NR	NS	NT	NU	OQ
NX	NY	NZ	OV
SC	SD	SE	TA	TB
SH	SJ	SK	TF	TG
SN	SO	SP	TL	TM
SR	SS	ST	SU	TQ	TR
SV	SW	SX	SY	SZ	TV

A	B	C	D
F	G	H	J
L	M	N	O
Q	R	S	T
V	W	X	Y
SM			
SQ			